MW01069568

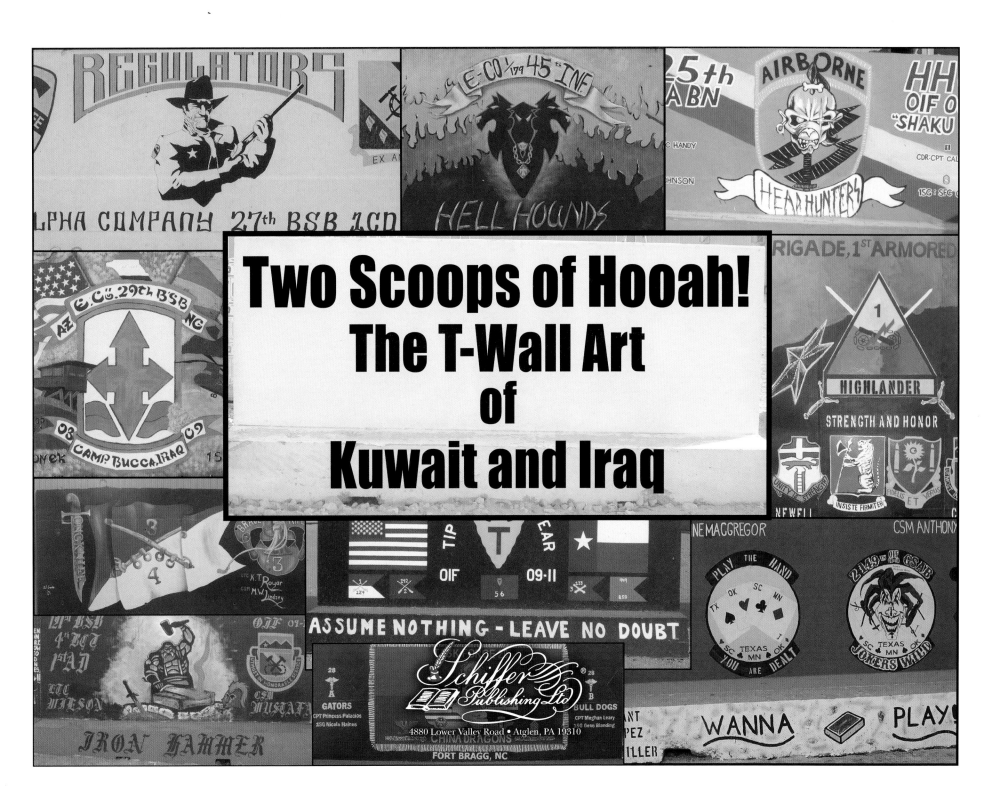

EDITOR'S NOTE

This book was created as a historical document, and as a means to help the wounded from the conflict in the Middle East. My late father, Captain (Dr.) Emanuel Hauer, a Surgeon with the 3rd Field Hospital, U.S. Army, won the Bronze Star for saving fourteen GIs who had been shot or stabbed in the chest during the invasion of Luzon, Philippine Islands, 1945. He told me in later years that those soldiers suffered life-altering injuries so my life would be secure, and that if a wounded soldier needed help, one should give it without being asked. Those brave men and women should never be forgotten. They have given too much. This book and effort to help the wounded are a tribute to my father's memory.

George Hauer

Text by Robin Whitney, Dedication by Chaplain (Col.) Craig N. Wiley, and Artist's Foreword by Warren Kimble

Graphic Design by Alan C. Ellis, Editor George Hauer

ACKNOWLEDGMENTS

We wish to acknowledge the assistance, advice, and encouragement of the following:
David T. Robertson and Thomas Loikith of Harwood Lloyd, LLC, Hackensack, NJ, for their assistance and advice on legal matters related to this project, Frank Duffin of Wiggin and Dana, LLP New Haven, CT, for assistance on copyright matters. Sarah F. White, former Deputy Assistant Secretary of the Army, James Ball, Col. (Dr.) Gerard P. Curran, Col. Stephen P. Jones, LTC Michael, S. Davis, LTC Norman C. Fox, Major Anthony F. Beatman, SPC Jeffrey T. Smith, Dr. Donald Rankin USAF (Ret), CIT-Services, LLC, Don Allen, Ethel Anne Chorney, Joseph FireCrow, Larry Kalbfeld, Daria Novak, Amaar Al-Hayder, Michael Paolini, CPA, Donald Peters, and Jose "Tony" Vega.

Published by Schiffer Publishing, Ltd.
4880 Lower Valley Road
Atglen, PA 19310
Phone: (610) 593-1777; Fax: (610) 593-2002
E-mail: Info@schifferbooks.com

For our complete selection of fine books on this and related subjects, please visit our website at www.schifferbooks.com. You may also write for a free catalog.

This book may be purchased from the publisher. Please try your bookstore first.

We are always looking for people to write books on new and related subjects. If you have an idea for a book, please contact us at proposals@schifferbooks.com.

Schiffer Publishing's titles are available at special discounts for bulk purchases for sales promotions or premiums. Special editions, including personalized covers, corporate imprints, and excerpts can be created in large quantities for special needs. For more information, contact the publisher.

DEDICATION

This beautiful book is dedicated to the thousands of American Service Members and Coalition Partner Nations who braved the battlefields of Kuwait and Iraq to fight against the enemies of freedom.

It has been said that a picture is worth a thousand words. Within the pages of this book, you will see how cement structures, intended for barriers, were transformed into pictorial walls that identified military units and honored service members who gave their lives for freedom. They provided an *esprit de corps* for their unit members who were forward deployed from their home base, post, or camp. The unit colors and insignias displayed on these walls commemorate the thoughts and memories of the men and women who have fought, including those who have died for freedom.

Some of these artistic wall paintings were created by Service Members of our Coalition Partner Nations. Throughout the War on Terror, they have fought and died alongside their American partners. We pay tribute to them and give thanks for their sacrifice.

You will see memorial walls that proclaim in silence the ultimate sacrifice of serving one's country. We must never forget the sacrifice that war brings.

These painted walls represent Soldiers, Sailors, Airmen, Marines, Coast Guard, and D.O.D. Civilians who answered the call of freedom and deployed far from home and family. These walls have now decayed and turned to rubble, so this book will become a lasting legacy to those who have served in Kuwait and Iraq.

Today, thousands of military members of our Armed Forces are battling the tragic wounds of war, both mental and physical. All of the royalties from the purchase of this book will be donated to Operation: Music Aid.

Let us give thanks to those whose vision it was to compile these pictures and make this fantastic book a reality. Your selfless service does not go unnoticed.

Chaplain (Colonel) Craig N. Wiley
United States Army

Foreword From An Artist's Perspective

I was pleased and honored to be asked by George Hauer—a fellow alumnus of Syracuse University Class of 1960—to help select the artistic images for this book about the murals on the T-walls of compounds in Kuwait and Iraq.

The art is the purest of folk art. Soldiers working as individuals, or as a team, created these depictions of everyday war that are so impermanent. Soldiers—men and women artists—may be untrained, have a relative who influenced them, have taken a school art class, or have been professional artists before arriving in a war zone. The well-established logos of a unit show a fine sense of design and use of color and execution. In observing these artists' work, note the excellence of design in the choice of lettering that evokes and enhances the spirit, strength and power of each wall.

Art is seeing and reproducing one's experiences. These paintings depict visual perceptions of the soldiers' past and present situations. I wonder how the experience of designing and painting these murals will affect their present and future creative works. Art surrounds us all our lives, no matter who we are or where we are. These warriors were expressing what was going on in their present environment through art.

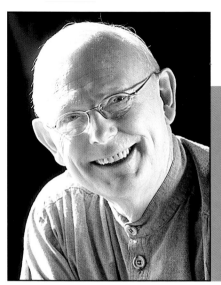

Warren Kimble

Contemporary folk art represented in many private and public collections worldwide

BFA Syracuse University, 1957

Honorary Doctor of Fine Arts, Green Mountain College

In the collection of Shelburne Museum, Shelburne, VT

George Arents Pioneer Medal. Syracuse University Outstanding Alumni Award

Units Included

(Some National Guard units appear in this section.)

Pages 10 through 149

ALAMO (THE)-JAG OFFICES CAMP ADDER
ANACONDA POWER AND LIGHT
(Power plant at Joint Base Balad)
ARMY TRANSPORTATION CORPS
Balad Association of Doctors
 Anaconda Surgical Society
BANDIT PRIDE
CATFISH AIR-Helicopter passenger terminal,
    Joint Base Balad
DEFENDER (THE)
FRA STRYKER/CAMP ANACONDA
G-FSC
JOINT BASE BALAD
LBA- ANACONDA LAW ENFORCEMENT
LVIS
MISSISSIPPI RIFLES
MORTARITAVILLE (USO)
MORTY'S GARAGE-BALAD
MOUNTAIN RANGERS
MRAP
NAVAL CUSTOMS DELTA CO.
NAVY PETROLEUM DETACHMENT
NPDB-5
PHIPPS TROOP CLINIC
Pittsburgh Steelers Terrible Towel
PT/OT JOINT BASE BALAD
RED CROSS

SEABEES 7+12 NMCB
SOLDIERS CREED
TASK FORCE JAYHAWK
TASK FORCE KEYSTONE
TASK FORCE SABER
TASK FORCE 26
TASK FORCE 34 COMBAT AVIATION
    BRIGADE
TASK FORCE118 MMB
TASK FORCE 163
TUSKEGEE AIRMEN
TUSKEGEE MEDICS
VETERANS DAY
VIKING WARRIOR
1/17 ARTILLERY
1-18TH INFANTRY
1-35 ARMOR (BAUMHOLDER, GERMANY)
152ND AVN
1-85TH AVIATION
1-100TH AVN
1-110TH INFANTRY
1-114TH INFANTRY
1-126 AVN REG. MEDEVAC
1-130TH ATTACK
1-131ST AIR BRIGADE
1-131ST ARMOR
1-137TH AHB

1-137TH E CO.
1-150TH AHB
1-151 LOGISTICS AVIATION
1-155TH INFANTRY/D CO.
1-159 AIRBORNE
1-161ST INFANTRY
1/179TH DELTA CO.
1/179TH 45TH INFANTRY/E CO. (OKLAHOMA)
186TH MP CO.
1-189TH AVN
1-200TH A & C CO.
1-244TH AVN
1-293RD INFANTRY
1ST ARMORED-4TH BRIGADE
1ST CAVALRY DIVISION
10TH CO. SUPPORT HOSPITAL
(FT. CARSON, CO)
10TH SBTB
11TH SIGNAL BRIGADE
16TH SUSTAINMENT BRIGADE
101ST ENGINEERS
102ND QM CORPS.
104TH MP BATTALION
106TH TC & 13TH CSSB/213TH
111TH POSTAL COMPANY
120TH FSC (HOBART, OK)
121ST BSB

122ND SUPPORT CORPS (SELMA, AL)

123RD MOBILE PUBLIC AFFAIRS DET.

126TH AVN-1ST BATTALION

130TH ENGINEER BN

130TH SIGNAL BN

133RD MEDICAL DET. (HANAU, GERMANY)

137TH AVN

138TH FIRE BRIGADE

142ND ENGINEERS

151 AVN

153RD MP CO.

162ND INFANTRY-HHC2

164TH SUPPORT GROUP

166TH REGIONAL SUPPORT GROUP

172ND INFANTRY

175TH INFANTRY

178TH MILITARY POLICE

182ND SAPPER

185TH AVN

188TH AVN

186TH ENG. CO. (DOTHAN, AL)

186TH SUPPORT CO. CSE

193RD AVN

194TH ENGINEERS

196TH TRANSPORTATION CO.

2ND TRANSPORTATION CO.
(FT. RICHARDSON, AK)

2-10TH AVN

2-104TH GSAB

2-104TH AVN

2-114 AVN

2-127TH INFANTRY BATTALION

2-149TH AVN B CO.

2-149TH AVN DELTA CO.

2-149TH CSAB

25TH COMBAT AVIATION BRIGADE

27TH BSB ALPHA CO.

28TH MED A & B

28TH CAB

29TH BSB

29TH FIELD ARTILLERY-3RD BATTALION

203RD MP CO.

209TH AREA SUPPORT BATTALION

213TH AREA SUPPORT

215TH ASMC

220TH MP CO.

223RD MEDICAL DETACHMENT

245TH AVIATION REG. TF SOONER

248TH ASMC MEDICS

259TH COMBAT AVIATION BRIGADE

259TH CSSB

277TH ASB

287TH SUSTAINMENT BRIGADE

296TH TRANSPORT CO.

3-6TH FIELD ARTILLERY

3-82ND FIELD ARTILLERY

3-158TH

3-297TH ASB

3-509TH

3RD ARMORED CAVALRY DIVISION

3RD CORPS SUPPORT COMMAND

30TH ENGINEERING BRIGADE

30TH SIGNAL BATTALION

31ST INFANTRY REGIMENT

34TH CAB

35TH SIGNAL BRIGADE

35TH SIGNAL BATTALION

36TH HHC

36TH SUSTAINMENT BRIGADE

37TH AIRBORNE SAPPER

37TH FINANCE

301ST ASG

304TH CHAPLAIN

304TH MP BN

304TH SUSTAINMENT BRIGADE

307TH MEDICAL CO.

314TH CSSB

325TH CSH

326TH ASG

332ND AIR EXPEDITIONARY WING

332ND ECES

332nd EFES

332ND ESFS

332ND EFCS

332ND EMDG

332ND VEHICLE MAINTENANCE

332ND TRANS. FLIGHT GROUP

345TH CSH

350TH HRC

351ST CSBN

354 MPAD

366TH AIRBORNE

377TH TRANSPORTERS

382ND FIELD ARTILLERY

3666 SMC

4-25TH RANGERS

4-27TH ARTILLERY

4-123RD AVN B CO.

4-159TH AVN REGIMENT

4TH BRIGADE ARMORED

4TH ENGINEERS

4TH SIGNAL BATTALION

40TH CORPS SUPPORT GROUP
40TH EXPED. SIGNAL BATTALION
40TH MP
44TH MEDICAL CO.
45TH AIRBORNE
45TH INF-1-179TH
45TH SUSTAINMENT BRIGADE
46TH EXPEDITIONARY SIGNAL BATTALION
402ND FIELD SUPPORT BRIGADE
415TH AVN REGIMENT
425TH AVIATION REG. 1ST BATTALION
425TH CABN
444TH AIRBORNE
463RD ENGINEER BATTALION
464TH MEDICAL CO.
5-509 RANGERS
55TH MEDICAL CO.
56TH INFANTRY-(FT. BRAGG)
56TH STRYKER
507TH CORP SUPPORT GROUP
510TH SAPPER ENGINEERS
536TH MAINTAINANCE CO.
(SCHOFIELD, HAWAII)
541ST PERSONNEL
546TH MAINTAINANCE CO.

551 MED CO (FT. LEWIS, WA)
557TH ERHS
557TH MED CO.
563RD SUPPORT AVIATION-A CO.
582ND MEDICAL LOGISTICS
64TH MEDICAL DETACHMENT (V.M.)
603 MP CO.
607TH MP BN
628TH ASB
639TH CS CO.
7TH CAVALRY-5TH SQUADRON
7TH MPBN
7TH SIGNAL BRIGADE
(MANHEIM, GERMANY)
7TH SUSTAINMENT BRIGADE
7-158TH AVN
72ND EXPEDITIONARY SIGNAL BATTALION
(MANHEIM, GERMANY)
76TH INFANTRY BRIGADE
716TH MILITARY POLICE
732ND AIR EXPEDITIONARY GROUP
732ND ECES
732ND ESCS
732ND ESFS
732ND INTEL. SQUAD

732ND MCT USAF
732ND MEDICAL MCT
735TH MSB A CO.
744TH MP CO.
769TH BATTALION ENGINEERS
770TH AIRBORNE
8TH CAVALRY
8TH MP BRIGADE
80TH ORD. BN (JACKSON, TN)
81ST MMT
89TH TRANSPORTATION CO.
810TH MILITARY POLICE
826TH ORD. CO.
834TH ASB
840TH DEPLOYMENT & DISTRIBUTION
864TH ASRB
887TH ESFS
9TH ENGINEER BN-B CO.
9TH SUPPORT BN-B CO.
90TH SUSTAINMENT BRIGADE
910 QM
957TH MRBC
1123RD TRANSPORTATION CO.
1387 QM (GREENVILLE, MISSISSIPPI)

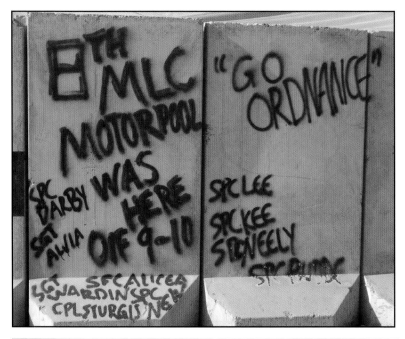

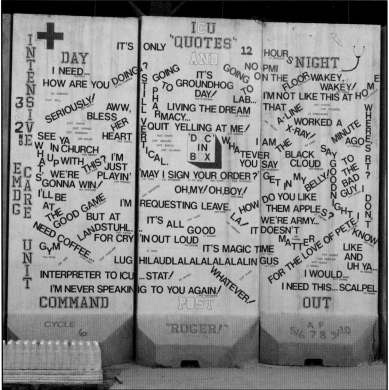

With his-first hand description, Colonel Curran gives a powerful introduction to the context of the murals photographed for this book:

"For much of the last six years, as a soldier arrives or departs Iraq, his first or last stop is a camp in Kuwait. Dependent on the time of year, you are usually hit in the face by a breeze that feels like a hair dryer, or hot coals near your face at a barbecue. In the summer, it is commonly 125–130 degrees Fahrenheit. This is real hot, like below zero is real cold. The next thing that is clearly different from home is how the desert is huge and flat. It reminds me of what I imagine the ocean floor would look like, without the water. While Iraq has more varied terrain, and even trees, Kuwait is strikingly stark. After the terrain and weather, the next striking thing about Kuwait is the large number of T-walls. T-walls are steel reinforced concrete molded barriers that are usually ten to fifteen feet tall and eight to ten feet wide. They were introduced into Iraq and Kuwait in the late 2004–2005 time period as blast protection against the common, poorly-aimed rockets and mortars in Iraq. Soldiers in that period typically lived in sand bag protected tents, which were quite vulnerable to these threats. T-walls provided real protection against the horizontal ripping shrapnel and concussive blast of a near miss to the areas where we lived, worked, and slept."

June 2010
Gerard P. Curran, Commander, COL, MC
118th MMB – Multifunctional Medical Battalion
Connecticut Army National Guard

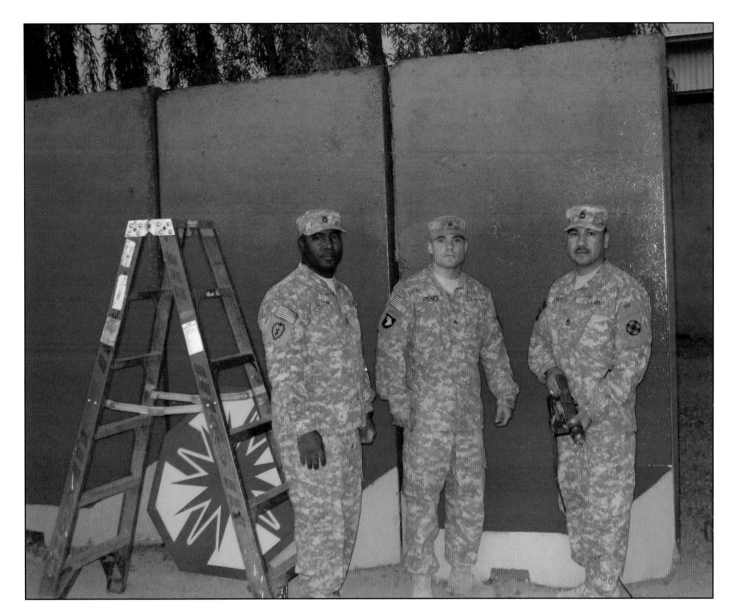

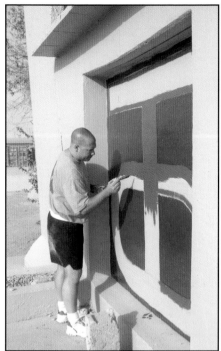

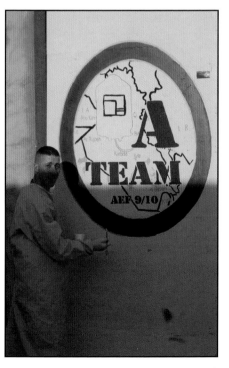

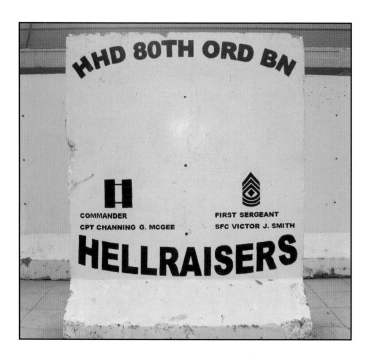

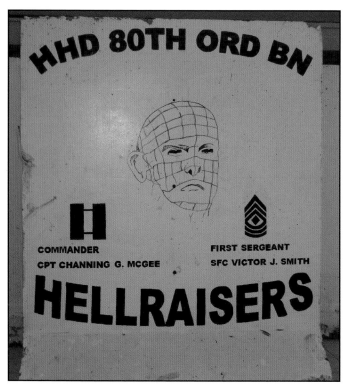

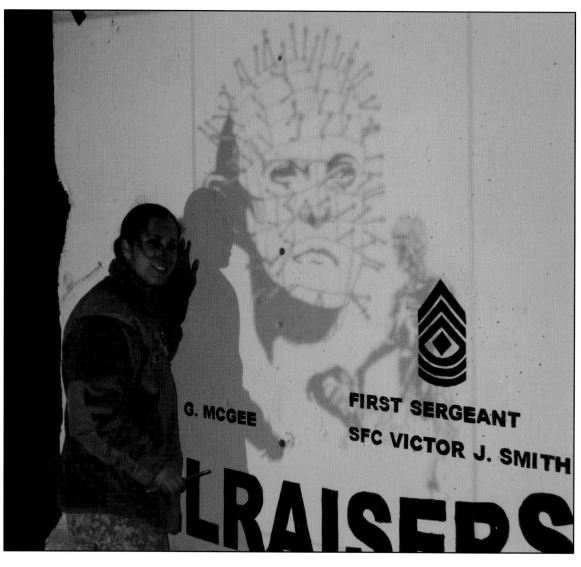

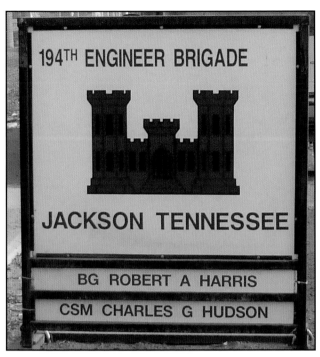

On a purely experiential level, these elaborate T-walls must surely shock. The photographs collected in this book challenge us to imagine this immense desert with eternally flat terrain and its truly monumental scale nearly bleached of color. In this exotic landscape, the impact of the sudden intrusion of thousands of bright, endlessly imaginative images must surely astound. Through these photographs, we can begin to experience the cacophony, action, colors, and the astonishing variety of activities that these vibrant images thrust upon the enormous, largely silent, and nearly featureless landscape that surrounds many of the military installations.

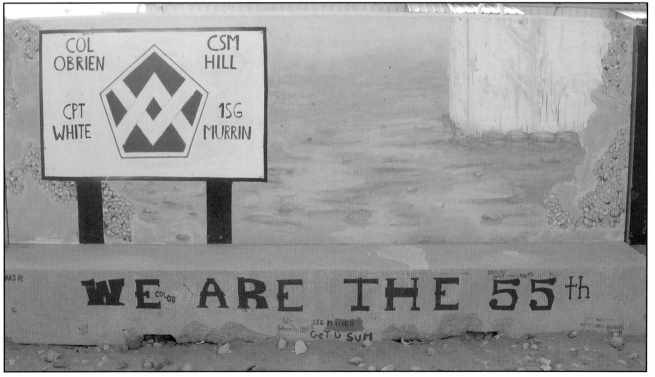

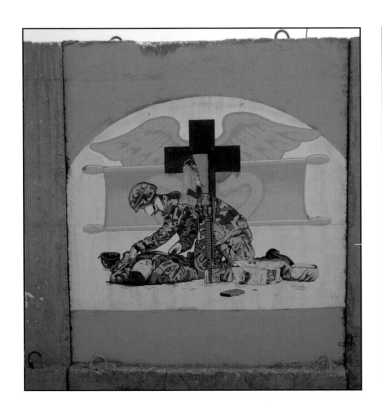 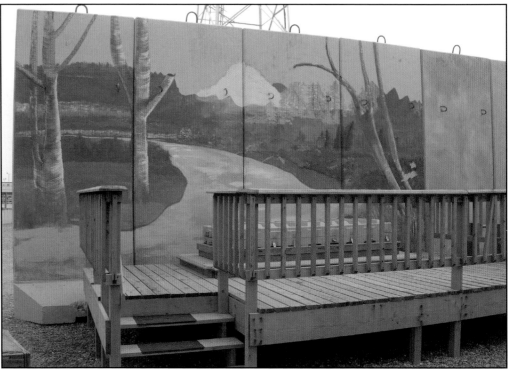

James Ball, Assistant Red Cross Station Manager, who took many of the photographs in this book, describes his experience at Joint Base Balad in Iraq:

"I want to emphasize that the T-wall cannot be taken out of the context of a war zone with incoming mortar and rocket attacks weekly, loud and impressive F-16 jets taking off at all hours of the day and night, camaraderie at the base cafeterias, standing at attention at the beginning of every movie shown at the base theater for the playing of the national anthem, and not least, the helicopters coming in with wounded soldiers to the base hospital. It is all one mosaic with T-walls representing one impressive part of the puzzle."

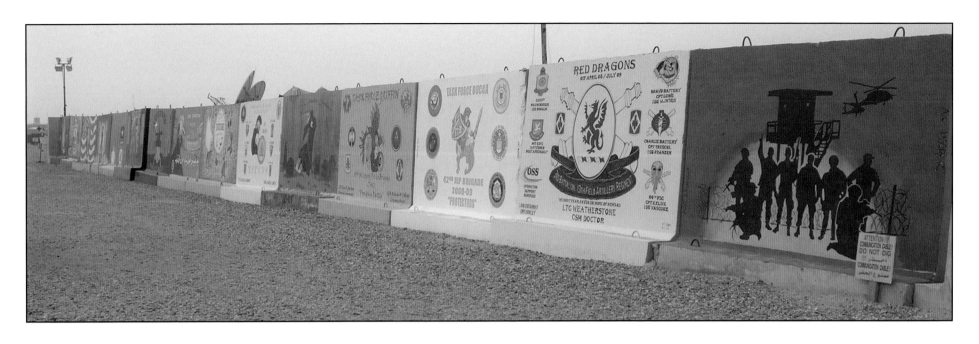

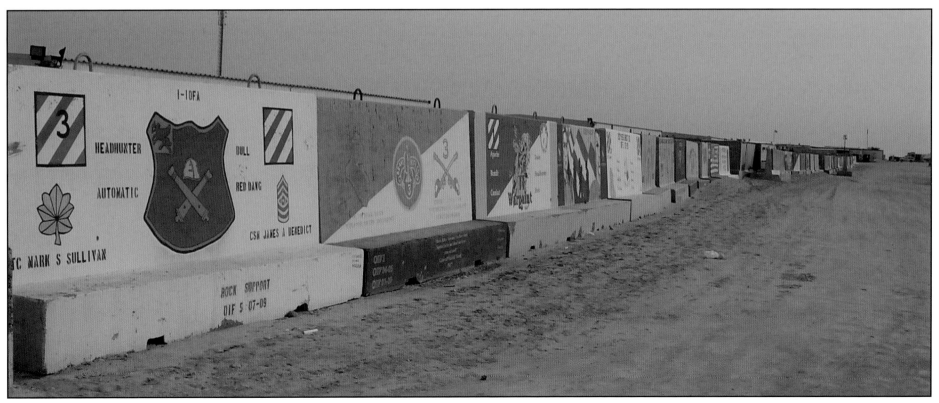

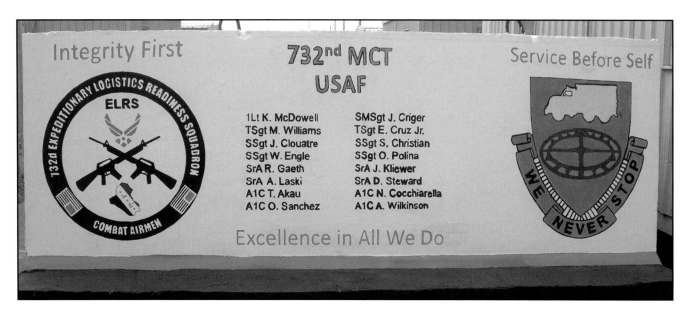

Integrity First

732nd MCT
USAF

Service Before Self

132d EXPEDITIONARY LOGISTICS READINESS SQUADRON
ELRS
COMBAT AIRMEN

1Lt K. McDowell
TSgt M. Williams
SSgt J. Clouatre
SSgt W. Engle
SrA R. Gaeth
SrA A. Laski
A1C T. Akau
A1C O. Sanchez

SMSgt J. Criger
TSgt E. Cruz Jr.
SSgt S. Christian
SSgt O. Polina
SrA J. Kliewer
SrA D. Steward
A1C N. Cocchiarella
A1C A. Wilkinson

WE NEVER STOP

Excellence in All We Do

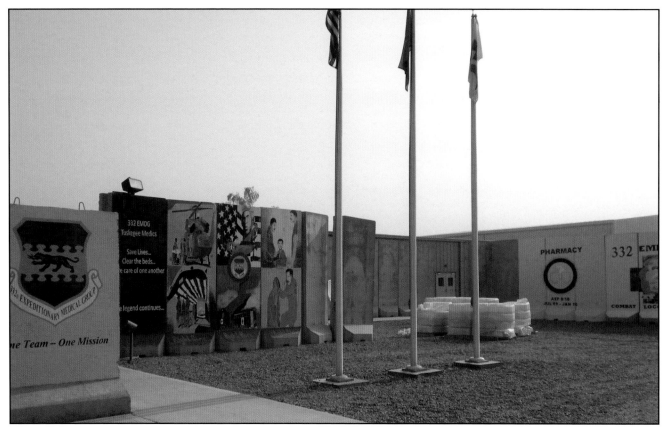

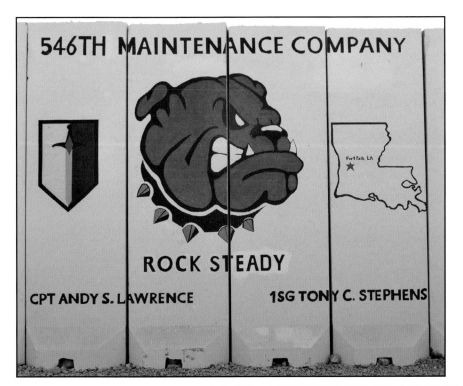

He describes many thousands of people living and working on this giant military installation. The population consists of thousands of military personnel from all branches of the U.S and Coalition armed forces, many of them women. The base also houses thousands of non-military private contractors and additional thousands of citizens from the developing world, many of whom do not speak English and are hired to clean, cook, and provide most of the unskilled labor of the base. He describes the Ugandan soldiers who guard the entrance to the main dining hall and the Nepalese man who does not speak

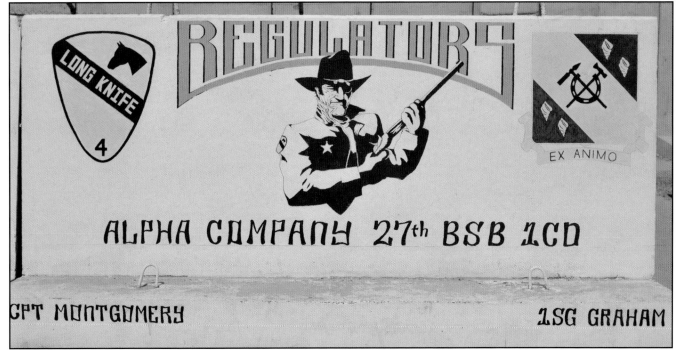

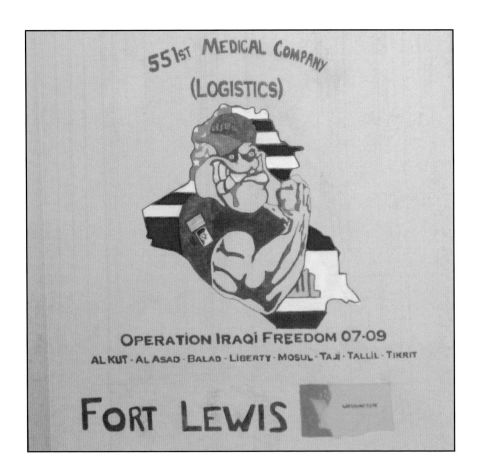

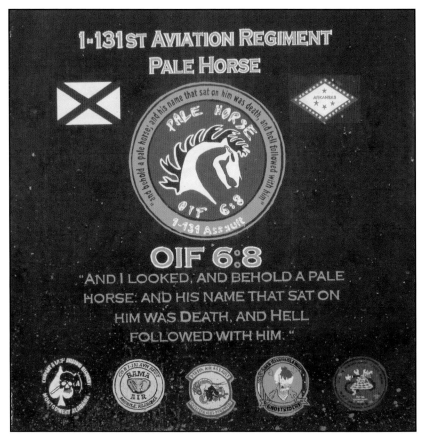

English, but who cleans the Red Cross office on the base. He describes the swimming pools and the many entertainments of the base, such as sports contests and holiday celebrations. The base is a place consisting largely of containerized housing and workspaces made up of shipping container-like structures. These are all surrounded by and interspersed with thousands of sections of steel reinforced concrete blast walls, known as

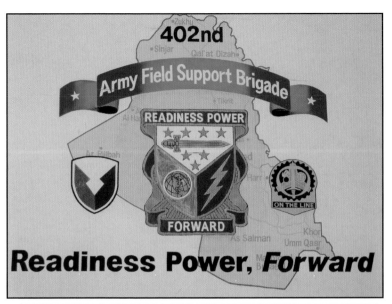

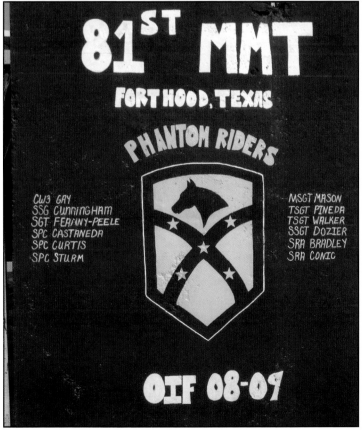

T-walls, many of which are twelve to fifteen feet high and many sections wide. It is these many acres of impersonal and blank concrete walls that the soldiers saw fit to fill with images and artwork, and which were used in such imaginative ways to personalize and transform their environment.

The general public, of course, is not the intended viewer of these works. The soldiers created these works by themselves and for themselves. They did not intend to communicate with anyone other than themselves and each other. But the images they chose, the subjects they selected, the fantasies they celebrate, and the memories they honor are powerful messages that speak to universal, timeless human impulses: identify with your particular group, make your surroundings distinctively your own, and reference your experience, your culture, and your time in this particular place and space. Many of the walls serve as memorials for fallen comrades and carry a powerful charge of grief, loss, and memory for some of the military units.

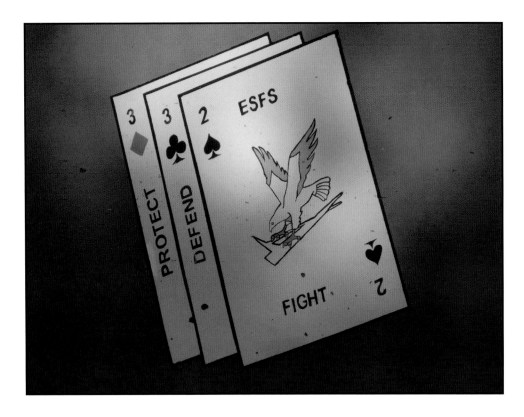

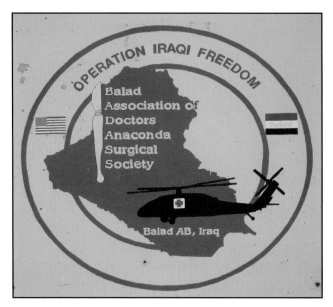

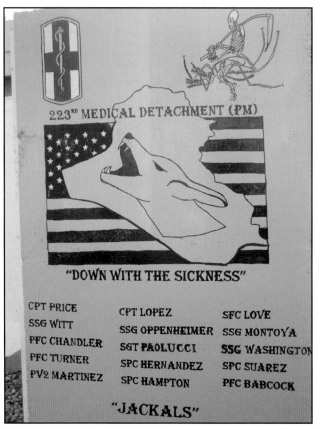

As outsiders, how many different ways can we approach these images to grasp the fullest possible impact of their meaning? Of course, soldiers and wayfarers from time immemorial have left their mark on the landscapes through which they passed. "Kilroy was here," and so was the Spanish explorer-soldier Juan de Oñate who carved his name and the date into a stone canyon wall in New Mexico when his expedition passed by on "16 of April 1605."

On the most elementary level, the decorated blast walls serve a similar purpose: to document in some way the presence and the experience of the unusual combination of people and purpose that

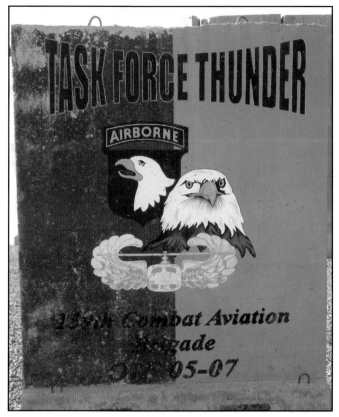

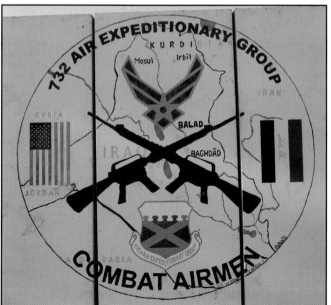

came together at this place. The steel reinforced concrete T-wall sections were designed for blast protection, rapid assembly, and transport. They serve a very necessary and vital purpose: to provide safety and protection to those behind them. Of course, the secure nature of these structures also demands that they serve to isolate inhabitants from the street and each other. The blank walls demand uniformity and lack distinguishing characteristics. With every wall identical to the next, unadorned, they would serve to disorient and confuse.

The actions of the soldier-artists powerfully overcome the disorientation and the uniformity inherent in a maze of anonymous cement walls. In the hands of the artists, the walls become distinctive, memorable, and meaningful through the art placed on them. The artwork erases any sense of anonymity, isolation, and disorientation. The paintings on the T-walls proudly announce and identify each unit, serve as powerful memorials,

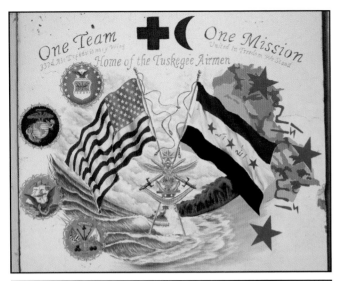

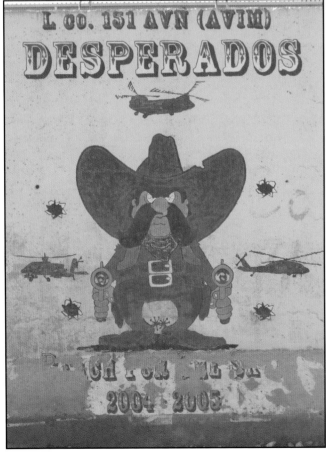

or celebrate and inspire. They make each sector unique and memorable, and bridge the gulf of isolation caused by the nearly impenetrable barrier of the wall itself.

Many of the walls tell us, and whoever passes by, useful and necessary information: who is where. The mechanics are here, the Kansas National Guard is there, and the military police are around the corner. In this regard, the works are strictly utilitarian and necessary, and provide information in a compelling way. The common element in much of this monumental wall art is in the purpose and intention to identify which group is located where. These "identification tags," in the early days of an American presence in these places, were rather simple and straightforward nametags. Quickly, they evolved into something much more complex and meaningful. They continued to identify the group in residence but, in addition, became a way to celebrate and honor these groups, their histories, their origins,

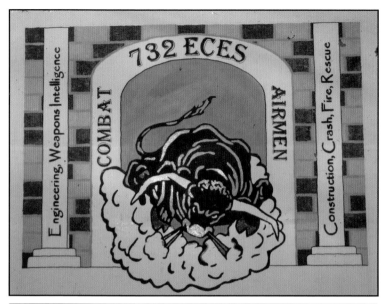

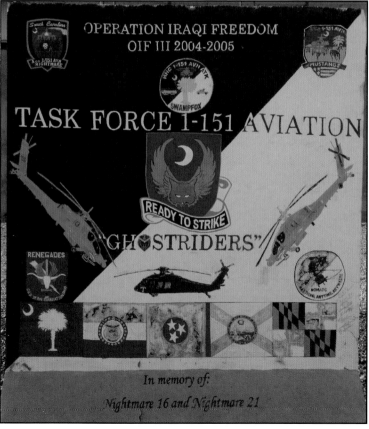

and their cultures. We find familiar local American icons taking up residence far from home. The Kansas Jayhawk and the familiar Native American warrior image are both endowed with new meaning and significance. Again and again, we see the art honoring the history and tradition of the past while it strives for new understandings, new expressions, and new symbols of inspiration and honor. We see memorial walls, too, and those that honor commanding officers and unit heraldry.

How is it that these artworks speak to us on so many levels? Looking at these works carries an immediate jolt of emotion, fascination, recognition, and intrigue that compels us to analyze our strong reactions and to try to understand why our response is so immediate and so visceral. Americans, of course, will bring to their experience of these works a strong sense of the current events that inform the works and their personal connections to the events and the people involved: the war in Iraq and the American soldiers who are direct participants in this history.

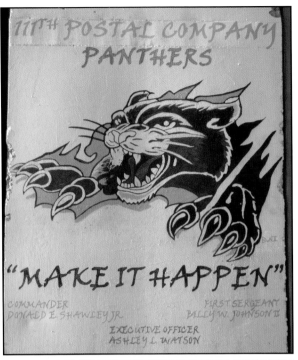

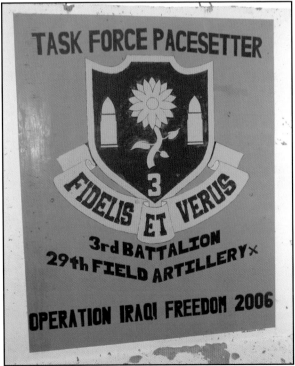

These artworks serve to change our perspective from watching history unfold on our television screens to a more ground-level appreciation of the location, the atmosphere, and the soldiers' impact on and interaction with their environment. Through these monumental murals, we somehow gain a sense that history and current events are happening around us and even through us on a level far more personal and immediate than we ever assumed or imagined.

These works may surprise or intrigue us, but through them, there is no doubt that our perspective shifts, and our minds and hearts are jolted into a more direct and visceral relationship to the soldiers and events. Through these works, we are honored to be invited to share some of the soldiers' most personal thoughts and feelings, their instincts, their priorities, some of their sense of their own identity, and their sense of their place in history and indeed, in time.

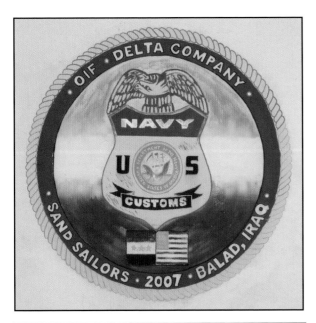

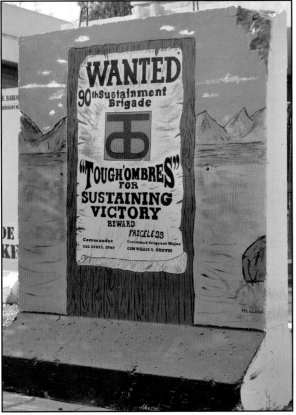

We are honored by the opportunity to experience their values, their creativity, their inspiration, and to come to see what these extraordinary soldiers honor, what they memorialize, and what they celebrate on a very personal, and somehow even intimate, level. We can appreciate the sense of humor and lament the losses. We can find here a sense of triumph and pride, as well as a sense of unrelenting loss and sacrifice.

The images on the T-walls thrust an astonishing variety of emotions, images, and information upon the very fabric of the built environment. Here at home, the one or two favorite wall murals in any city can become favorite icons of place. It is an entirely different concept for the murals to be nearly contiguous and to be themselves the defining feature of both street and building. The murals seem somehow stunningly American, while at the same time—like all great art—speak to common human themes and experiences. The environment they create when

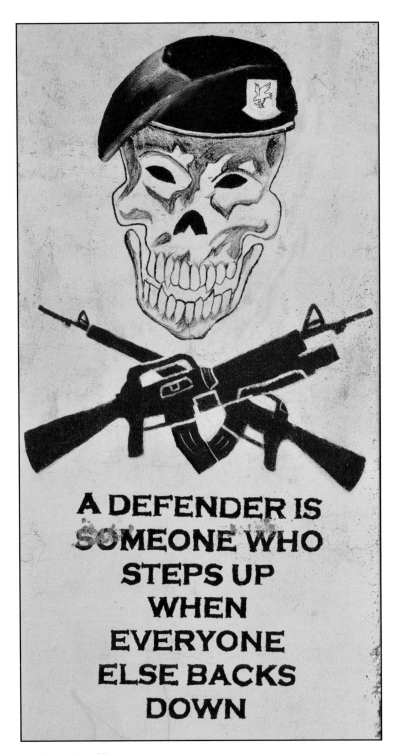

A DEFENDER IS
SOMEONE WHO
STEPS UP
WHEN
EVERYONE
ELSE BACKS
DOWN

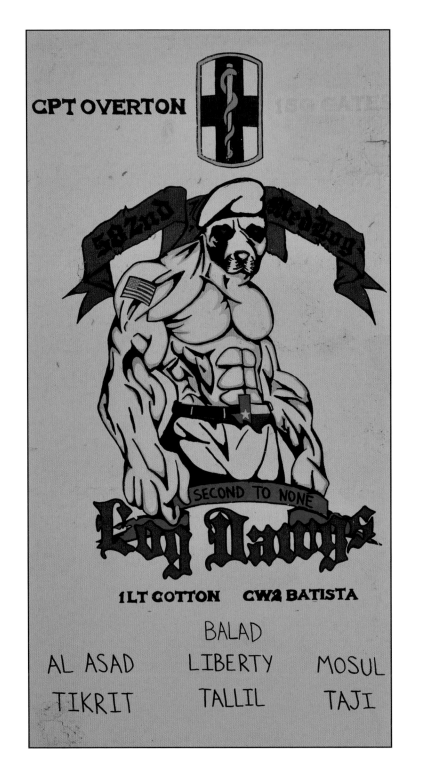

CPT OVERTON

582nd MedLog

SECOND TO NONE

Log Dawgs

1LT COTTON   CW2 BATISTA

BALAD
AL ASAD   LIBERTY   MOSUL
TIKRIT   TALLIL   TAJI

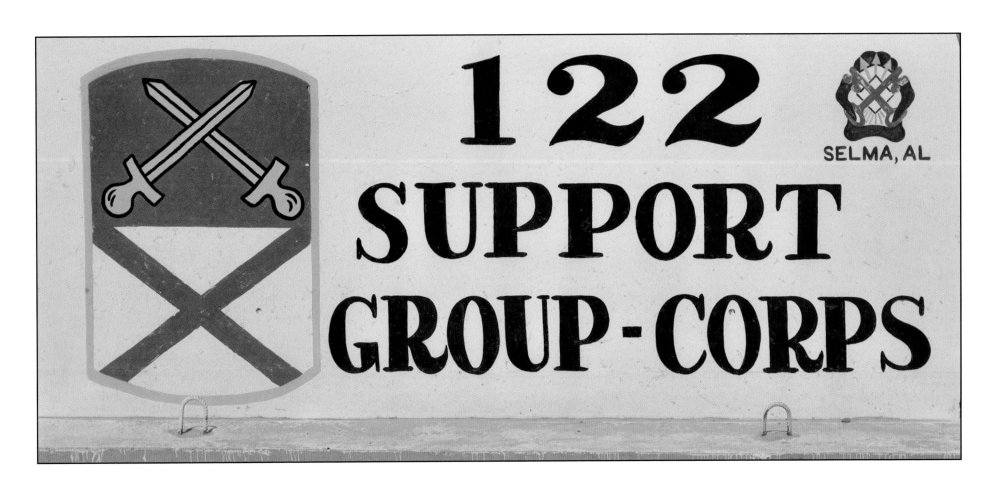

122 SUPPORT GROUP - CORPS

SELMA, AL

experienced as a whole must be somehow truly new and daunting. If the city is considered a living organism, then we must surely recognize that with these military installations, the city has evolved to a new level of meaning and experience. From a culture of billboards, advertising, commerce, and popular culture, the soldiers have taken the techniques, impact, and the scale, and have achieved a truly powerful re-imagining of the American tradition of promotion and entertainment. They have used familiar materials— and many times familiar images— monumental scale, and attention-grabbing graphic design techniques, and have fundamentally transformed them in their use, expression, purpose, and meaning.

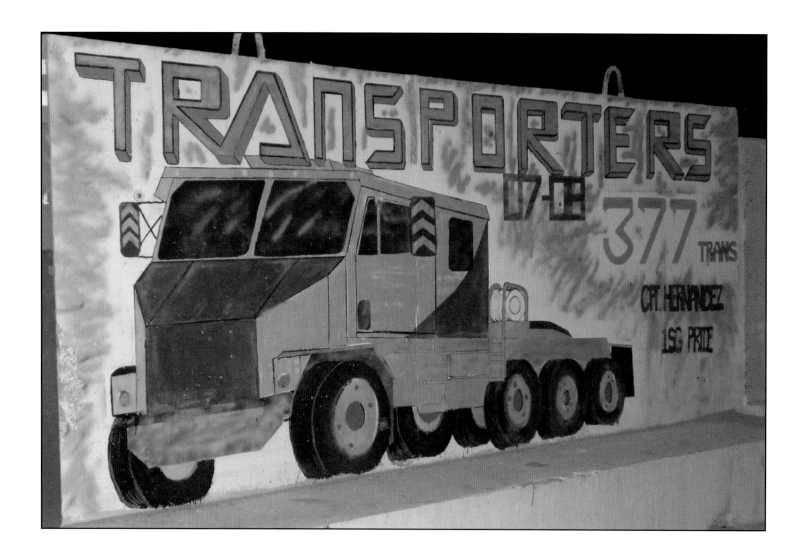

In addition, this art makes it clear that a new generation is on the scene. Contrast this art to that of our World War II soldiers. At that time, pin-up girls seemed to dominate the subject matter and there was a strong sexual content to much of the work. Are military censors at work in Kuwait and Iraq, or have the sensibilities of the soldiers changed this dramatically? Does the presence of so many female troops—a defining characteristic of twenty-first century U.S. military life—contribute to the change in sensibility? In addition, the soldier art of the 1940s frequently taunted the

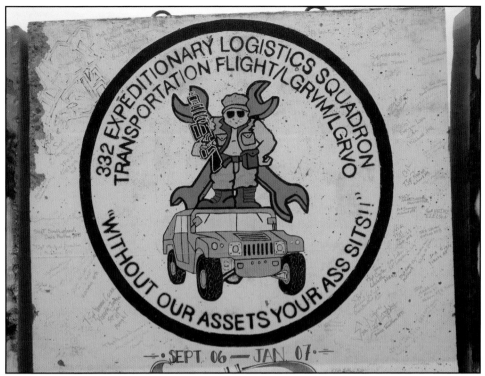

enemy, and much of the art was placed on the exceedingly transitory structure of the airplanes or, indeed, the bombs themselves. As Colonel Curran writes: "T-walls are similar to the nose art of the bombers of World War II, but I think they are more complicated in their themes, mostly due to the larger area the artists have to express themselves and the diversity of the artists. They are especially similar, in that they're perishable. These T-walls will eventually be ground into pebbles, or the art will literally be 'sand blasted' away by nature. This book of photos is an attempt to help convey their

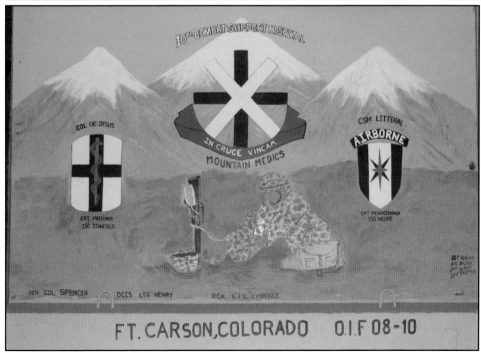

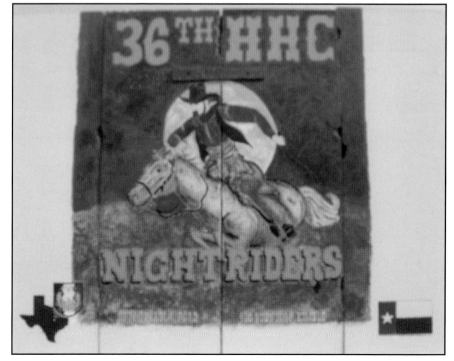

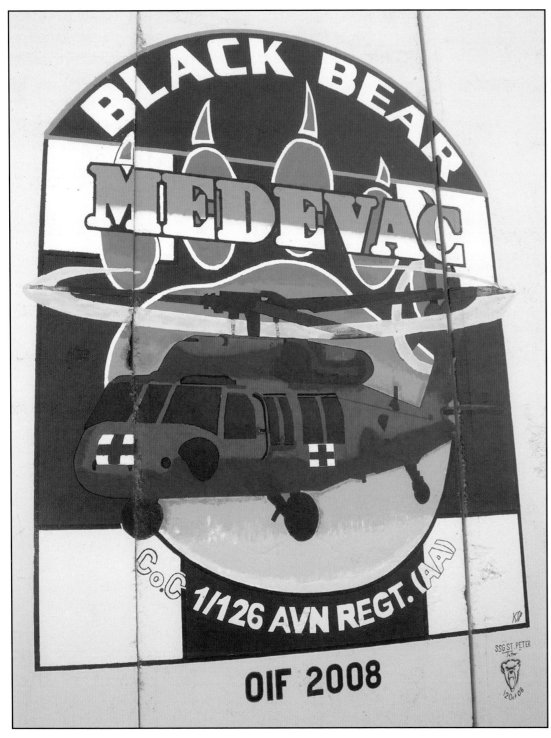

messages, and to allow our fellow Americans to see the art that expresses the feelings of common people facing a serious challenge on a personal and group level."

We may lament that these works cannot be a permanent mark on the landscape. They are created on multi-sectional cement blast walls that are designed to be transported and are easily disassembled. The T-walls are outdoor features covered with delicate paint, and by force of circumstance, are required to endure one of the harshest climates on Earth. They endure searing heat, bleaching, unrelenting sun, and ferocious scouring sandstorms, not to mention the occasional rocket or mortar blast. They are transitory, and this adds to their power. Like life itself, the seasons,

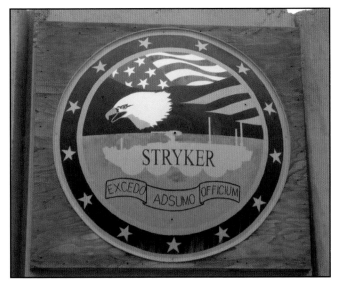

and both war and peace, the works do not merely tell us about the transitory nature of human reality, but are themselves a powerful visual example of one moment in human history, as they inevitably fade, bleach, chip, and are slowly or quickly eroded or dismantled. Their presence in a remote, dangerous location also adds to their power, since few will experience them directly and can only know them through photographs. Of course, this isolation, in itself, dilutes their reach and modulates their meaning.

Perhaps we should be grateful for this inevitable distance and separation. We recognize that few of us could withstand the actual experiences and living conditions common to these

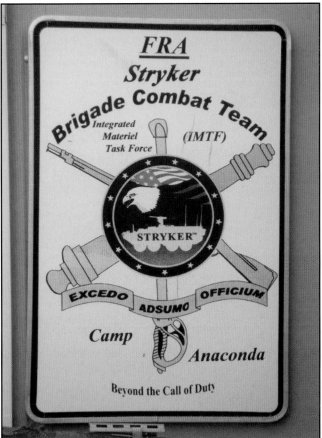

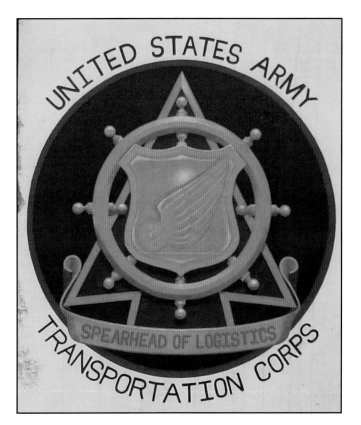

35th SIGNAL BRIGADE

OIF 10-12

Commander
COL Marc D. Harris

Command Sergeant Major

CSM Angel J. Ramos

TASK FORCE LION

warriors: the climate, battle, and the separation from loved ones that grieve them, and the fierce, bonding brotherhoods that sustain them. History and experience require a new imagining of time and place, and these artworks are powerful proof that a new time and a new place have indeed come into existence, at least for these uncommon men and women in a very exotic and forbidding place and circumstance. We are honored to be allowed a glimpse into their world through these photographs.

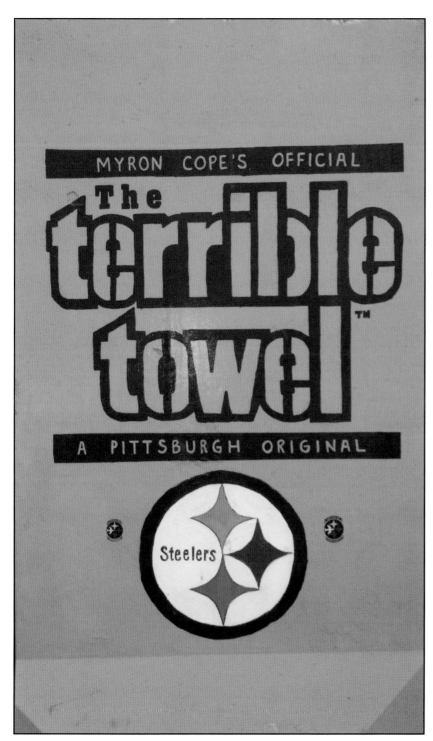

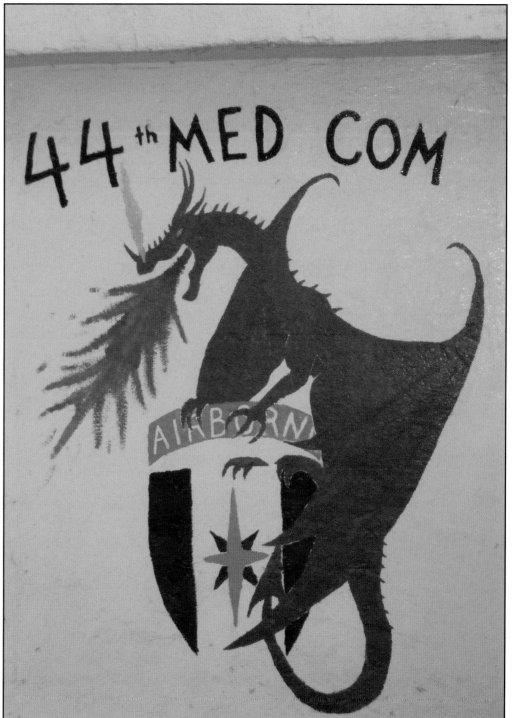

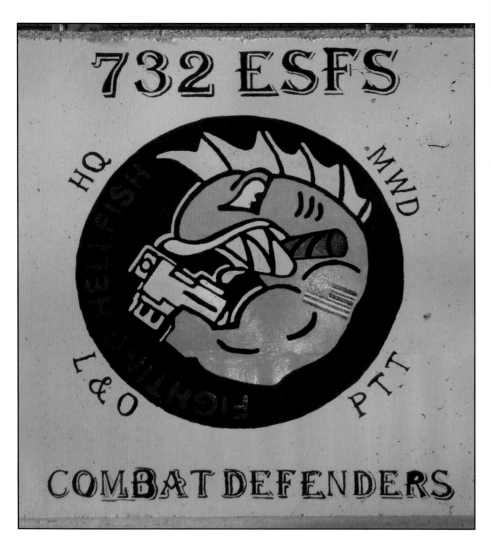

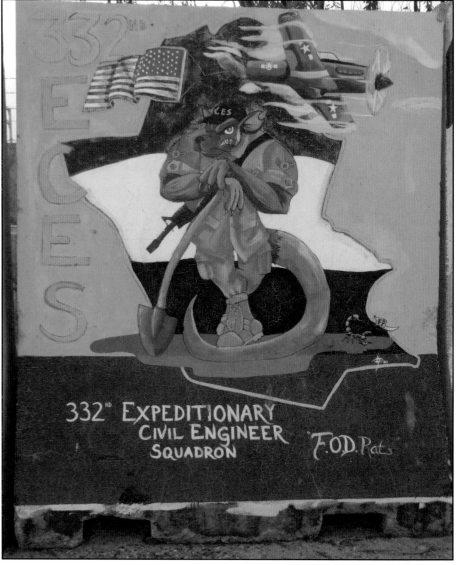

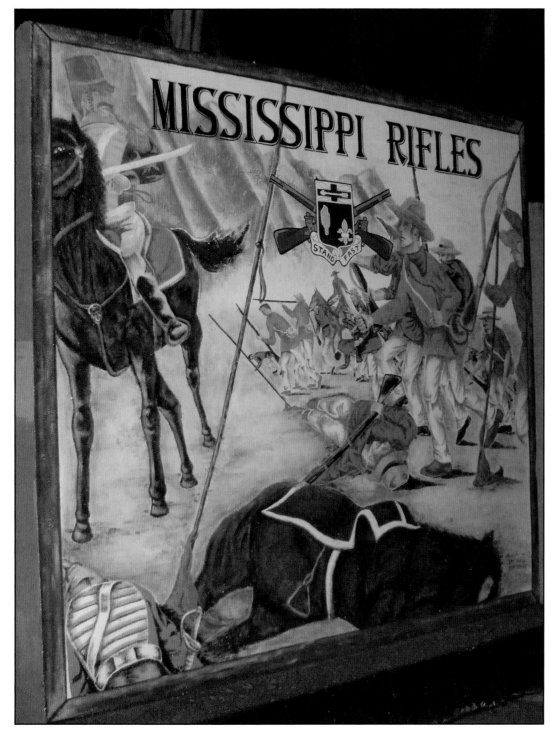

MISSISSIPPI RIFLES

STAND FAST

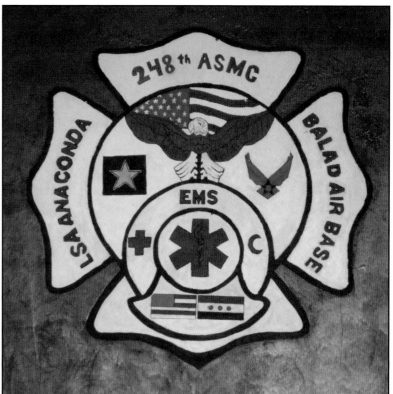

248th ASMC

LSA ANACONDA

BALAD AIR BASE

EMS

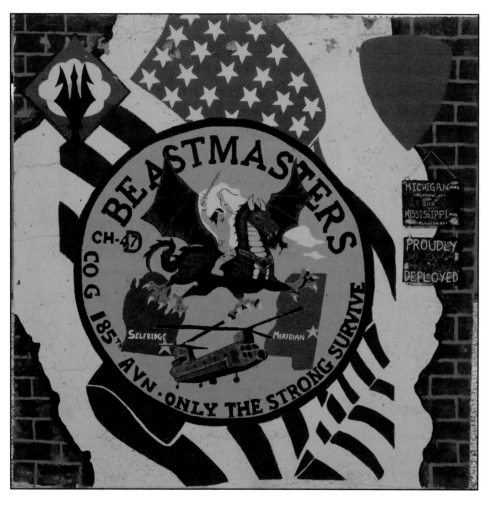

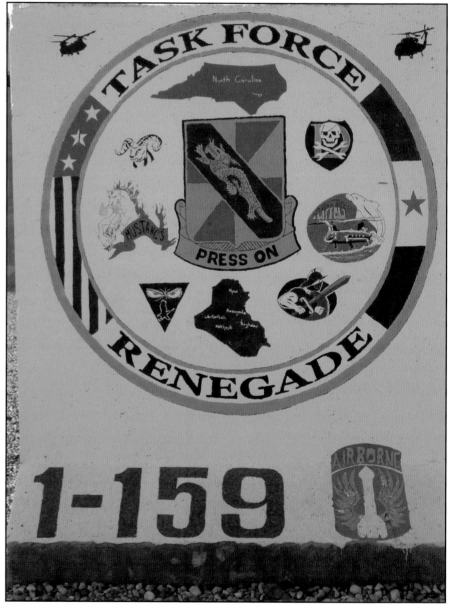

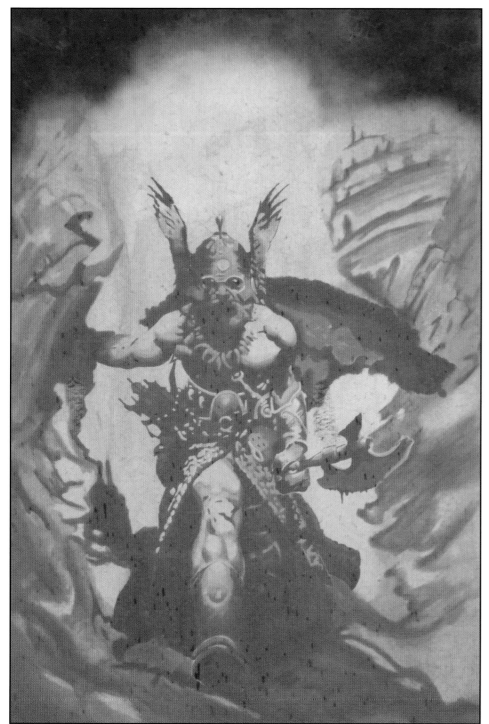

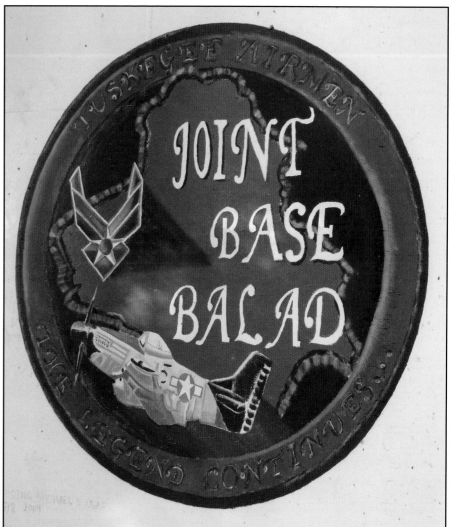

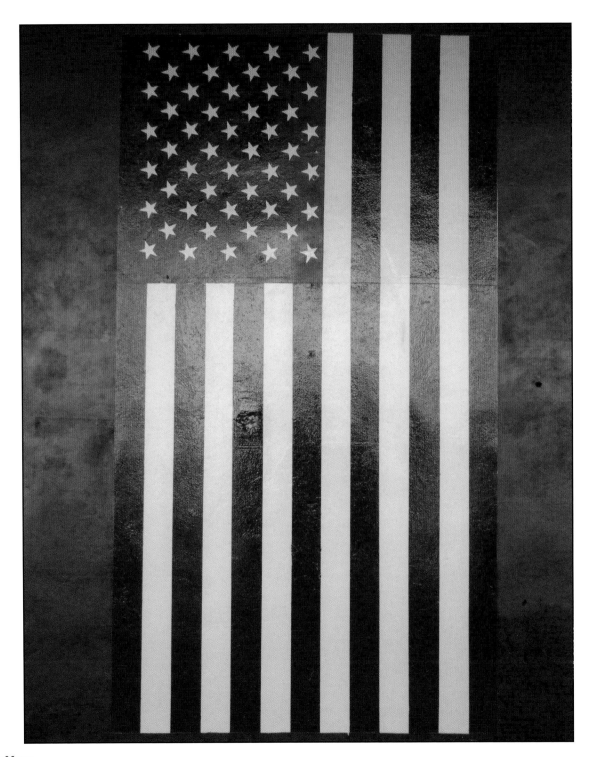

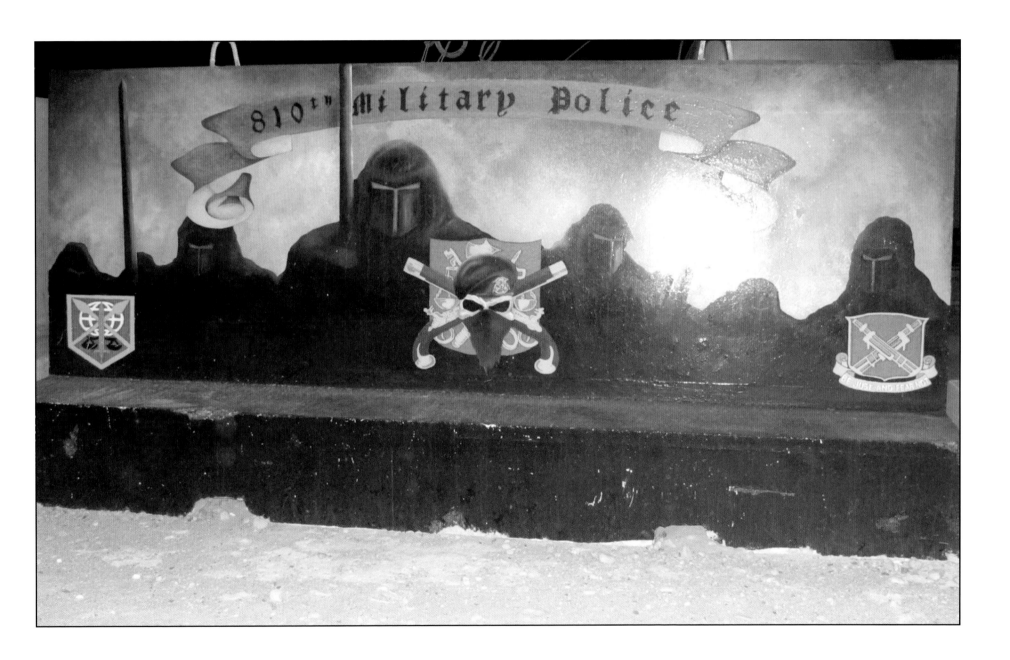

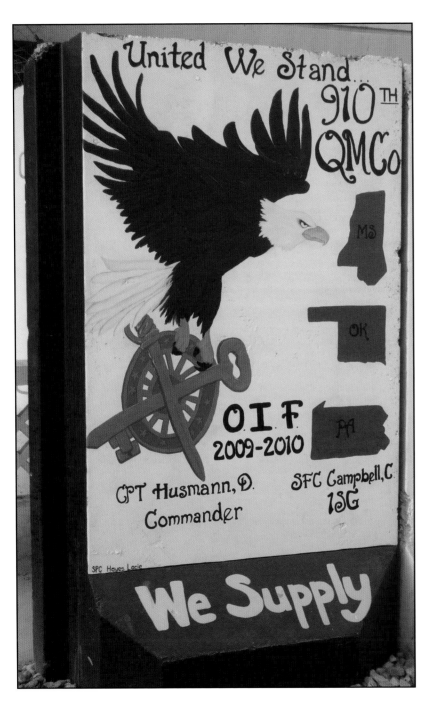

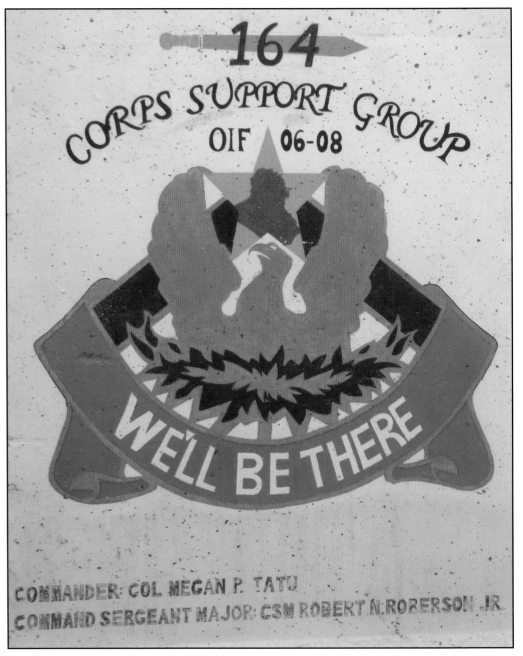

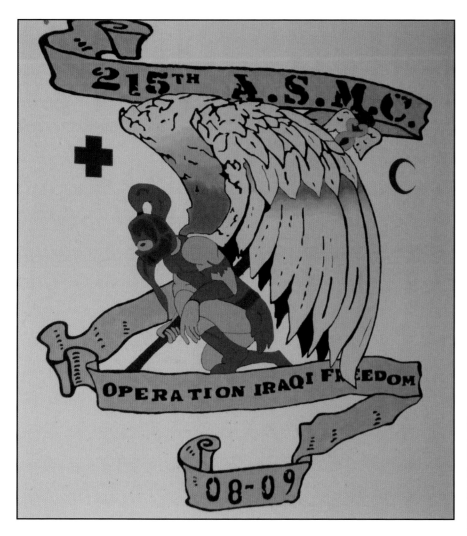

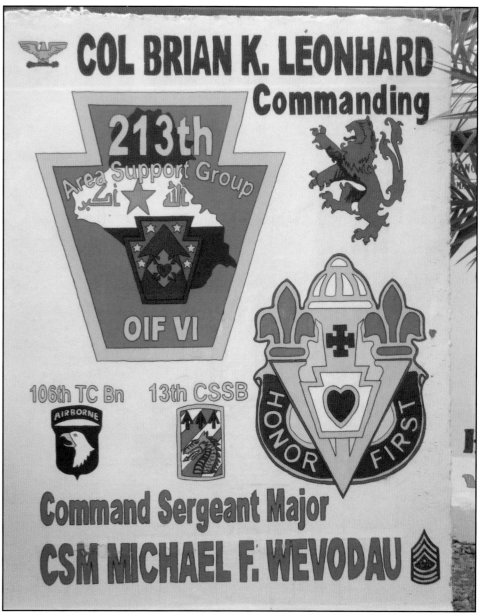

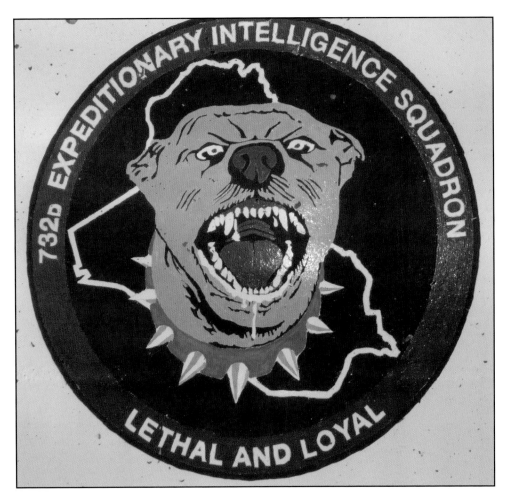

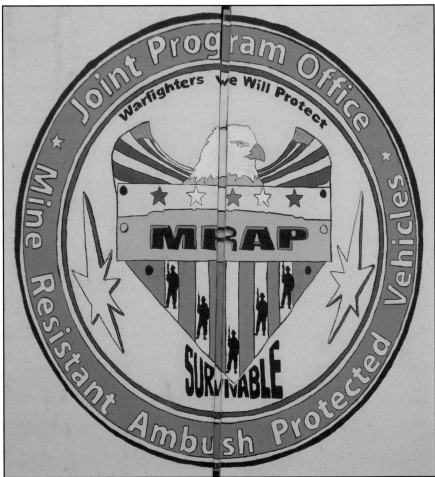

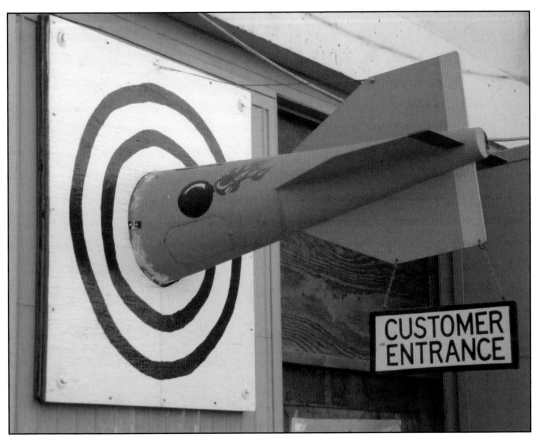

CUSTOMER ENTRANCE

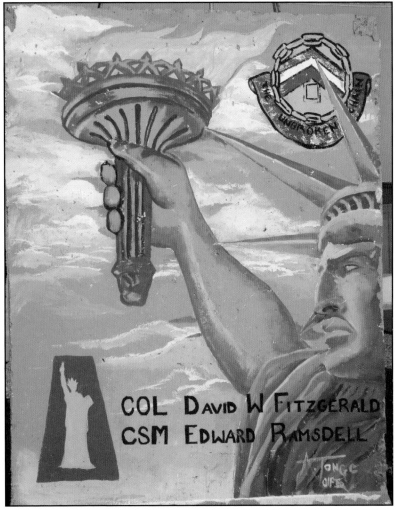

COL David W Fitzgerald
CSM Edward Ramsdell

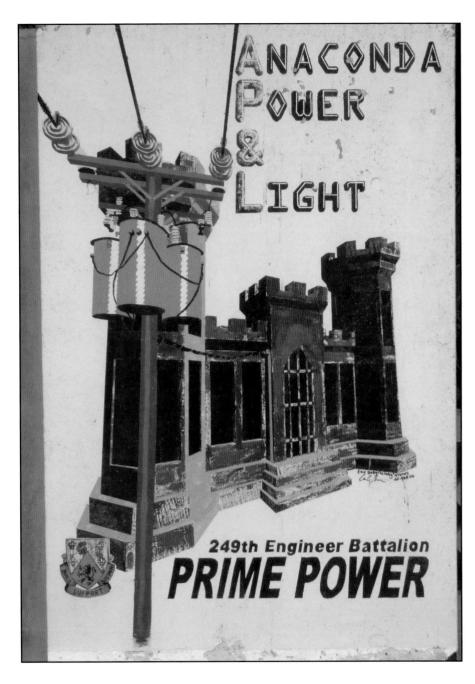

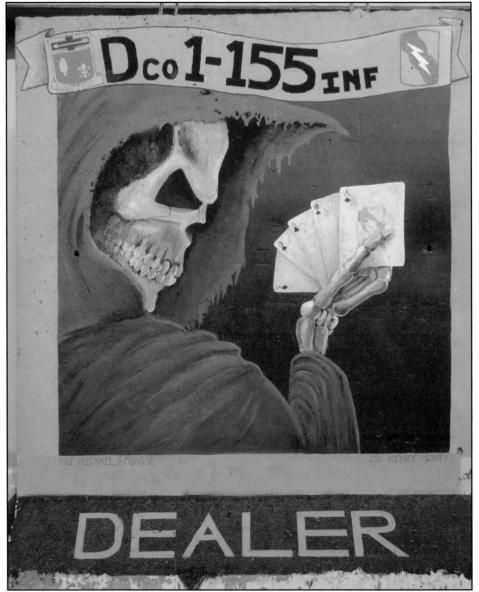

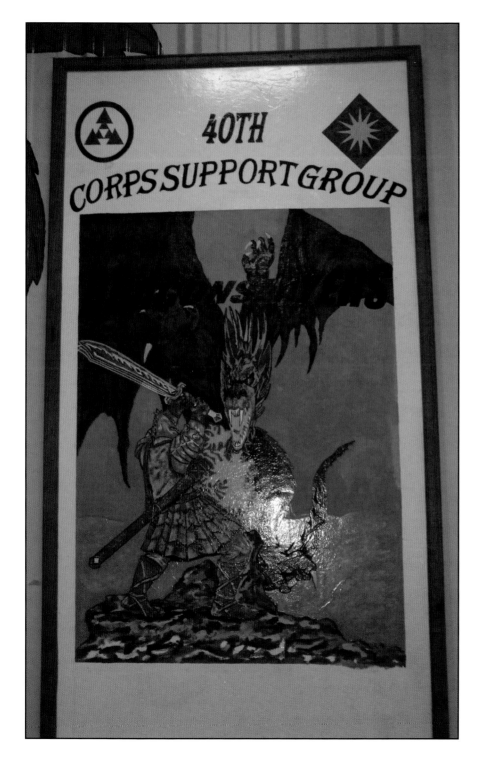

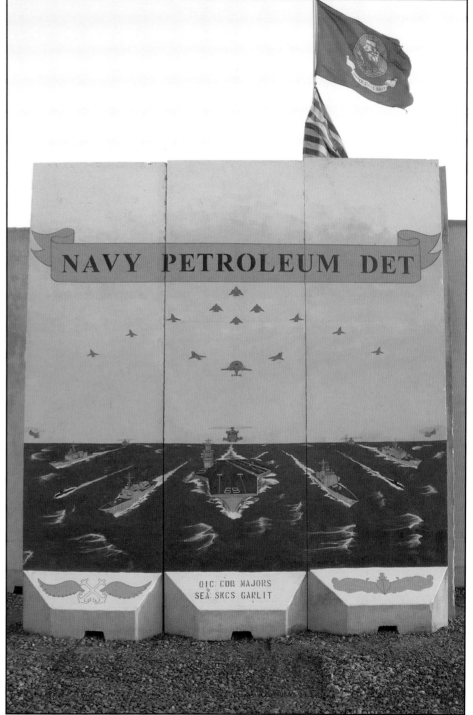

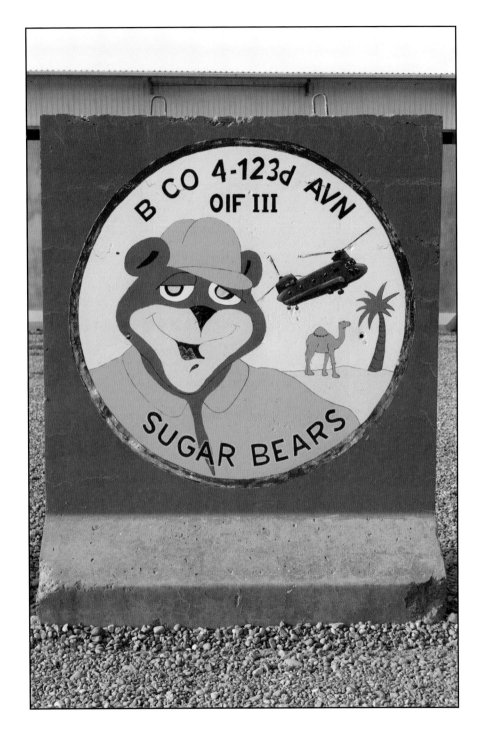

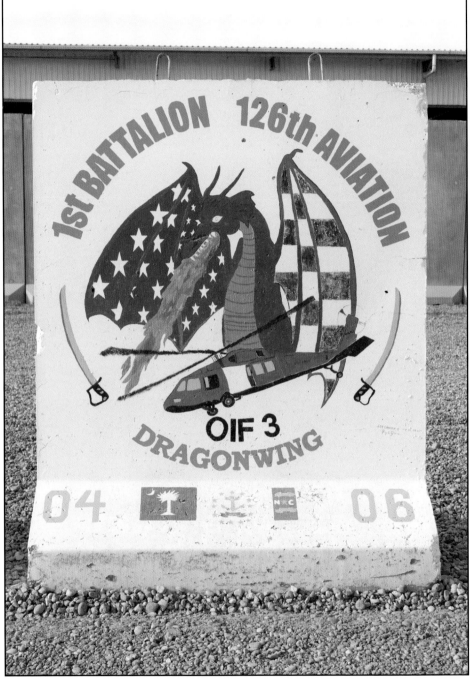

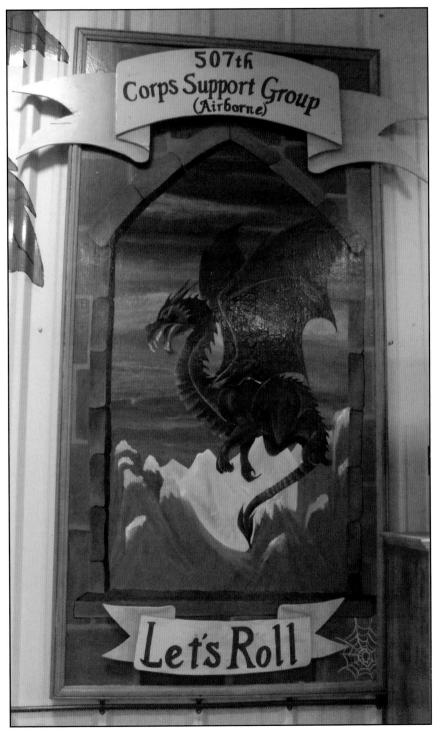

507th
Corps Support Group
(Airborne)

Let's Roll

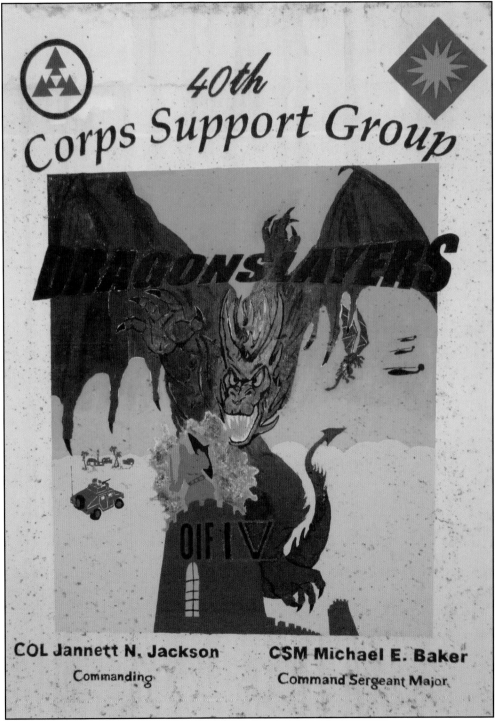

40th
Corps Support Group

DRAGONSLAYERS

OIF IV

COL Jannett N. Jackson
Commanding

CSM Michael E. Baker
Command Sergeant Major

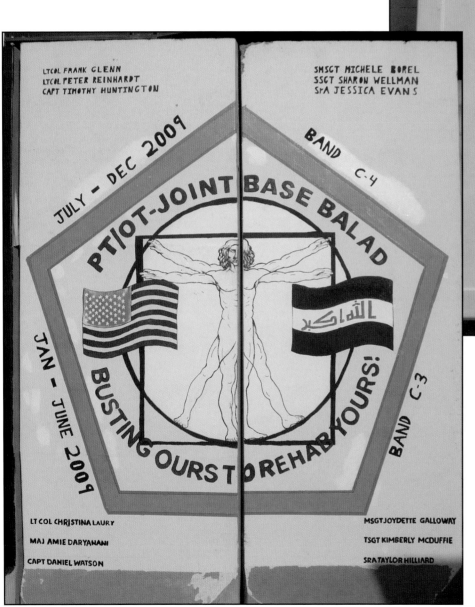

LTCOL FRANK GLENN
LTCOL PETER REINHARDT
CAPT TIMOTHY HUNTINGTON

SMSGT MICHELE BOREL
SSGT SHARON WELLMAN
SrA JESSICA EVANS

JULY – DEC 2009

BAND C-4

PT/OT-JOINT BASE BALAD

JAN – JUNE 2009

BUSTING OURS TO REHAB YOURS!

BAND C-3

الله أكبر

LT COL CHRISTINA LAURY

MAJ AMIE DARYANANI

CAPT DANIEL WATSON

MSGT JOYDETTE GALLOWAY

TSGT KIMBERLY MCDUFFIE

SRA TAYLOR HILLIARD

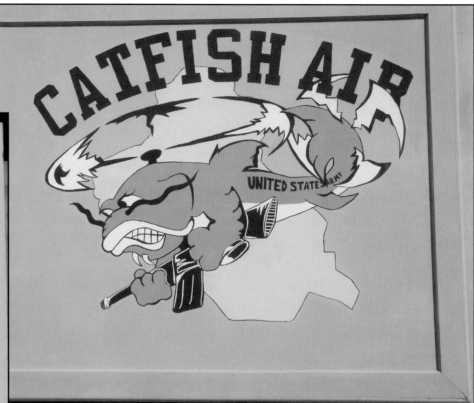

CATFISH AIR

UNITED STATES ARMY

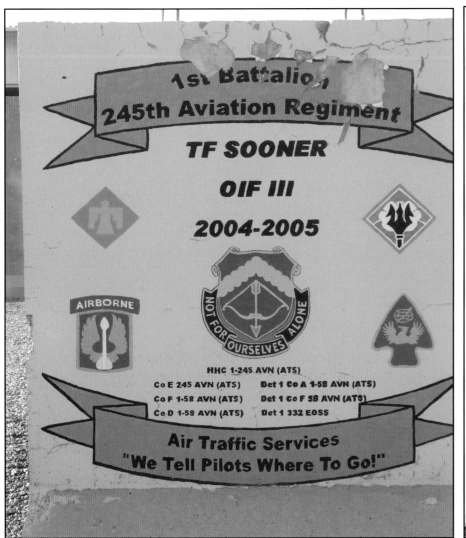

1st Battalion
245th Aviation Regiment

TF SOONER

OIF III

2004-2005

NOT FOR OURSELVES ALONE

AIRBORNE

HHC 1-245 AVN (ATS)

Co E 245 AVN (ATS)   Det 1 Co A 1-58 AVN (ATS)

Co F 1-58 AVN (ATS)   Det 1 Co F 58 AVN (ATS)

Co D 1-58 AVN (ATS)   Det 1 332 EOSS

Air Traffic Services
"We Tell Pilots Where To Go!"

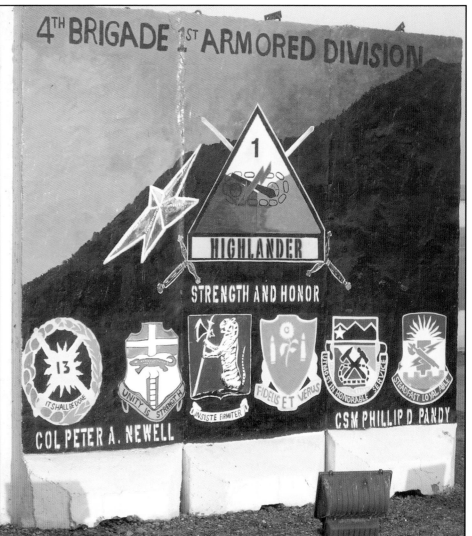

4TH BRIGADE 1ST ARMORED DIVISION

1

HIGHLANDER

STRENGTH AND HONOR

13

IT SHALL BE DONE

UNITY IS STRENGTH

INSISTE FIRMITER

FIDELIS ET VERUS

UTMOST IN HONORABLE SERVICE

STEADFAST LOYAL ABLE

COL PETER A. NEWELL

CSM PHILLIP D. PANDY

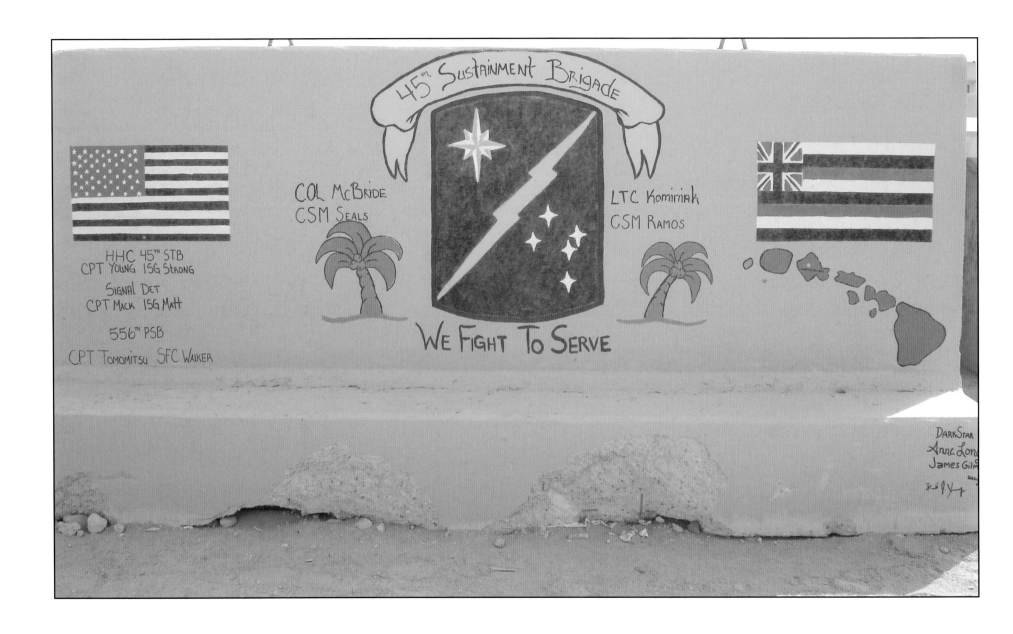

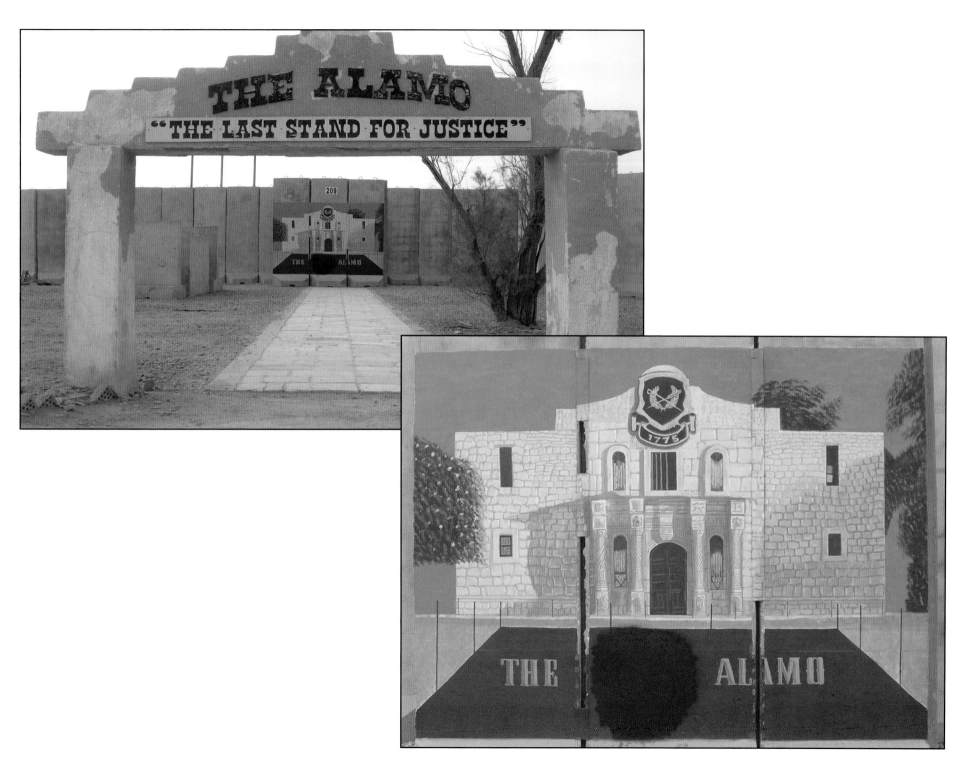

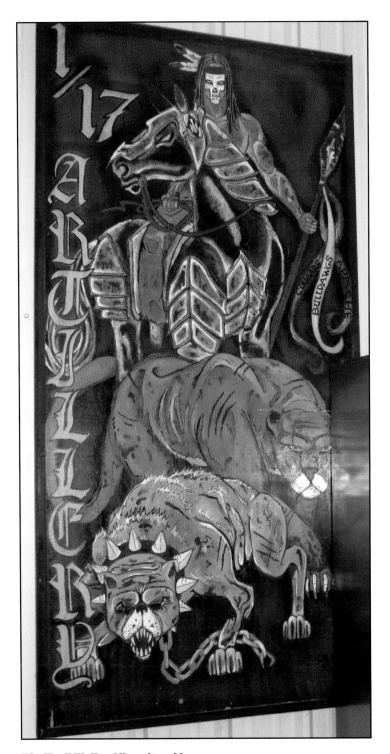

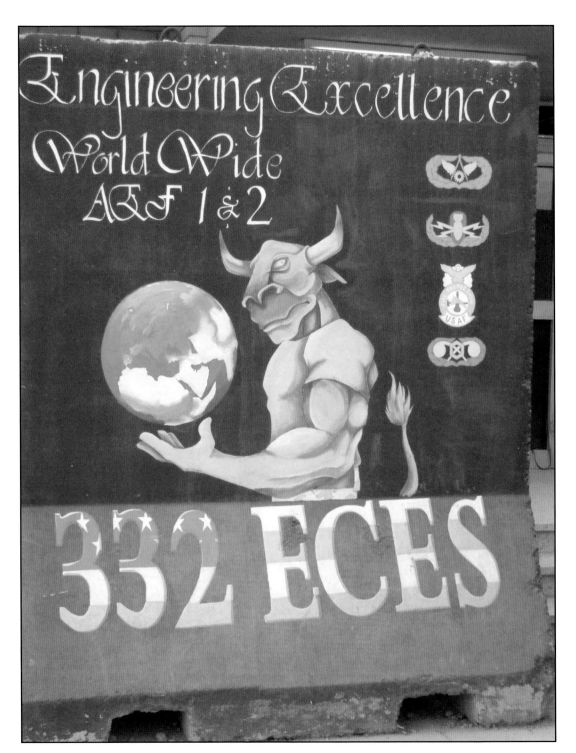

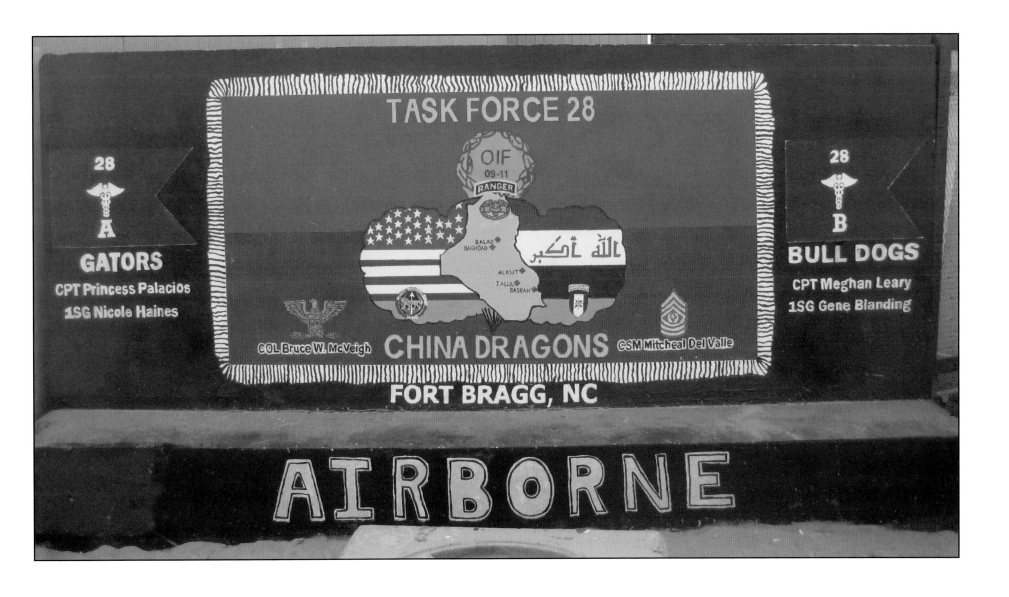

TASK FORCE 28

OIF 09-11

RANGER

28

A

GATORS

CPT Princess Palacios

1SG Nicole Haines

28

B

BULL DOGS

CPT Meghan Leary

1SG Gene Blanding

COL Bruce W. McVeigh

CHINA DRAGONS

CSM Mitcheal Del Valle

FORT BRAGG, NC

AIRBORNE

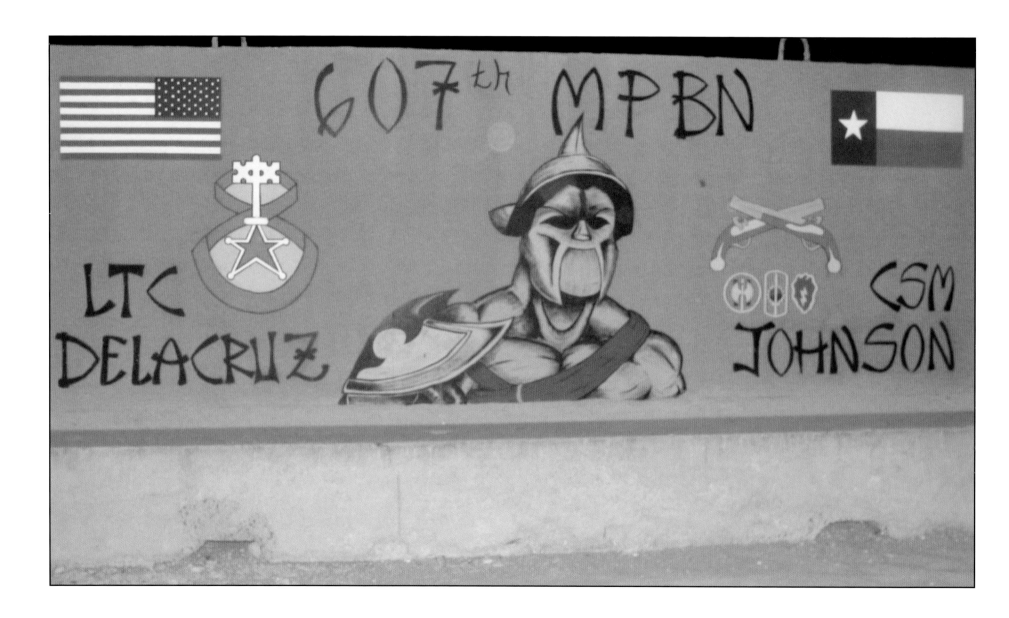

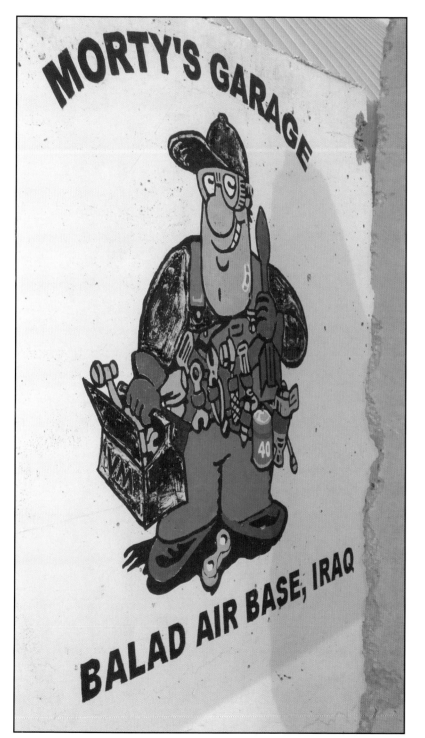

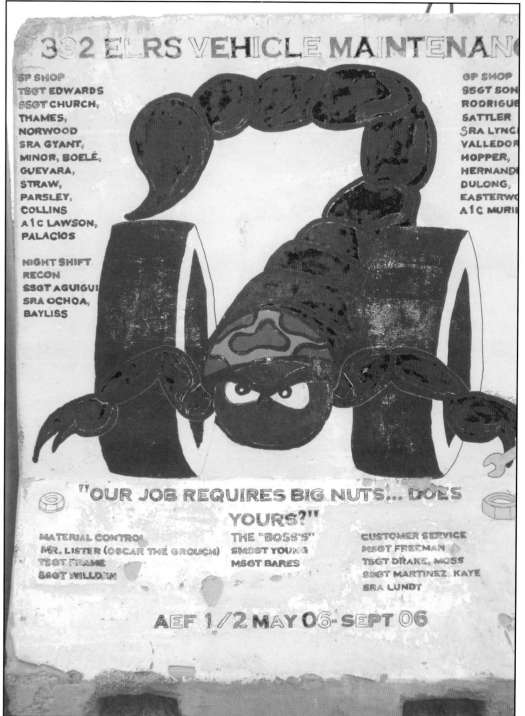

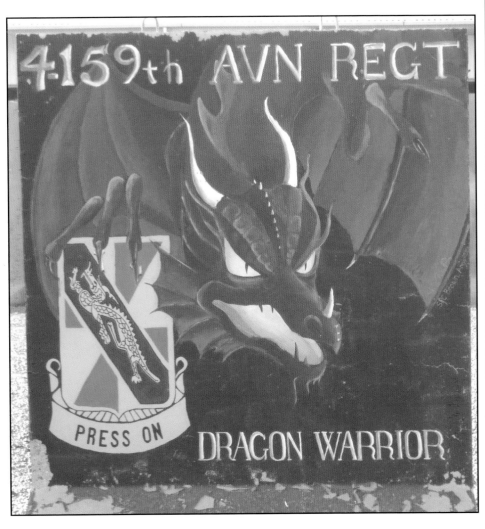

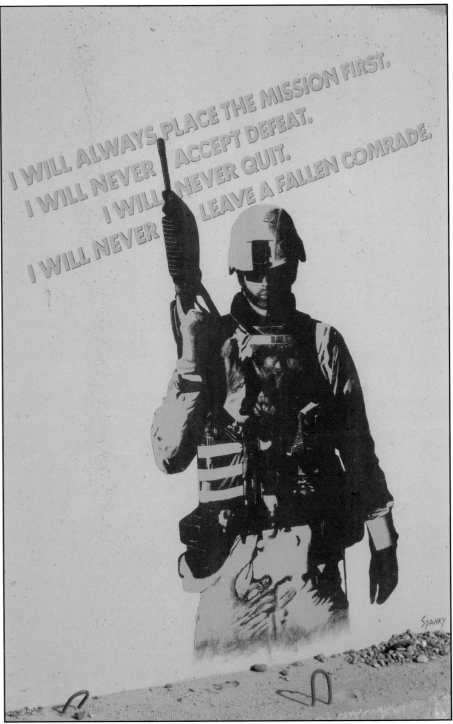

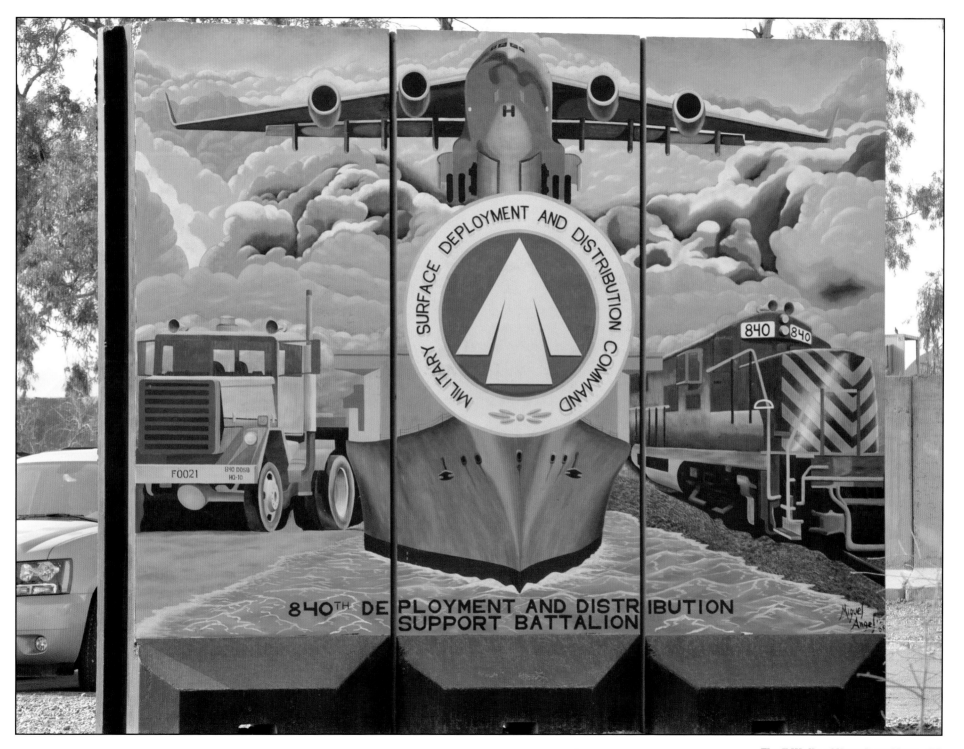

840TH DEPLOYMENT AND DISTRIBUTION SUPPORT BATTALION

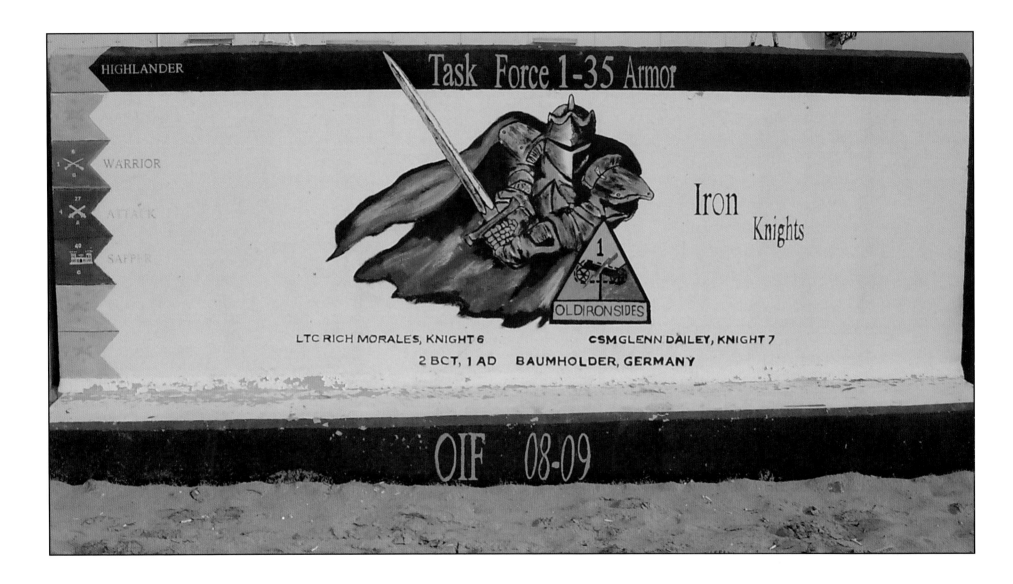

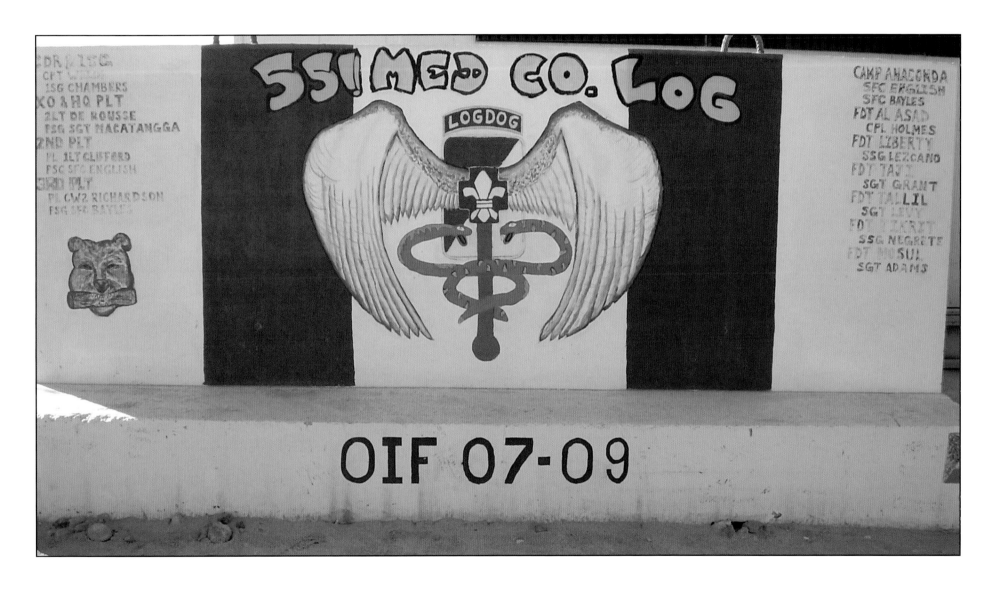

551 MED CO. LOG

LOGDOG

OIF 07-09

CDR/1SG
CPT WILSON
1SG CHAMBERS
XO & HQ PLT
2LT DE ROUSSE
FSG SGT MACATANGGA
2ND PLT
PL 1LT CLIFFORD
FSG SFC ENGLISH
3RD PLT
PL CW2 RICHARDSON
FSG SFC BAYLES

CAMP ANACONDA
SFC ENGLISH
SFC BAYLES
FOT AL ASAD
CPL HOLMES
FOT LIBERTY
SSG LEZCANO
FOT TAJI
SGT GRANT
FOT TALLIL
SGT LEVY
FOT TIKRIT
SSG NEGRETE
FOT MOSUL
SGT ADAMS

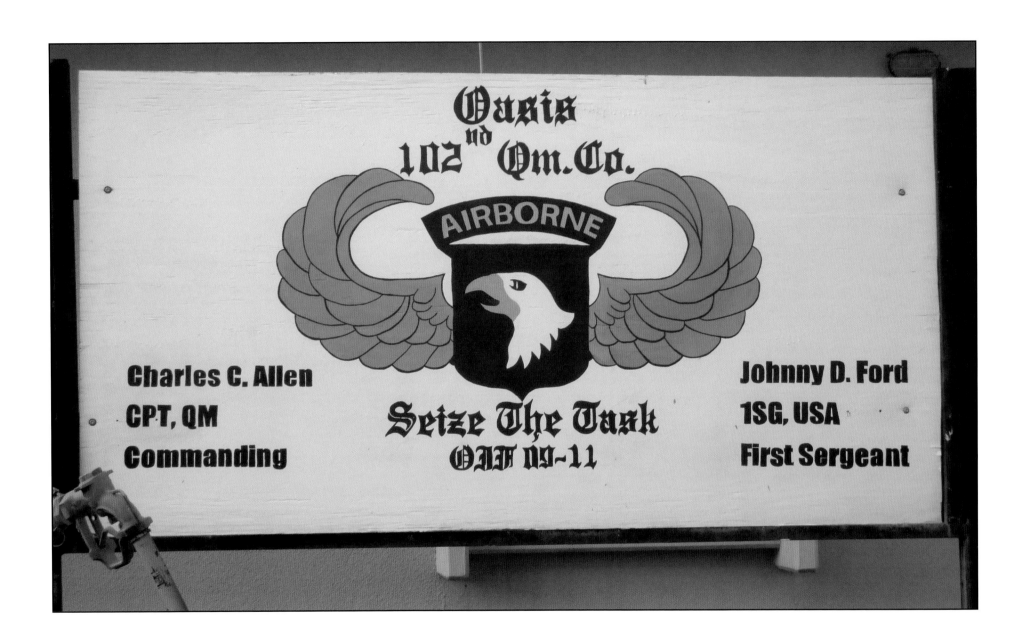

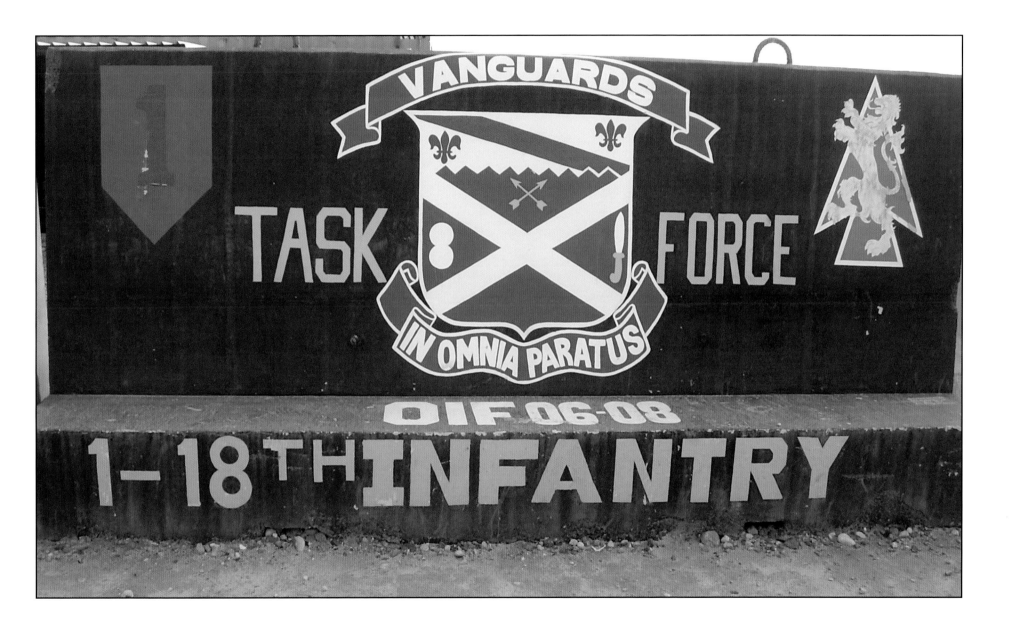

VANGUARDS

TASK FORCE

IN OMNIA PARATUS

OIF 06-08

1-18TH INFANTRY

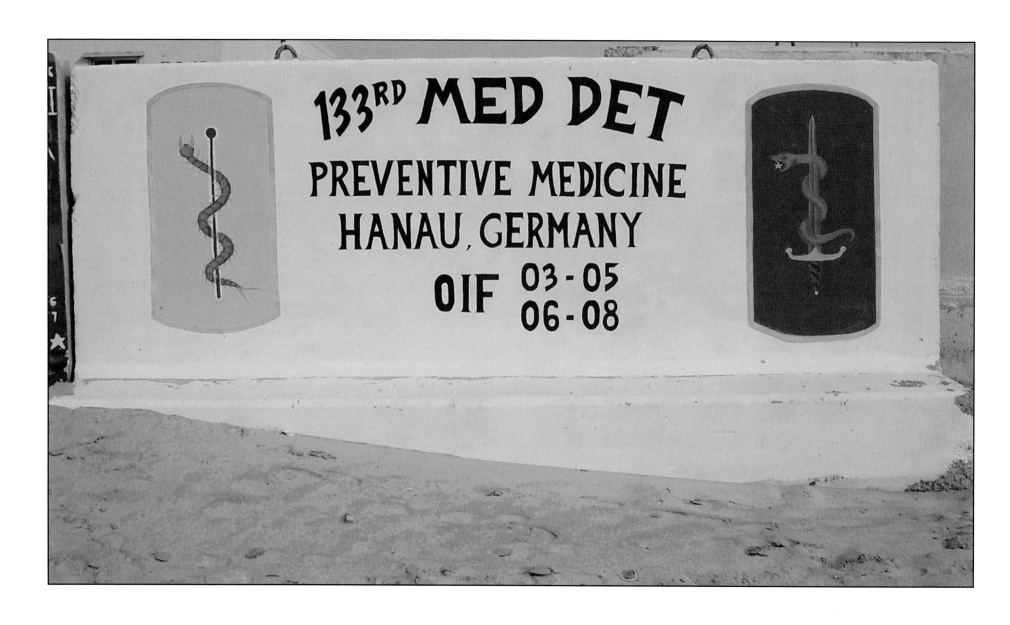

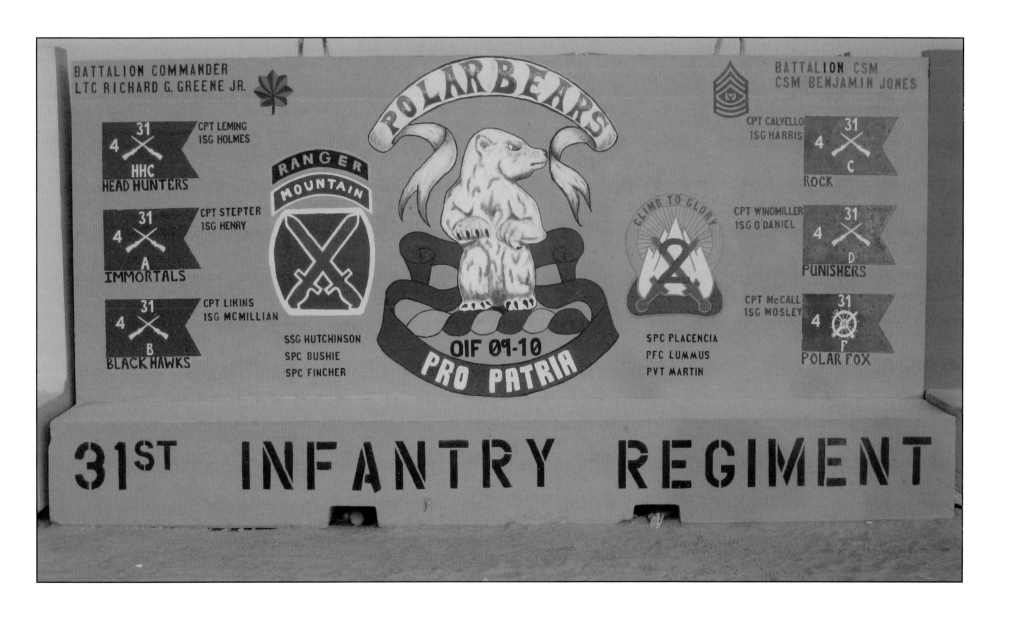

BATTALION COMMANDER
LTC RICHARD G. GREENE JR.

BATTALION CSM
CSM BENJAMIN JONES

POLAR BEARS

RANGER
MOUNTAIN

CLIMB TO GLORY

OIF 09-10
PRO PATRIA

4 31
HHC
HEAD HUNTERS

CPT LEMING
1SG HOLMES

4 31
A
IMMORTALS

CPT STEPTER
1SG HENRY

4 31
B
BLACK HAWKS

CPT LIKINS
1SG MCMILLIAN

SSG HUTCHINSON
SPC BUSHIE
SPC FINCHER

SPC PLACENCIA
PFC LUMMUS
PVT MARTIN

CPT CALVELLO
1SG HARRIS

4 31
C
ROCK

CPT WINDMILLER
1SG O DANIEL

4 31
D
PUNISHERS

CPT McCALL
1SG MOSLEY

4 31
F
POLAR FOX

31ST INFANTRY REGIMENT

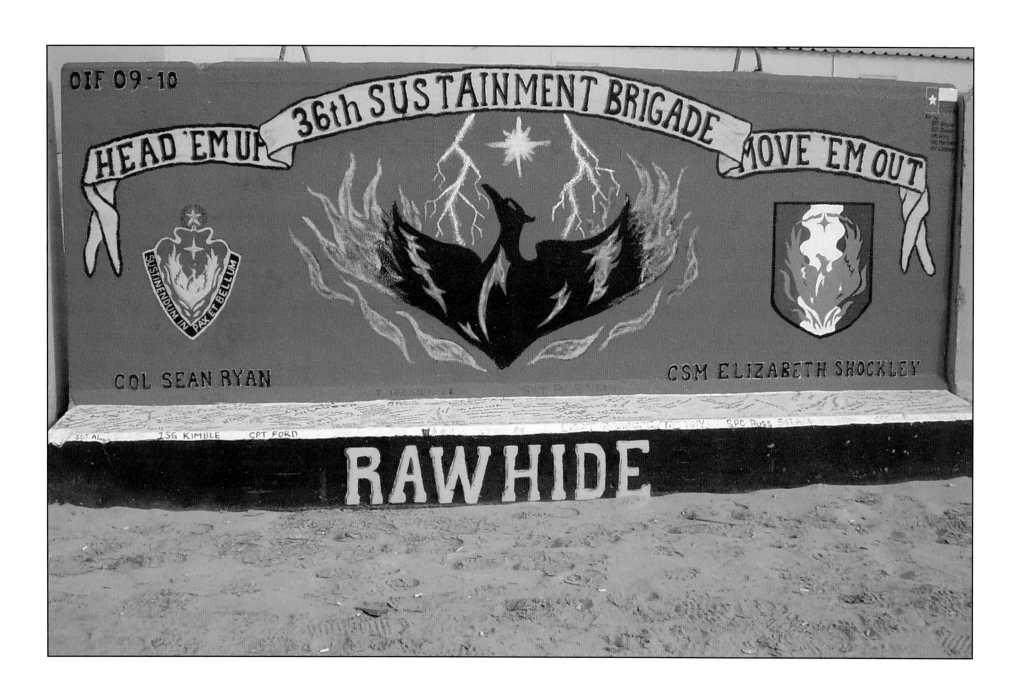

OIF 09-10

36th SUSTAINMENT BRIGADE

HEAD 'EM UP   MOVE 'EM OUT

SUSTINENDUM IN PAX ET BELLUM

COL SEAN RYAN   CSM ELIZABETH SHOCKLEY

1SG KIMBLE   CPT FORD

RAWHIDE

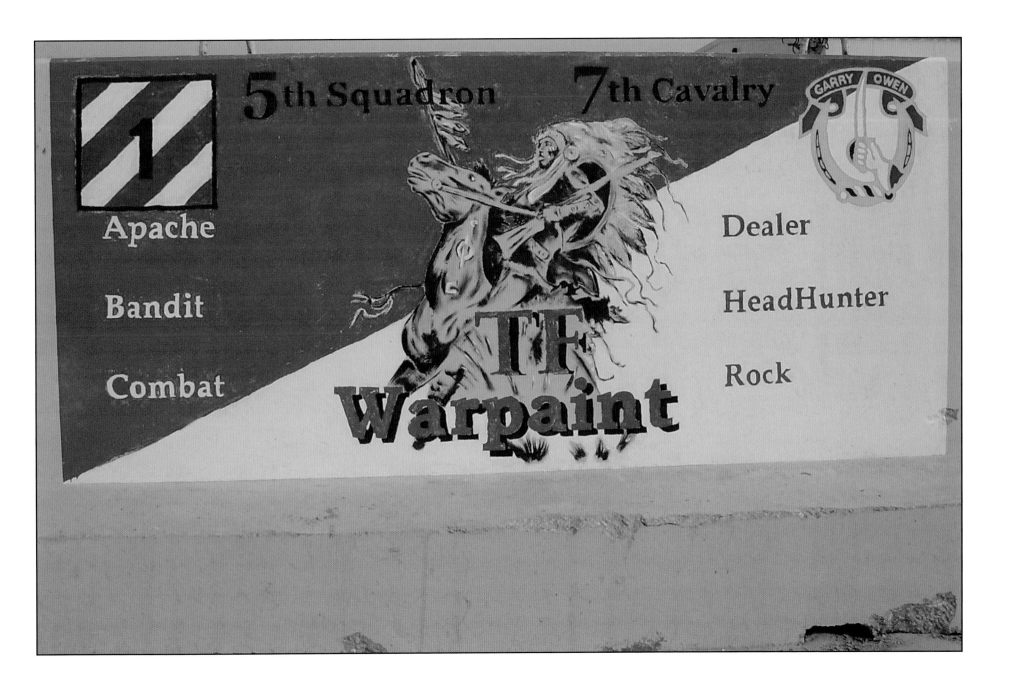

5th Squadron 7th Cavalry

Apache

Bandit

Combat

TF Warpaint

Dealer

HeadHunter

Rock

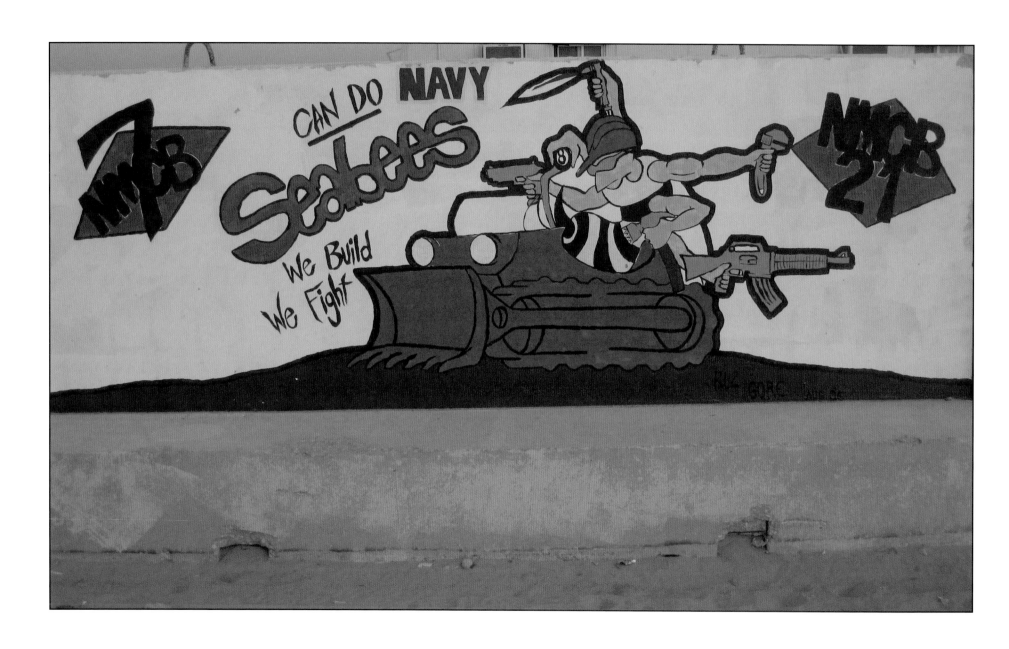

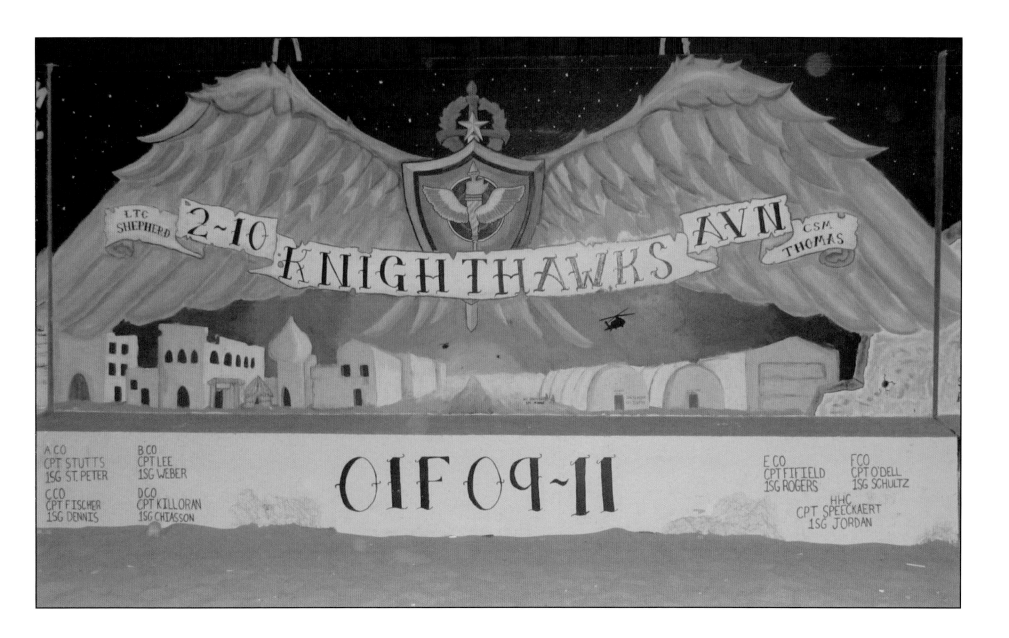

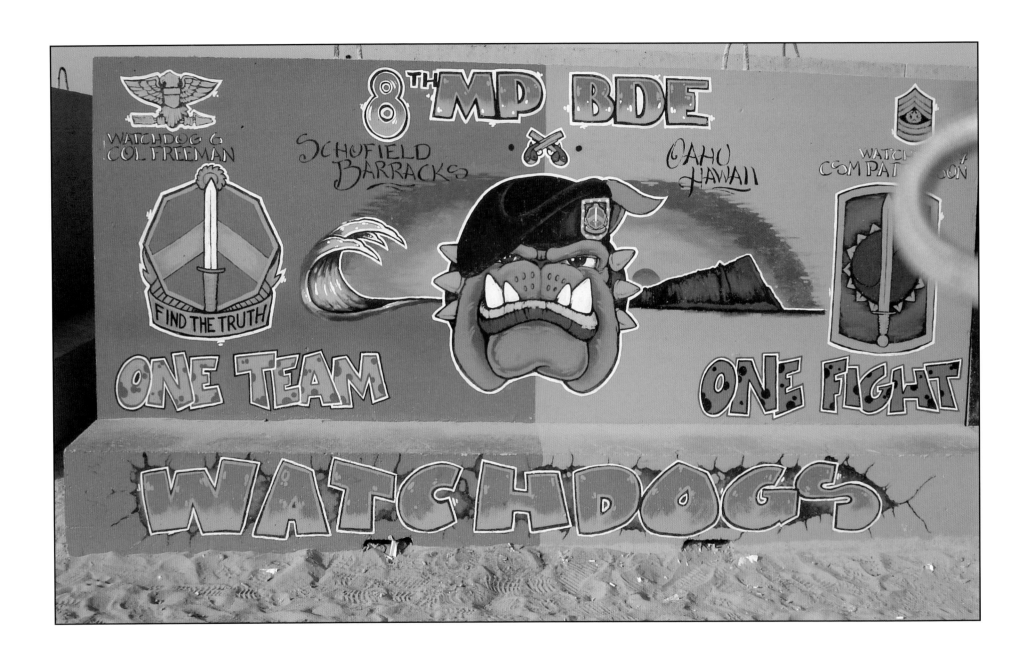

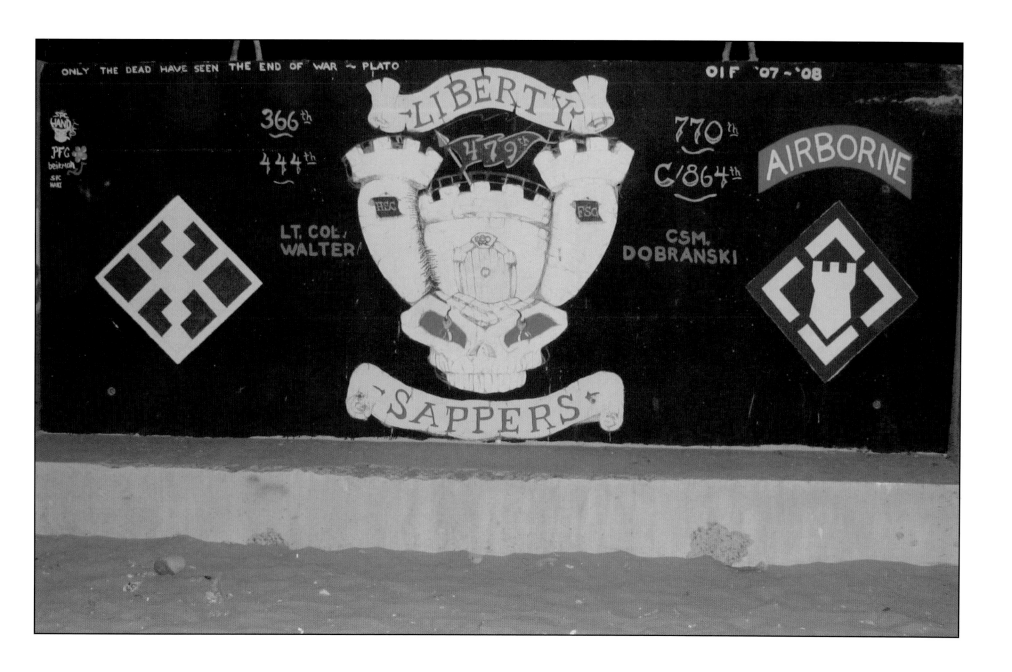

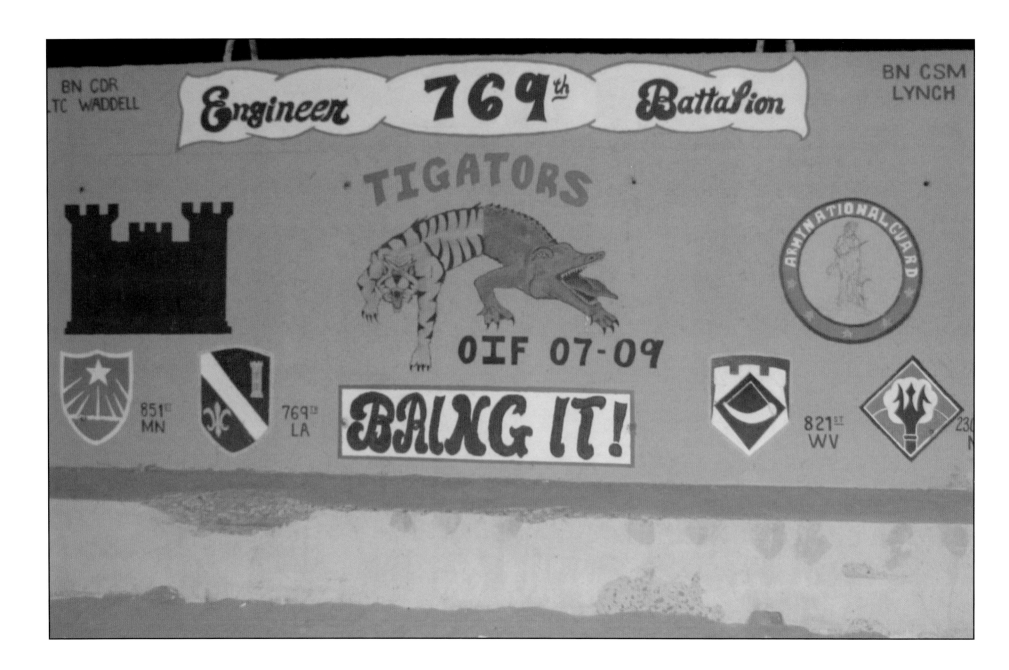

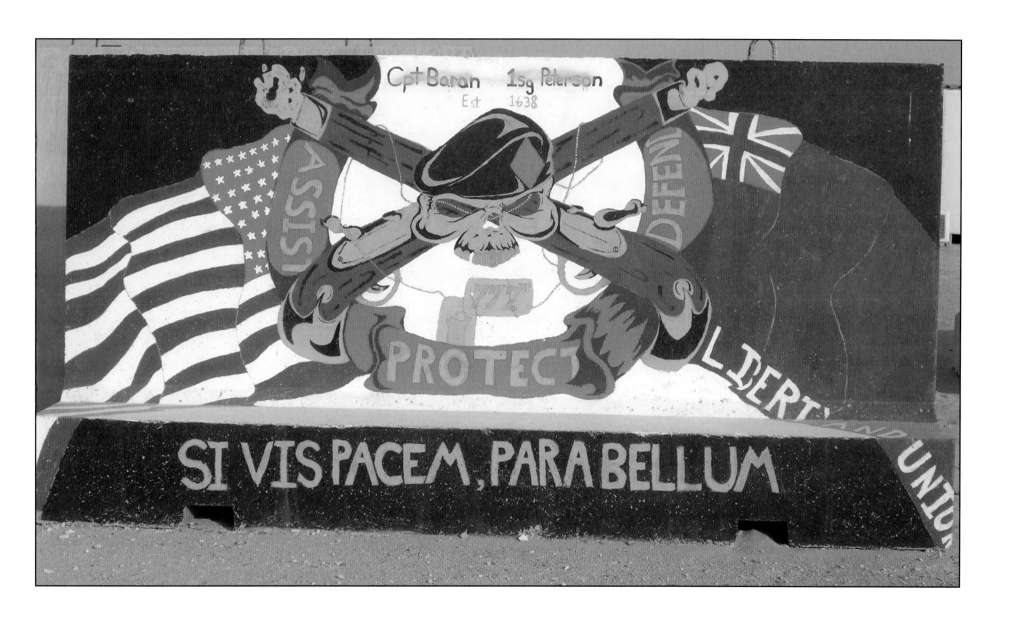

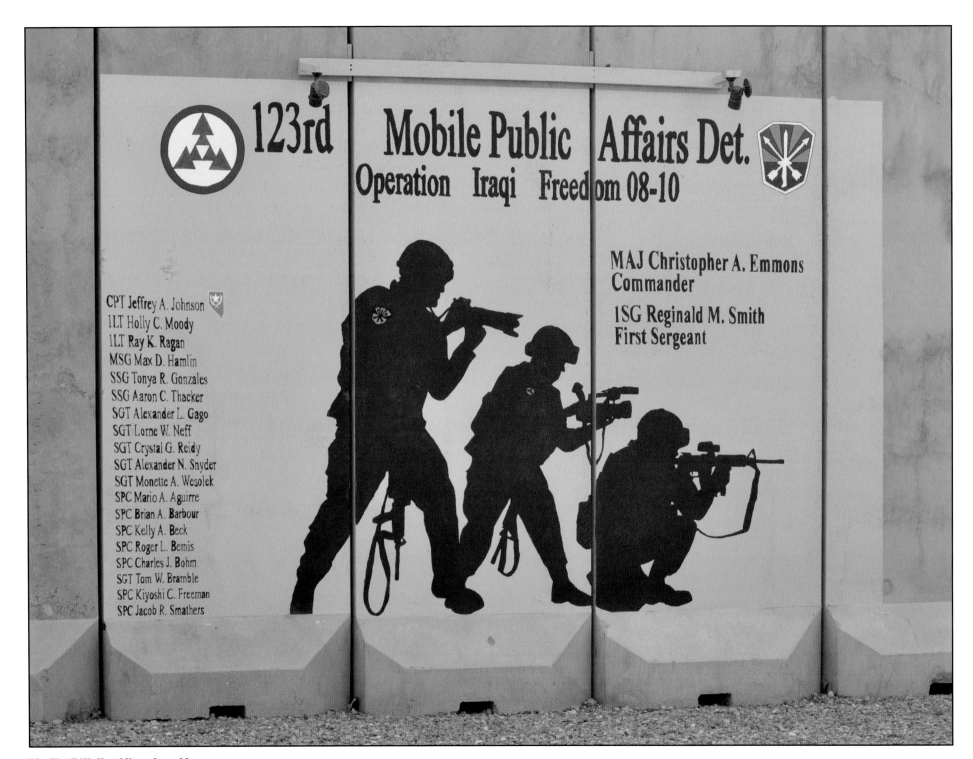

123rd Mobile Public Affairs Det.
Operation Iraqi Freedom 08-10

CPT Jeffrey A. Johnson
1LT Holly C. Moody
1LT Ray K. Ragan
MSG Max D. Hamlin
SSG Tonya R. Gonzales
SSG Aaron C. Thacker
SGT Alexander L. Gago
SGT Lorne W. Neff
SGT Crystal G. Reidy
SGT Alexander N. Snyder
SGT Monette A. Wesolek
SPC Mario A. Aguirre
SPC Brian A. Barbour
SPC Kelly A. Beck
SPC Roger L. Bemis
SPC Charles J. Bohm
SGT Tom W. Bramble
SPC Kiyoshi C. Freeman
SPC Jacob R. Smathers

MAJ Christopher A. Emmons
Commander

1SG Reginald M. Smith
First Sergeant

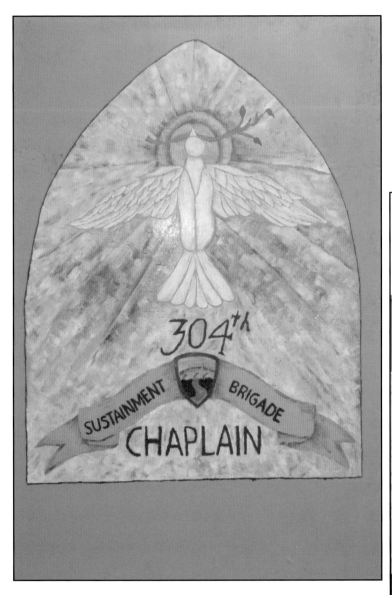

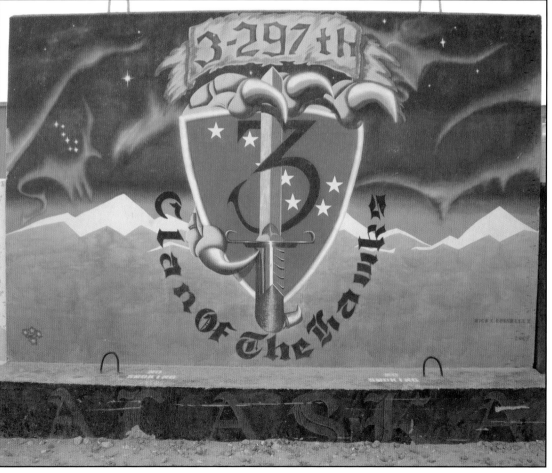

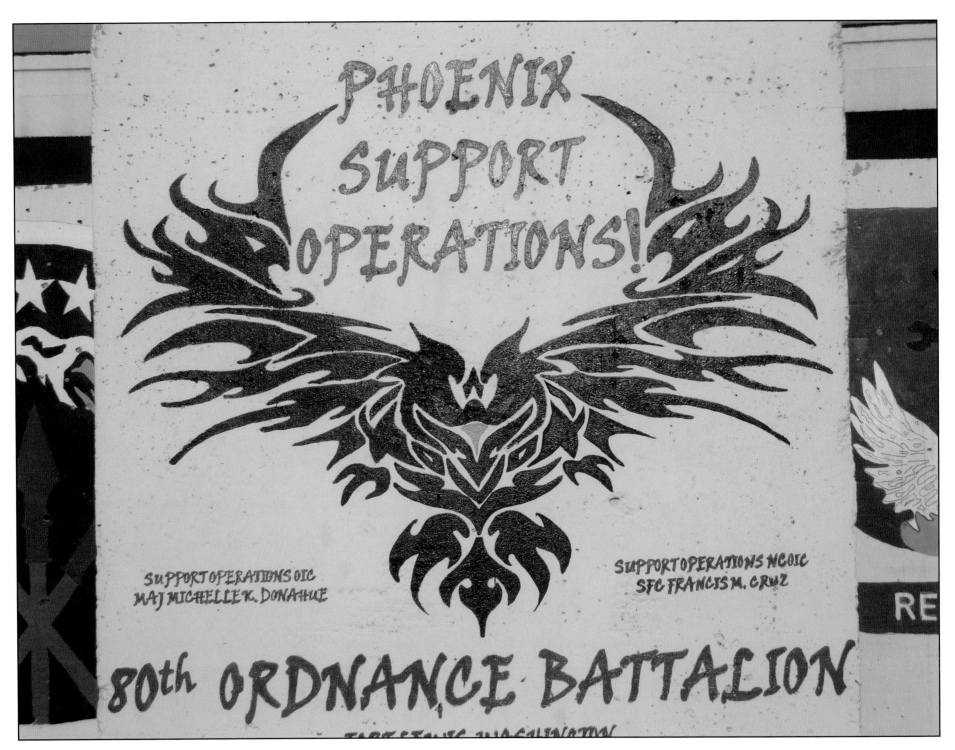

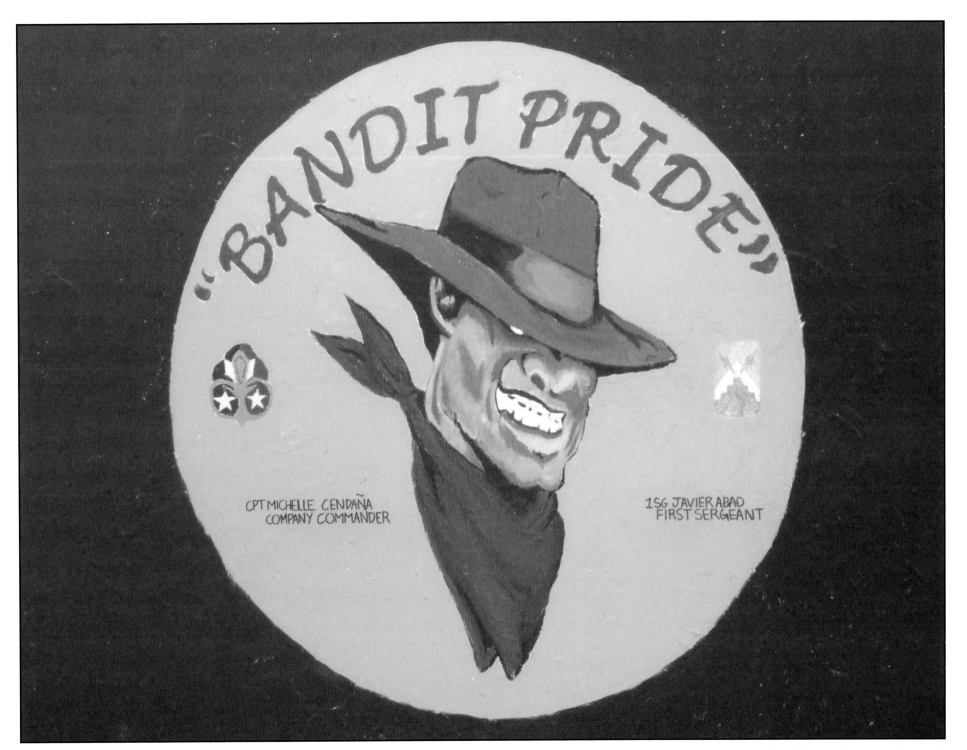

"BANDIT PRIDE"

CPT MICHELLE CENDAÑA
COMPANY COMMANDER

1SG JAVIER ABAD
FIRST SERGEANT

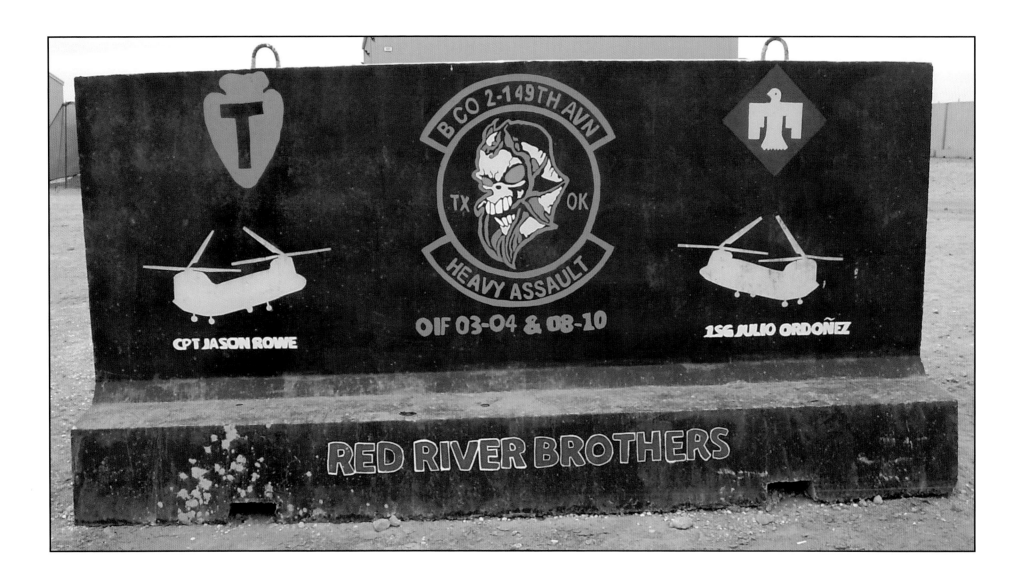

B CO 2-149TH AVN
TX OK
HEAVY ASSAULT
OIF 03-04 & 08-10

CPT JASON ROWE

1SG JULIO ORDOÑEZ

RED RIVER BROTHERS

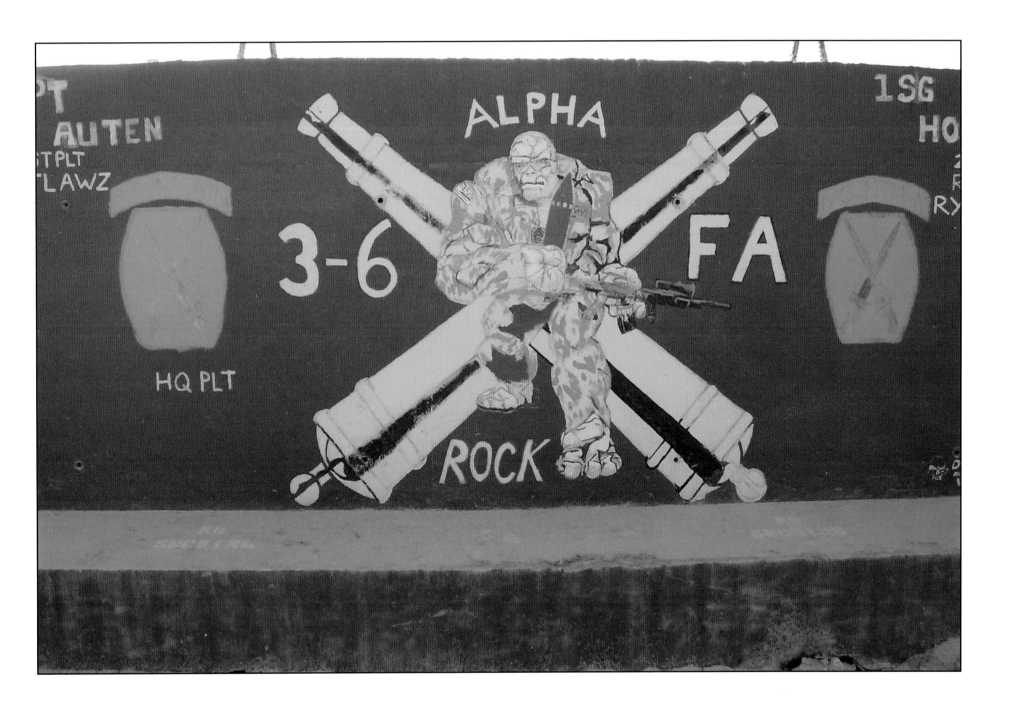

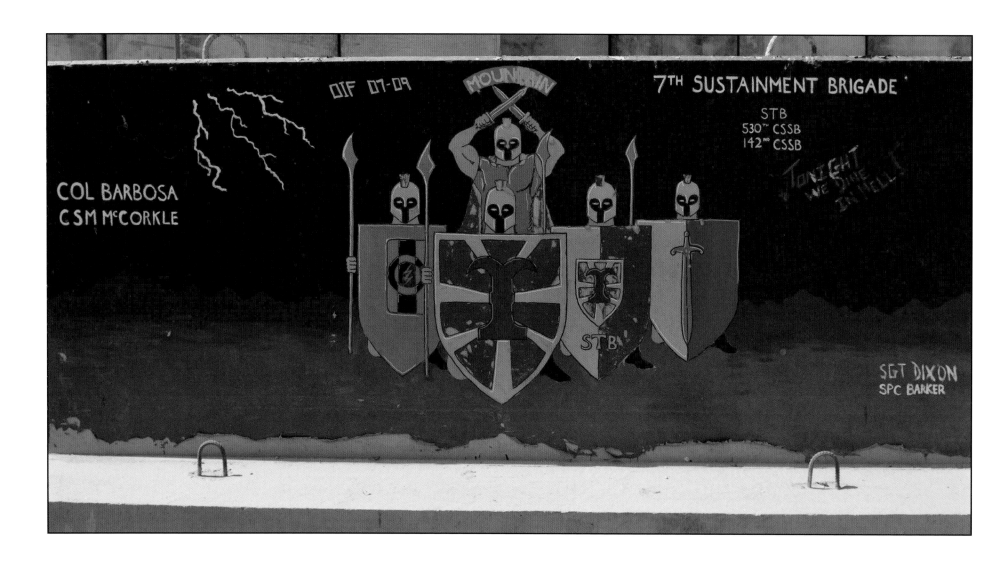

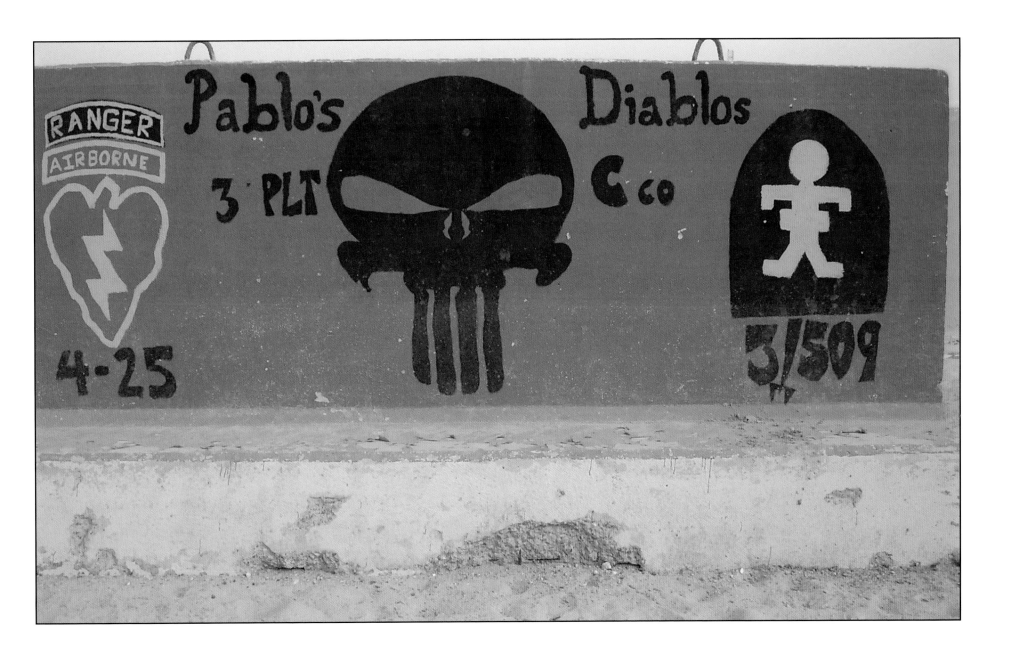

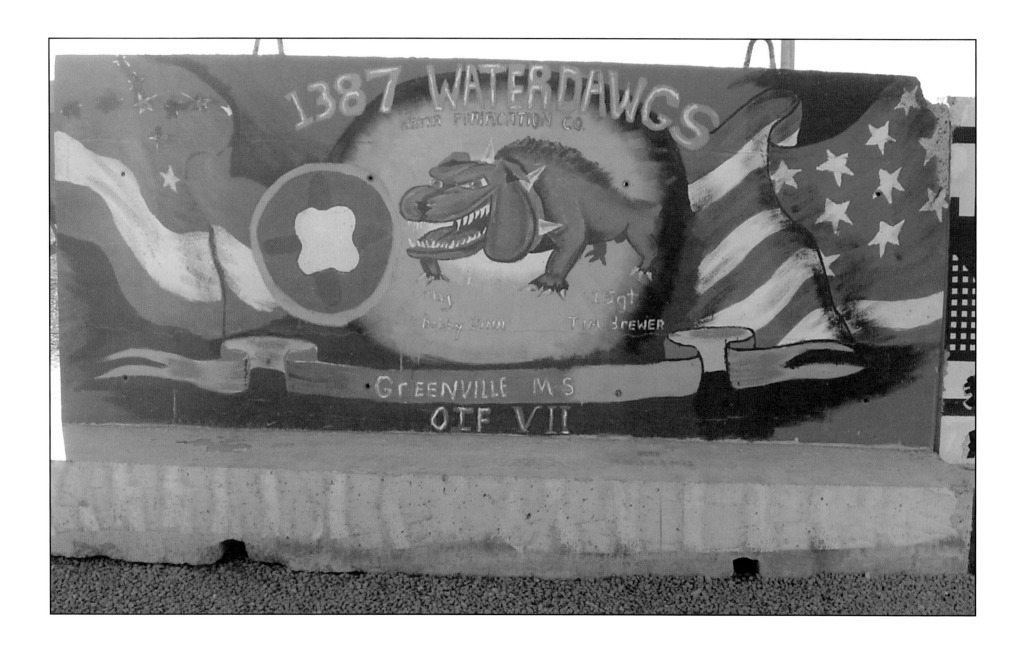

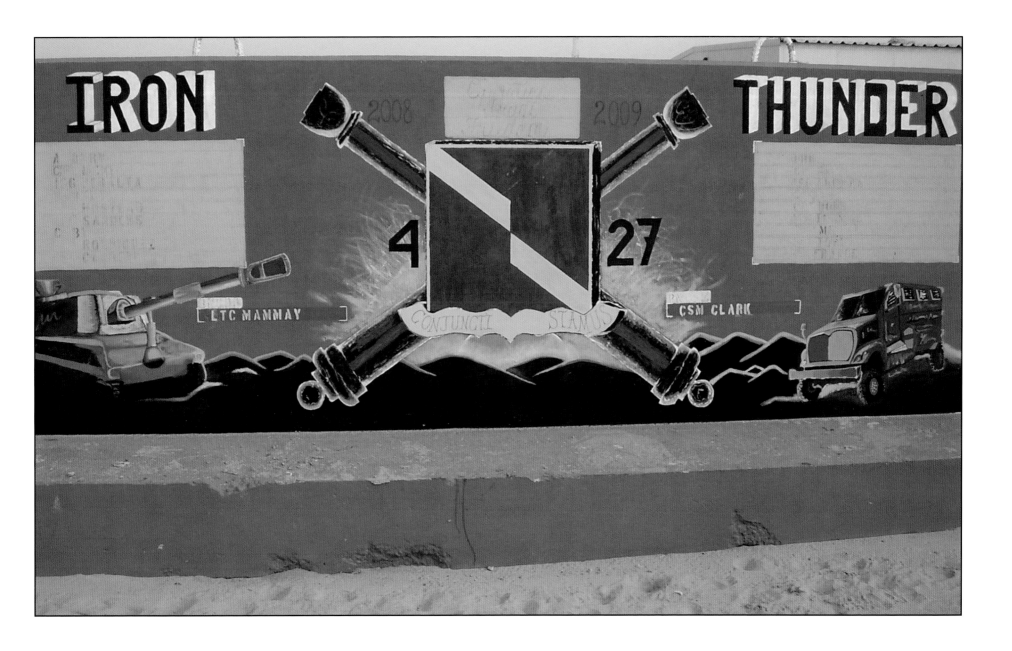

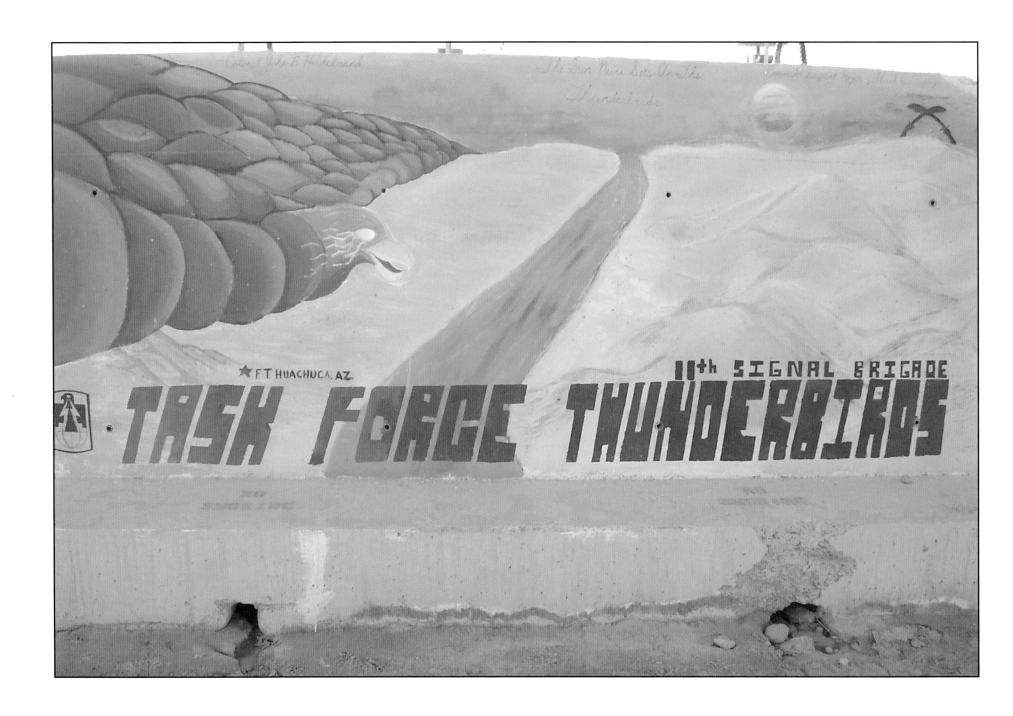

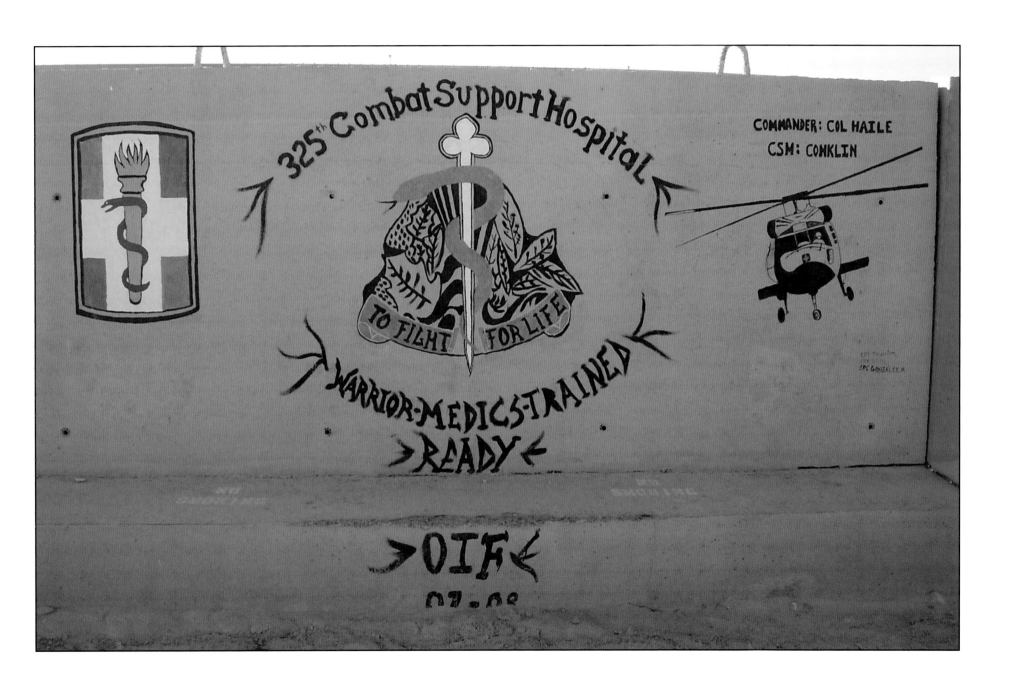

325ᵗʰ Combat Support Hospital

COMMANDER: COL HAILE
CSM: CONKLIN

TO FIGHT FOR LIFE

WARRIOR·MEDICS·TRAINED

READY

OIF

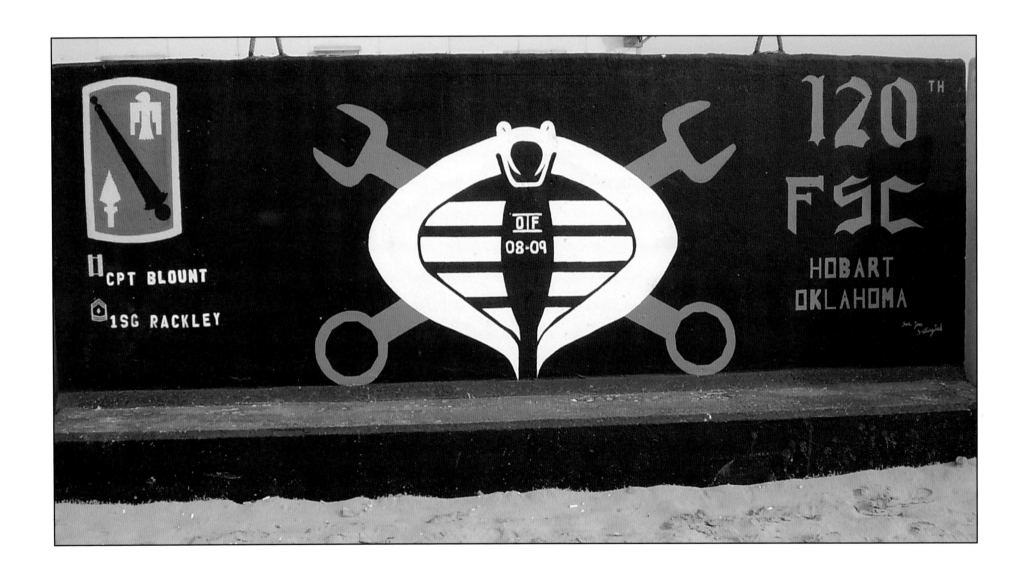

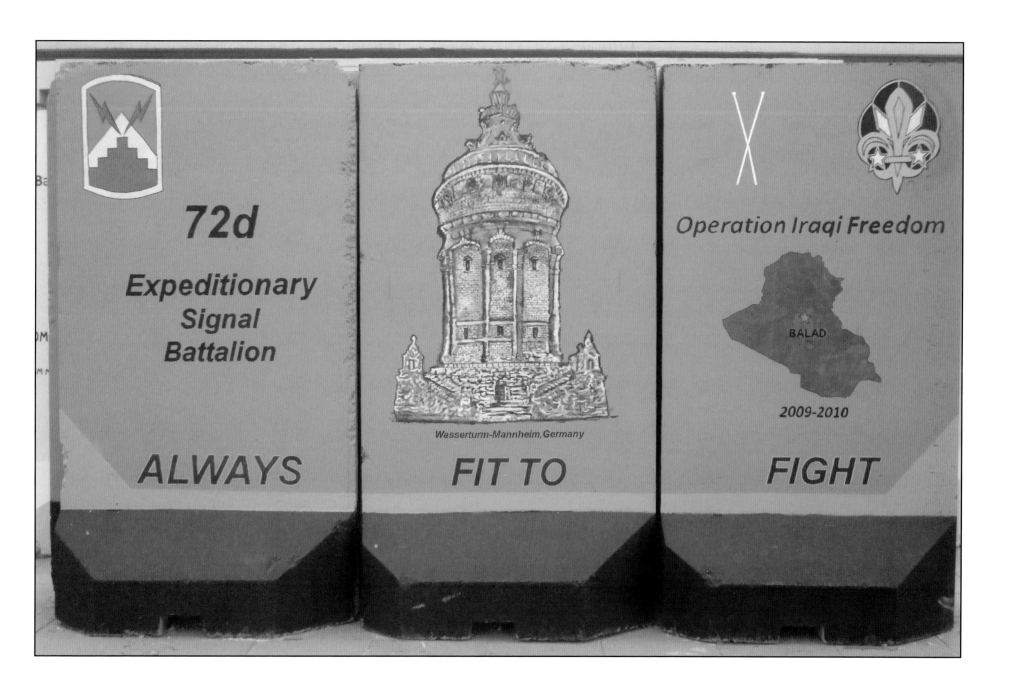

72d Expeditionary Signal Battalion

ALWAYS

Wasserturm-Mannheim, Germany

FIT TO

Operation Iraqi Freedom

BALAD

2009-2010

FIGHT

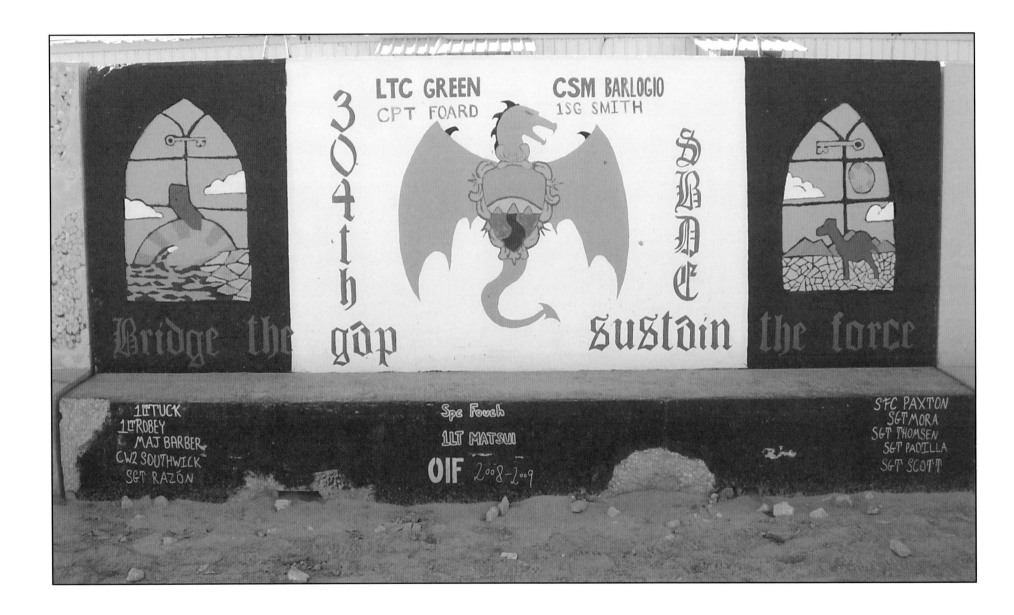

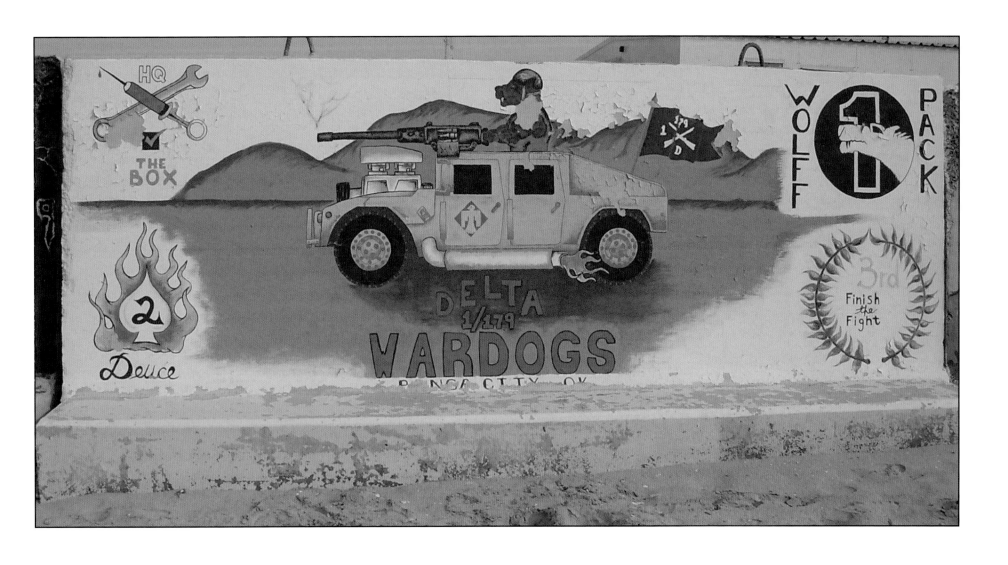

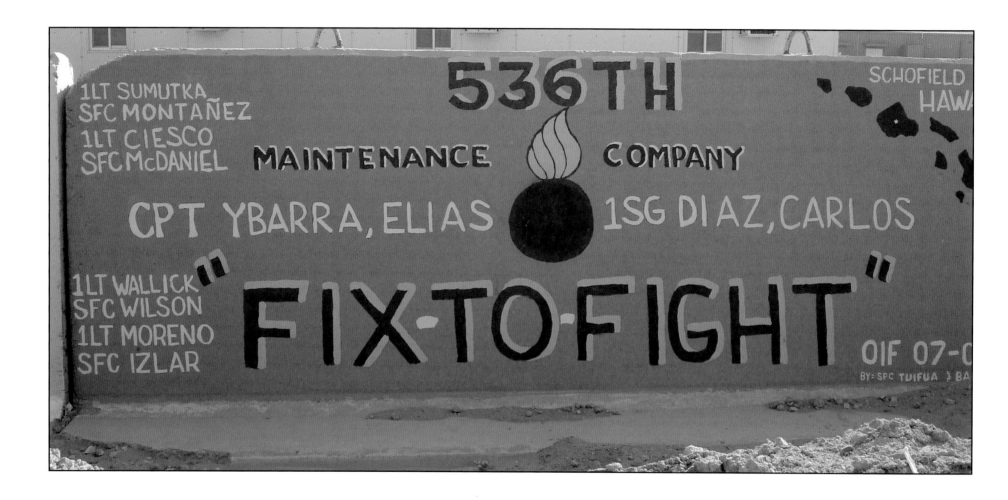

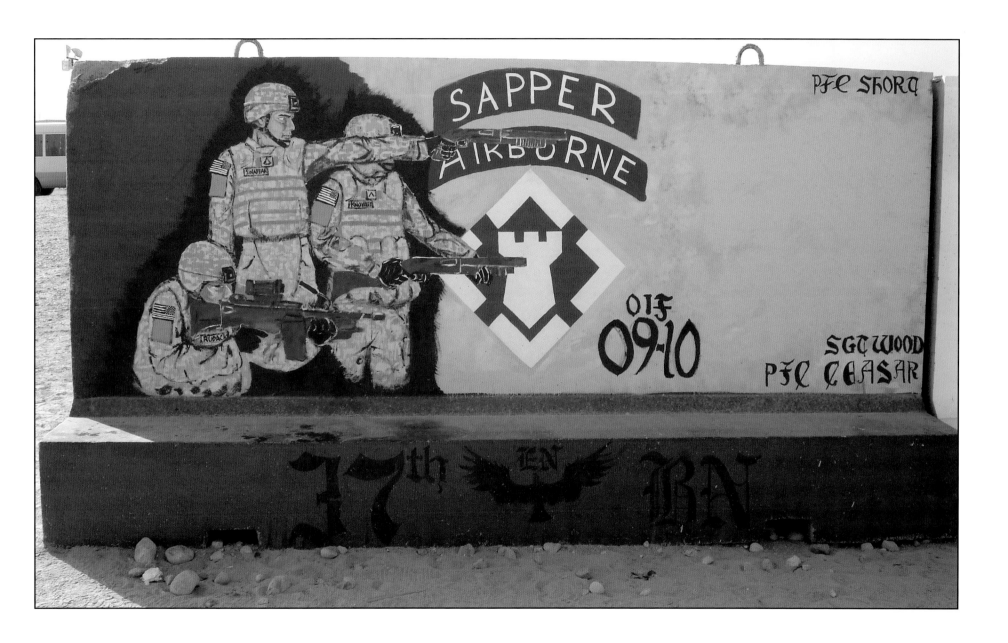

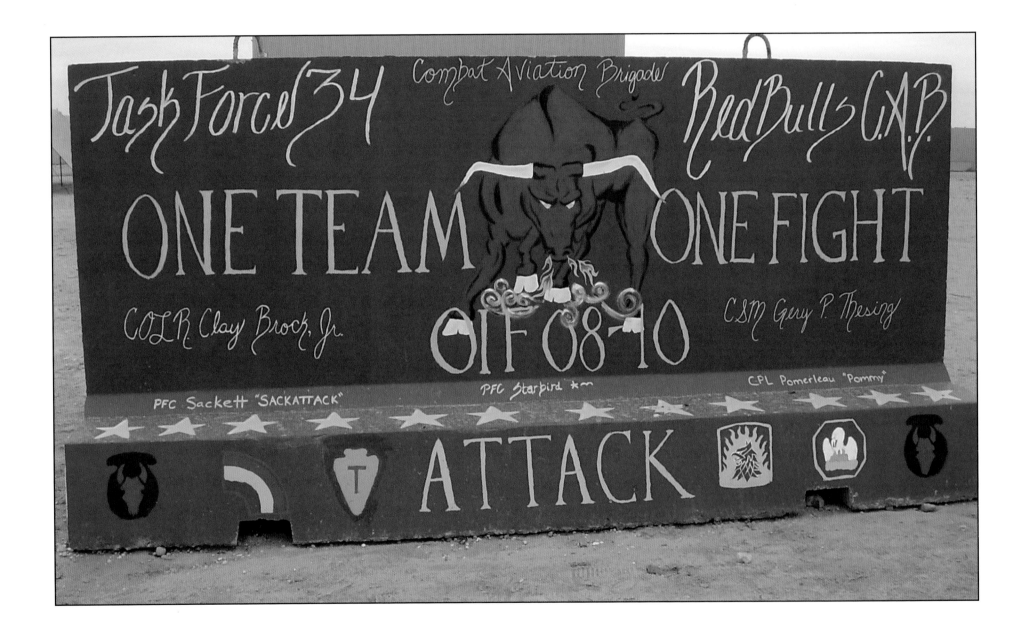

Task Force 34 Combat Aviation Brigade Red Bulls C.A.B.

ONE TEAM ONE FIGHT

COL R. Clay Brock, Jr. OIF 08-10 CSM Gary P. Thesing

PFC Sackett "SACKATTACK" PFC Starbird *m CPL Pomerleau "Pommy"

ATTACK

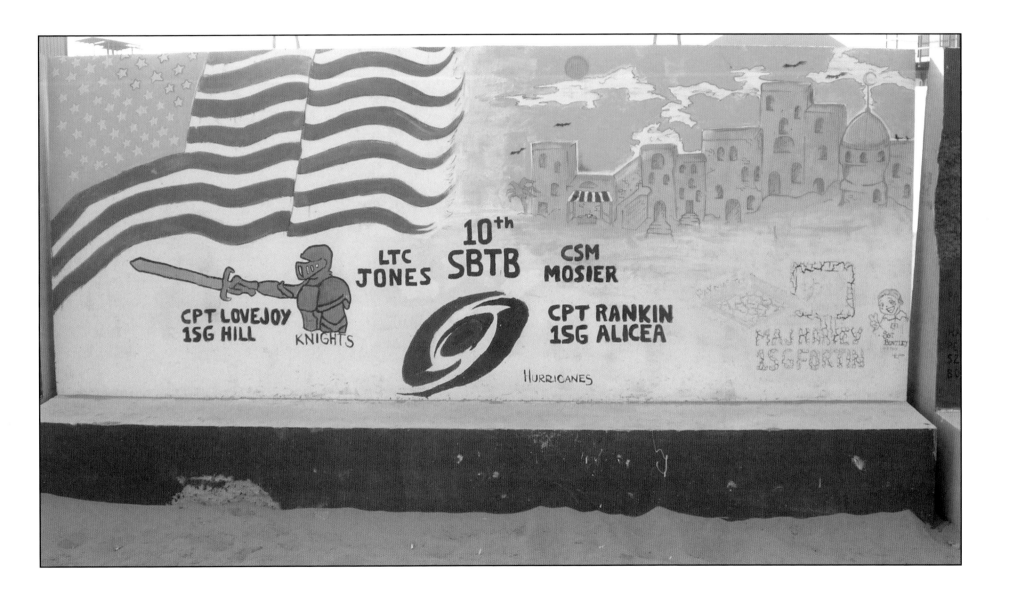

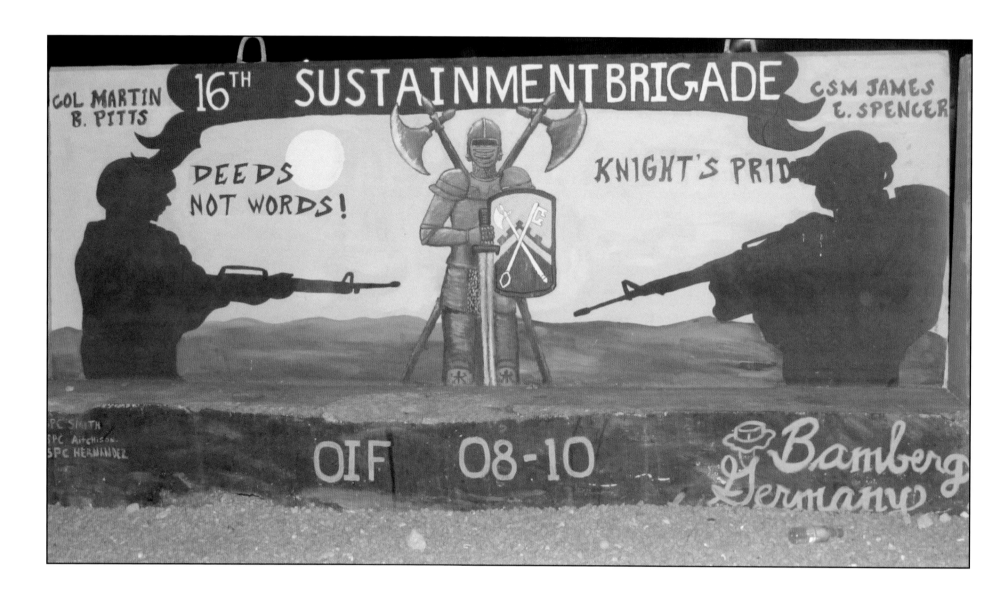

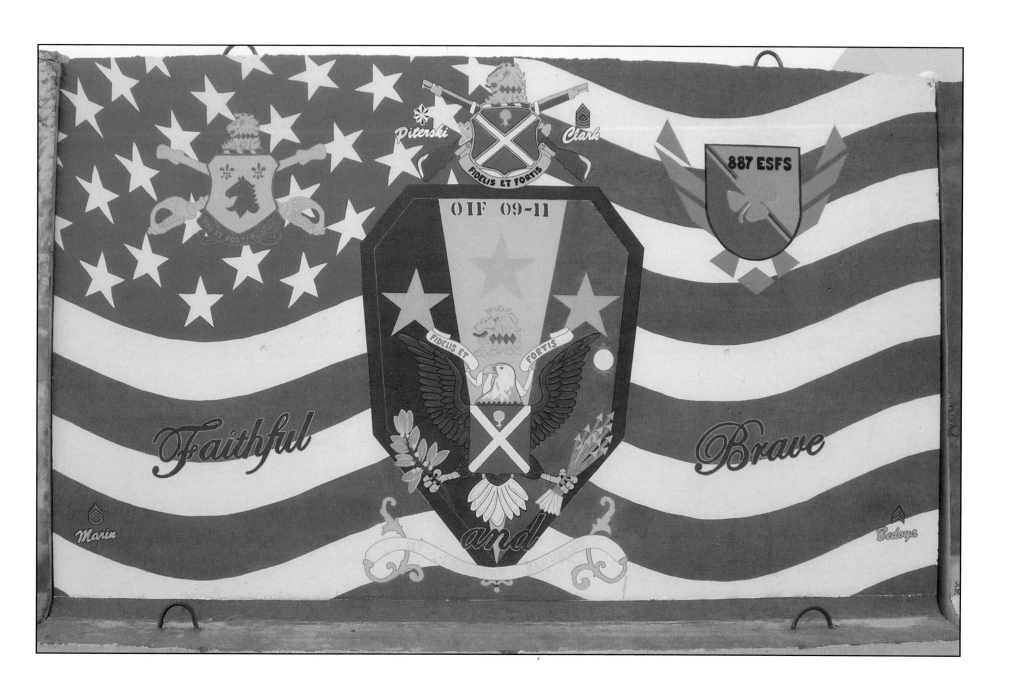

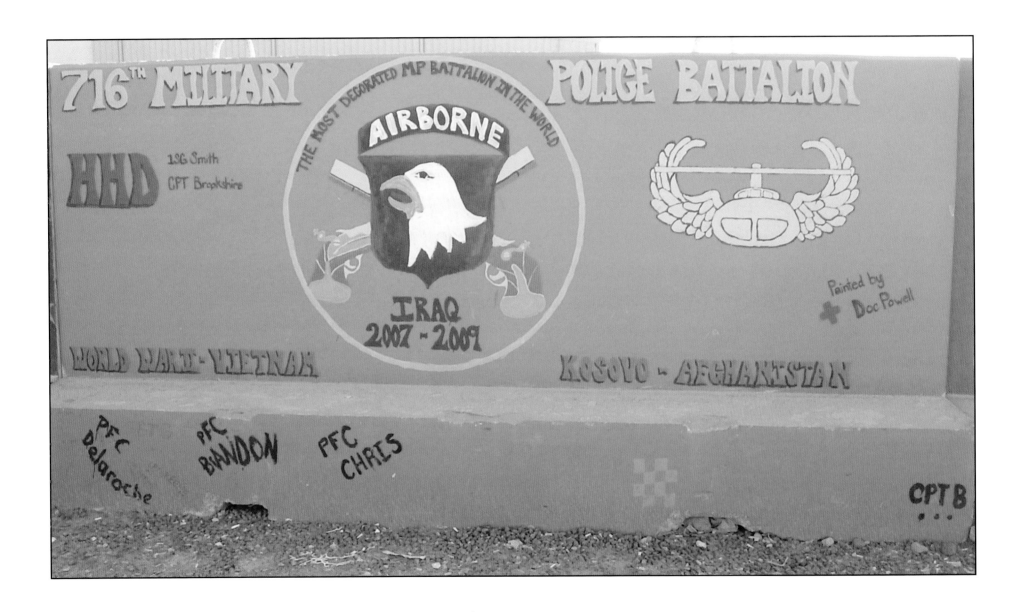

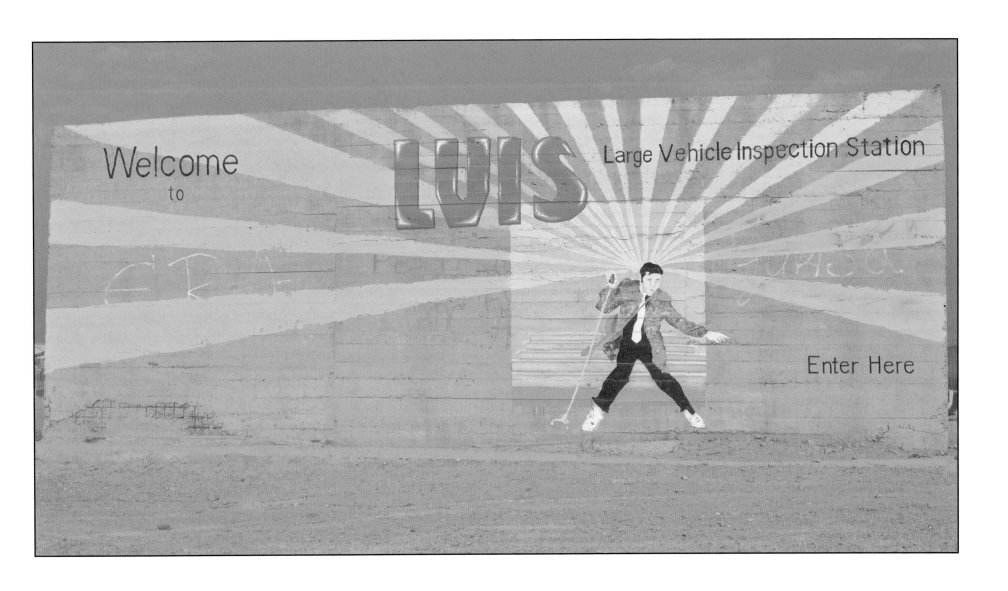

Welcome to **LVIS** Large Vehicle Inspection Station

Enter Here

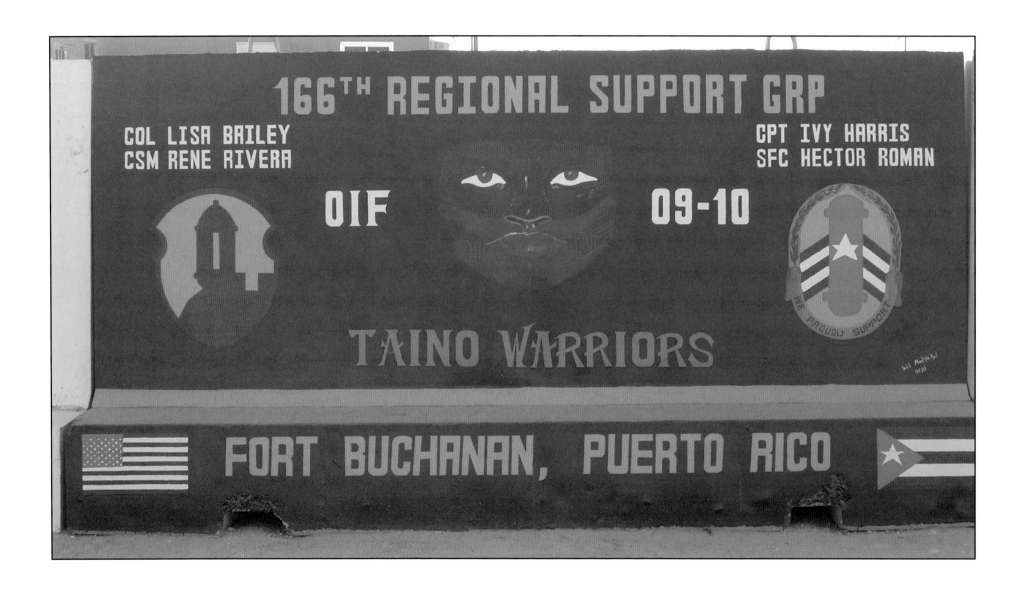

166TH REGIONAL SUPPORT GRP

COL LISA BAILEY
CSM RENE RIVERA

CPT IVY HARRIS
SFC HECTOR ROMAN

OIF

09-10

TAINO WARRIORS

FORT BUCHANAN, PUERTO RICO

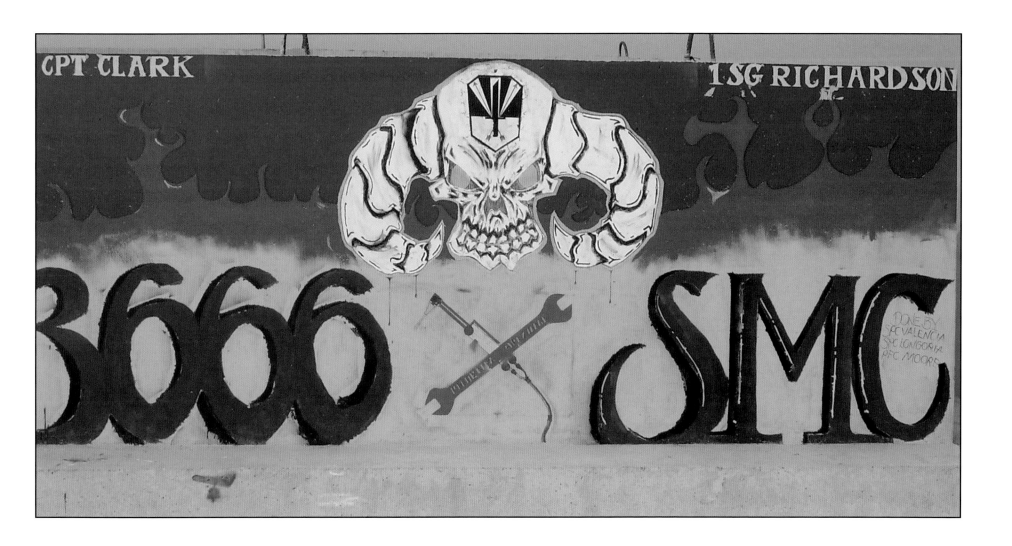

CPT CLARK

1SG RICHARDSON

3666

SMC

DONE BY
SPC VALENCIA
SPC LONGORIA
PFC MOORE

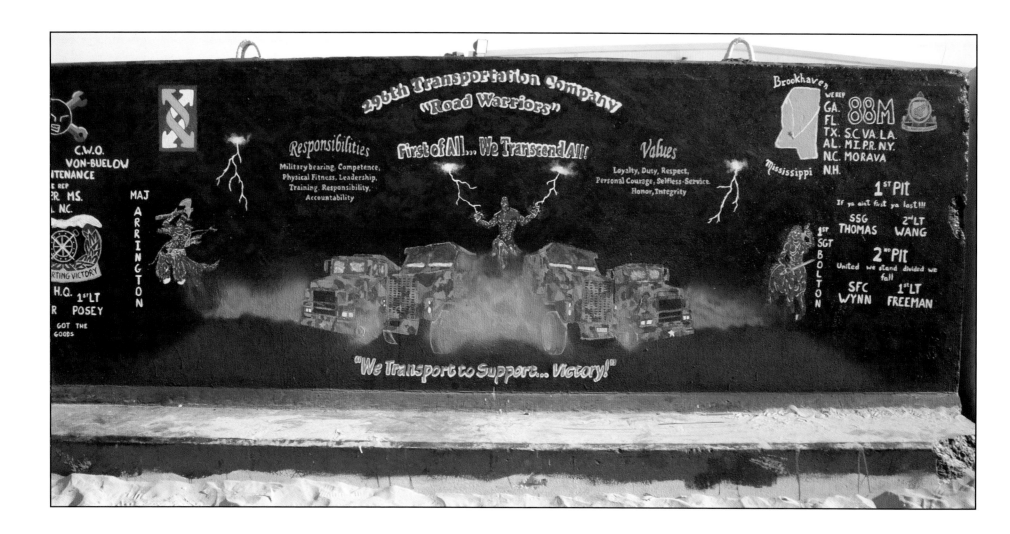

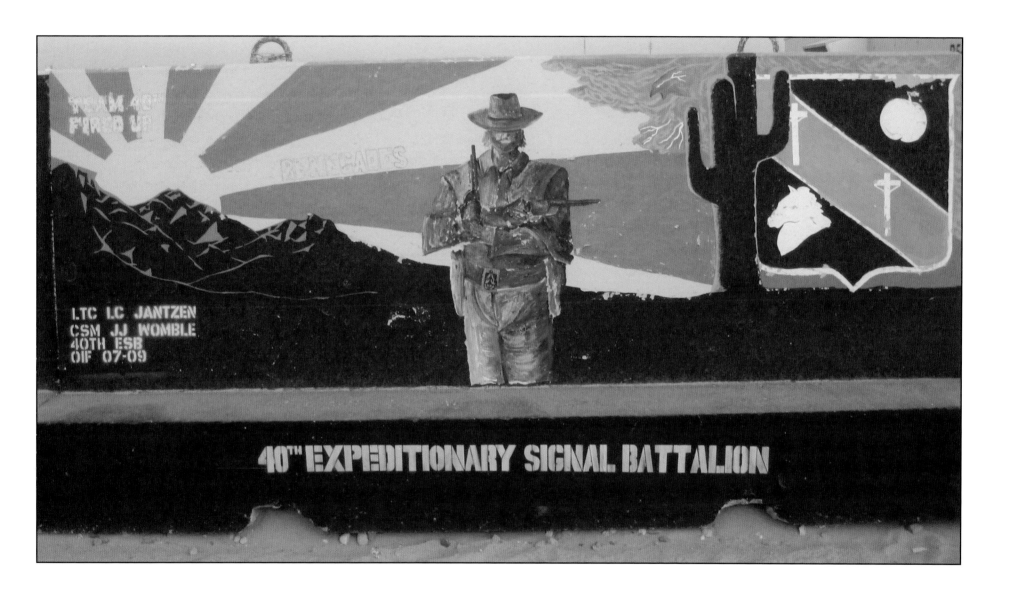

TEAM 40
FIRED UP

RENEGADES

LTC LC JANTZEN
CSM JJ WOMBLE
40TH ESB
OIF 07-09

40TH EXPEDITIONARY SIGNAL BATTALION

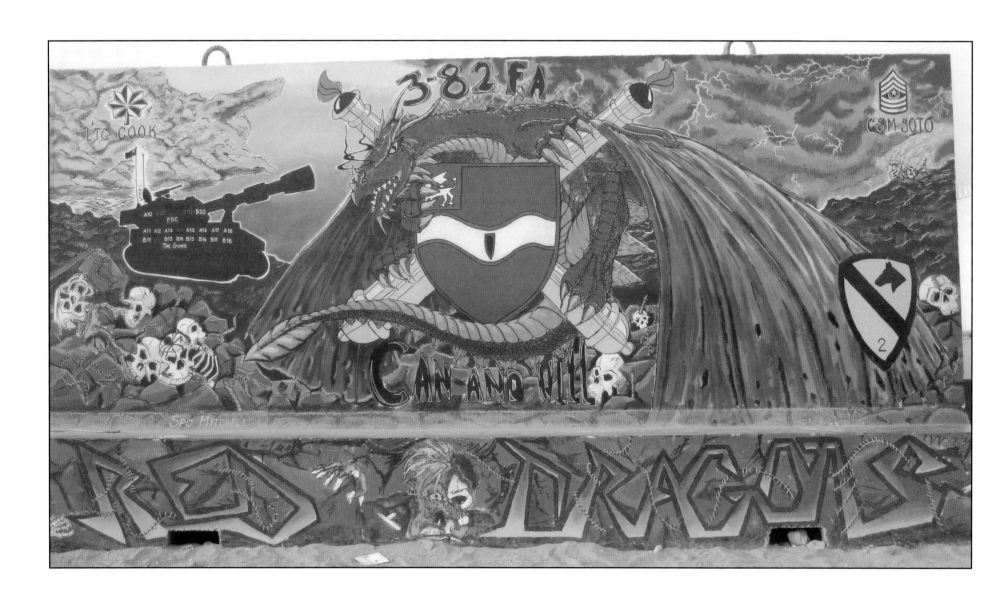

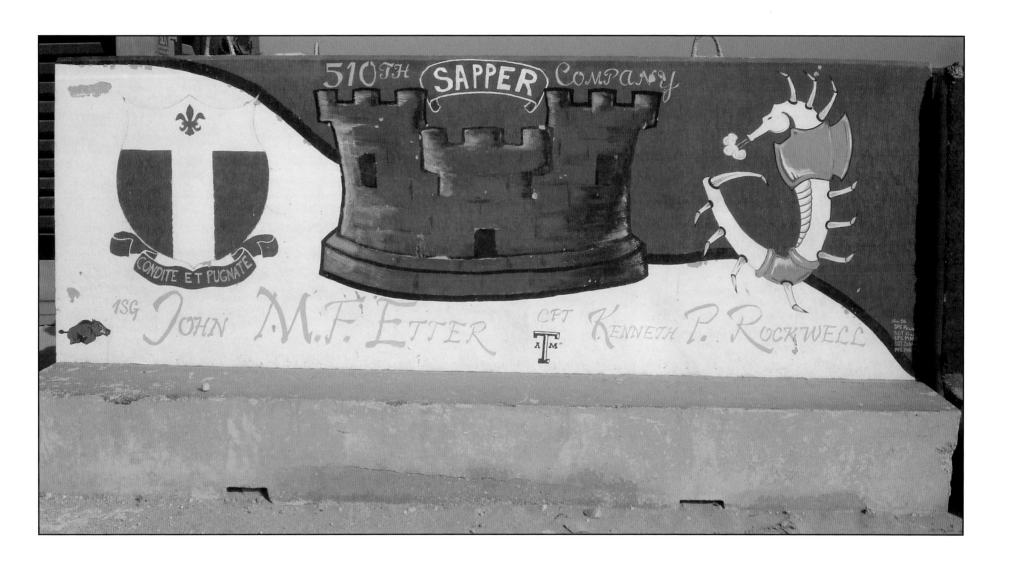

510TH SAPPER COMPANY

CONDITE ET PUGNATE

1SG JOHN M.F. ETTER   CPT KENNETH P. ROCKWELL

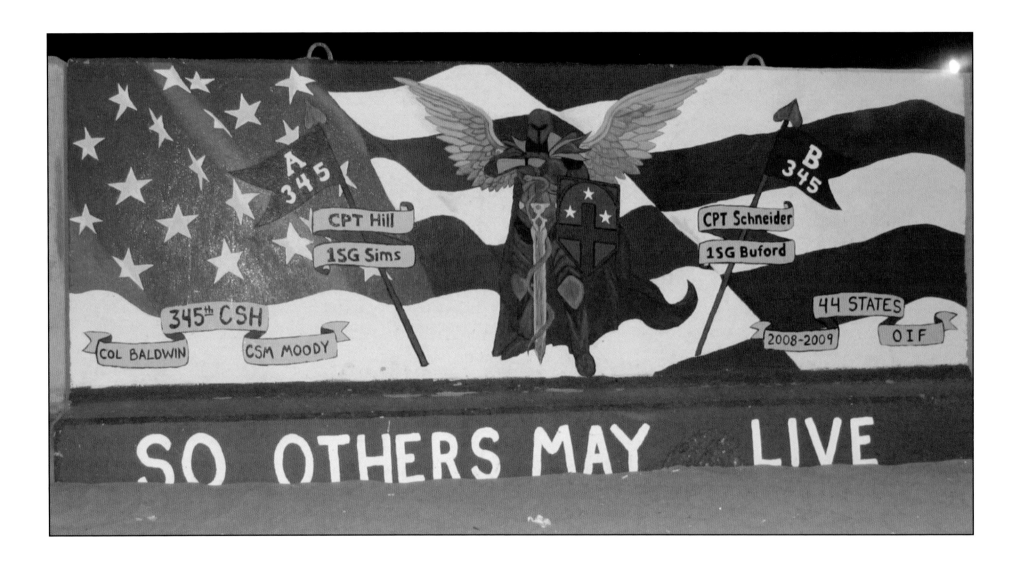

SO OTHERS MAY LIVE

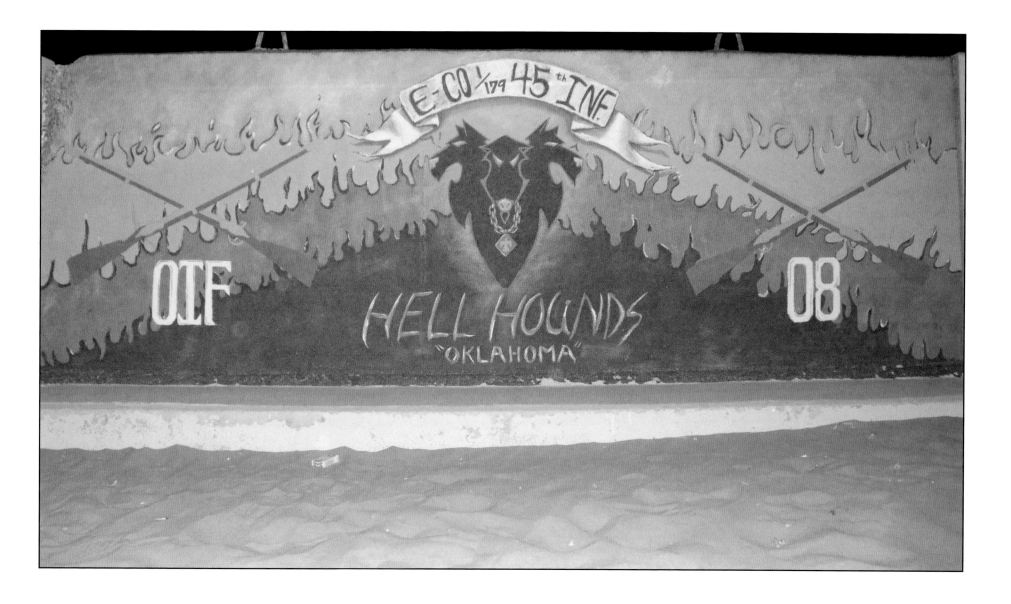

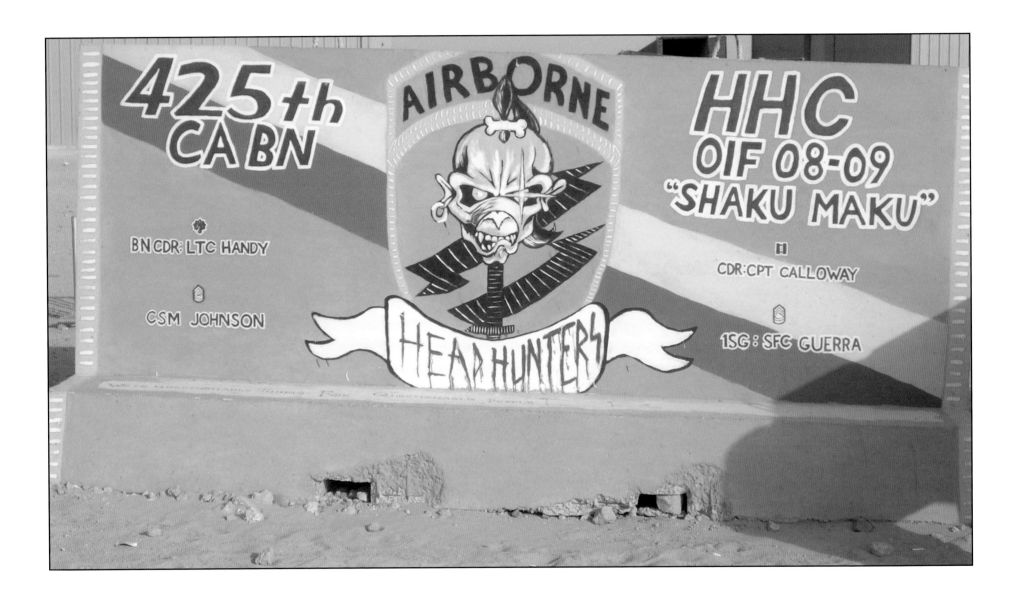

425th CA BN

BN CDR: LTC HANDY

CSM JOHNSON

AIRBORNE

HEAD HUNTERS

HHC
OIF 08-09
"SHAKU MAKU"

CDR: CPT CALLOWAY

1SG: SFC GUERRA

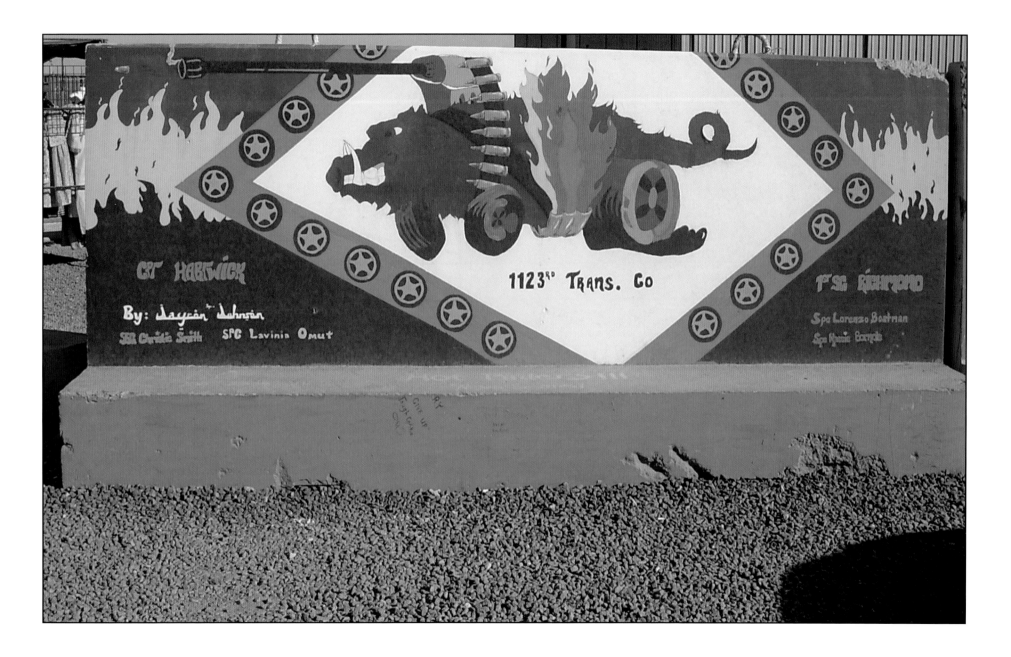

CPT HARTWICK

By: Jayson Johnson

SGT Christie Smith   SPC Lavinia Omut

1123ᴿᴰ TRANS. CO

FSG RICHMOND

Spc Lorenzo Boatman

Spc Rosie Baryeh

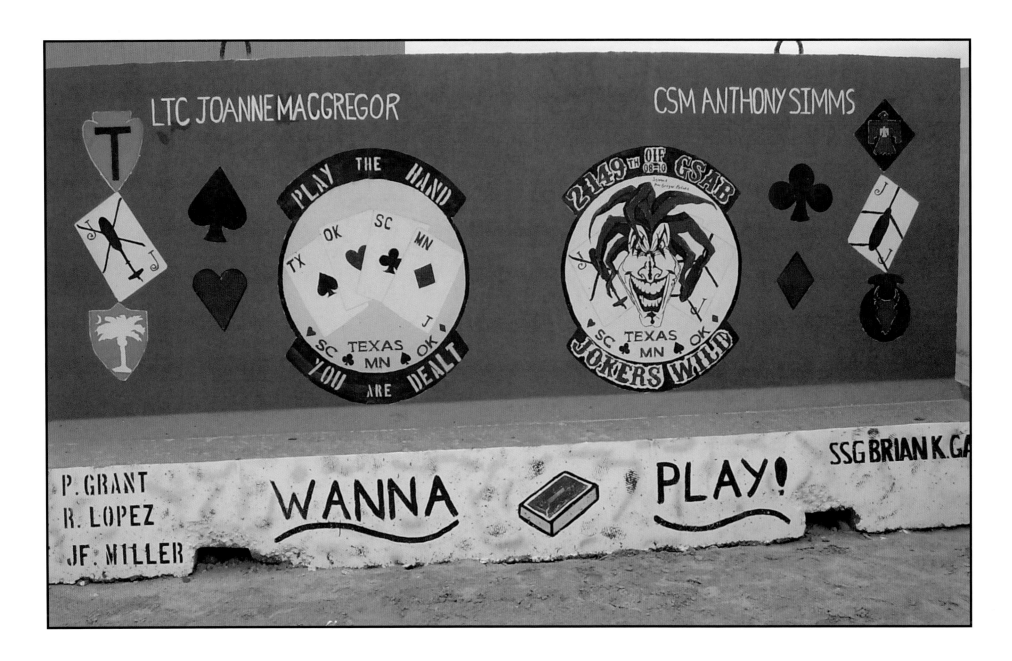

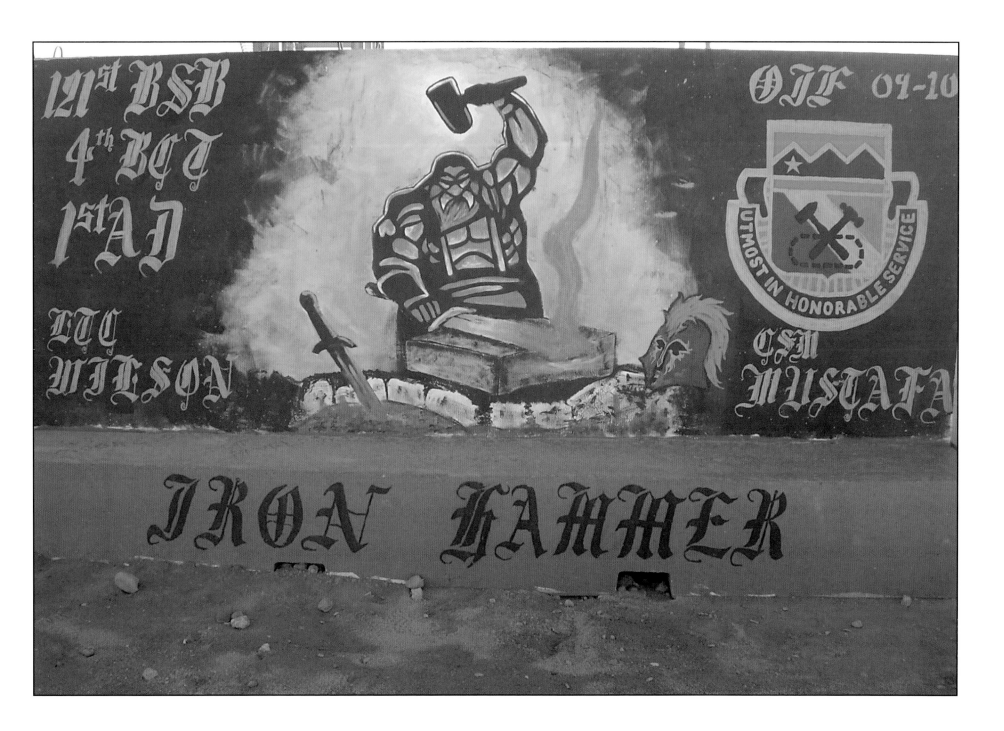

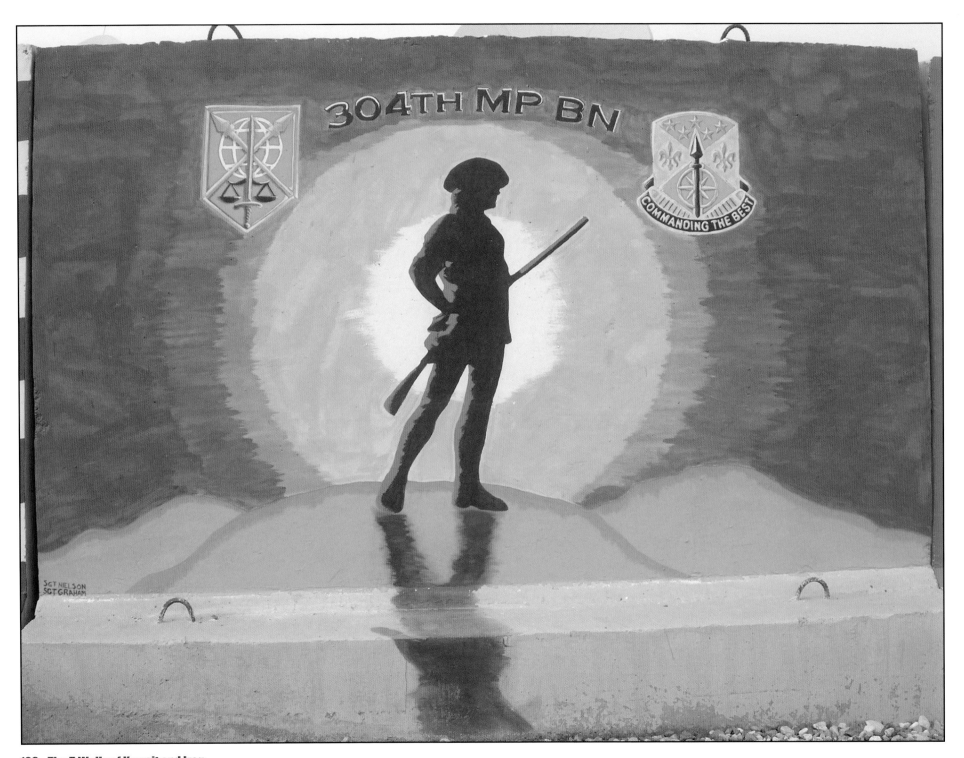

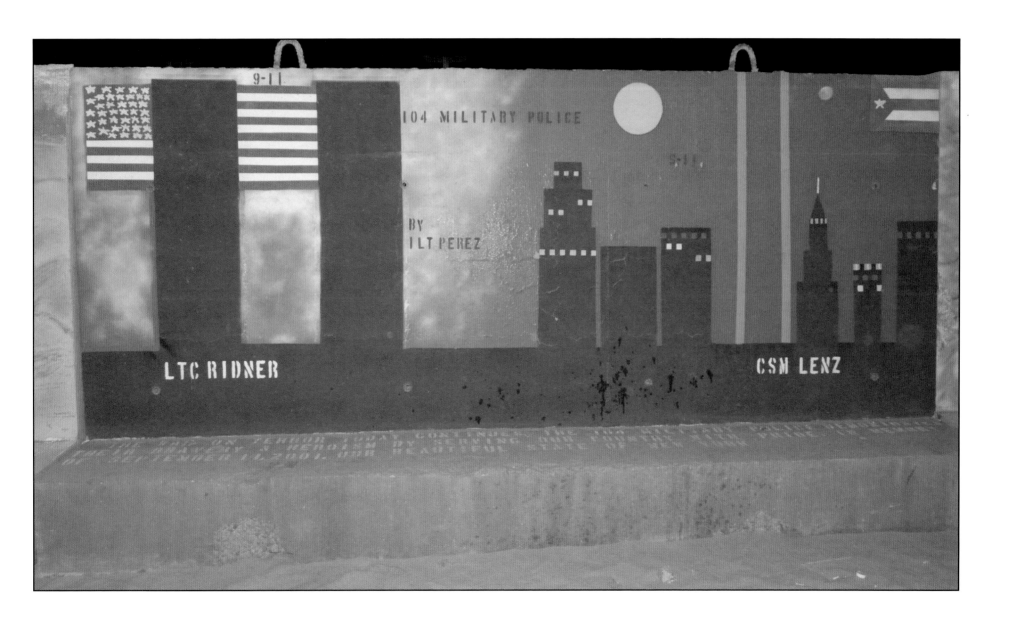

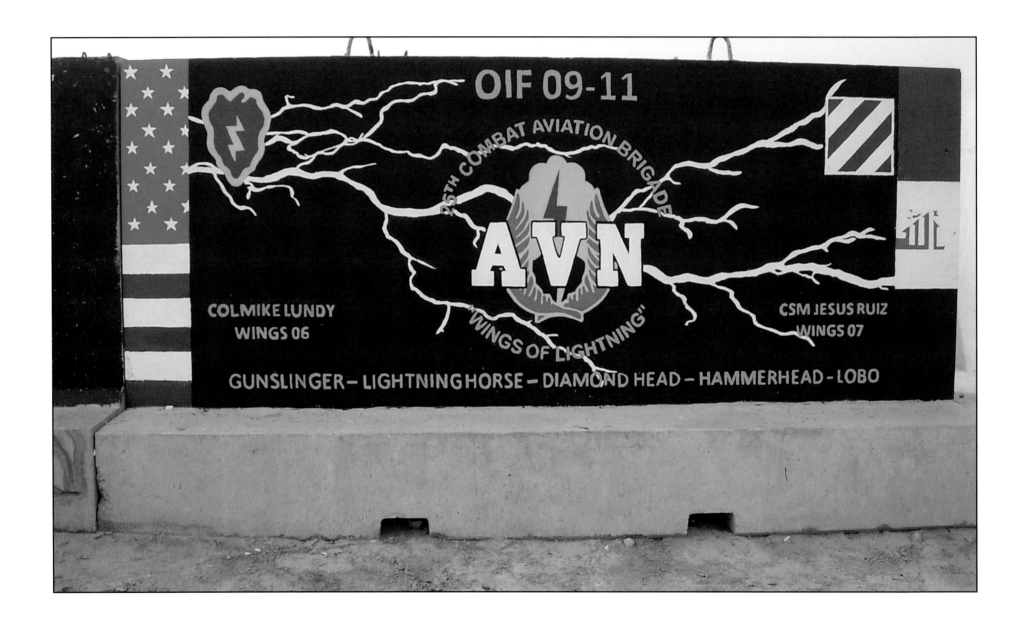

OIF 09-11

25TH COMBAT AVIATION BRIGADE

AVN

"WINGS OF LIGHTNING"

COL MIKE LUNDY
WINGS 06

CSM JESUS RUIZ
WINGS 07

GUNSLINGER – LIGHTNING HORSE – DIAMOND HEAD – HAMMERHEAD - LOBO

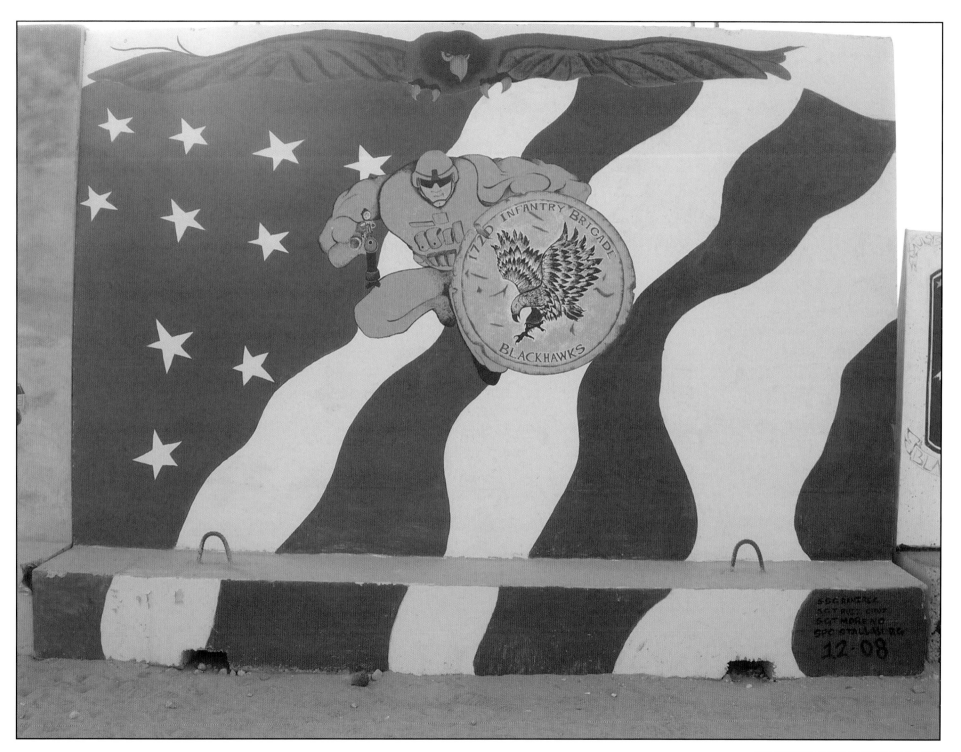

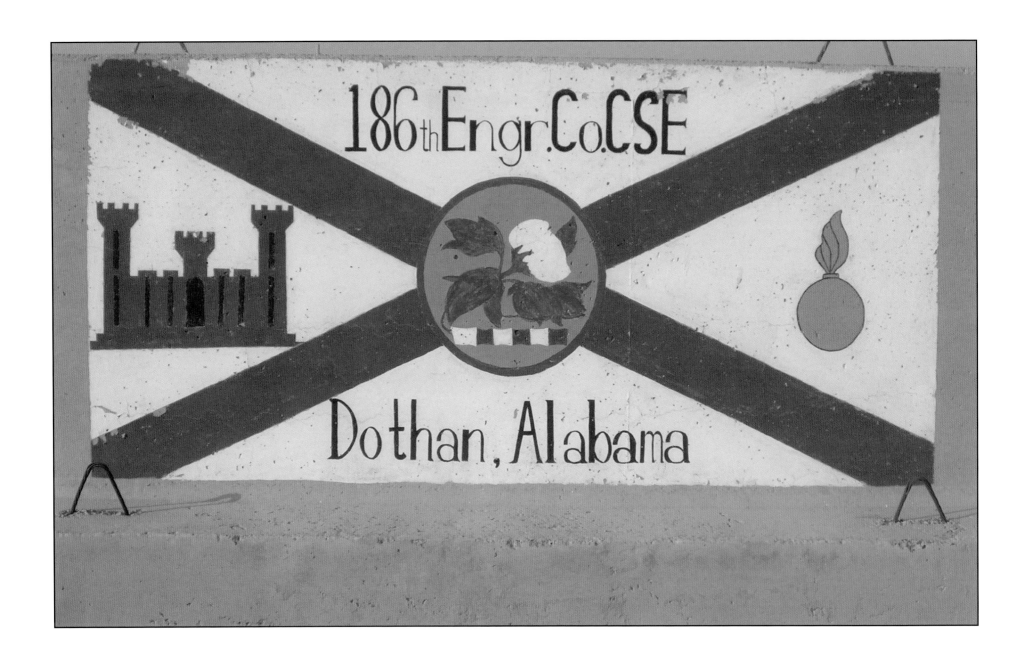

186th Engr. Co. CSE

Dothan, Alabama

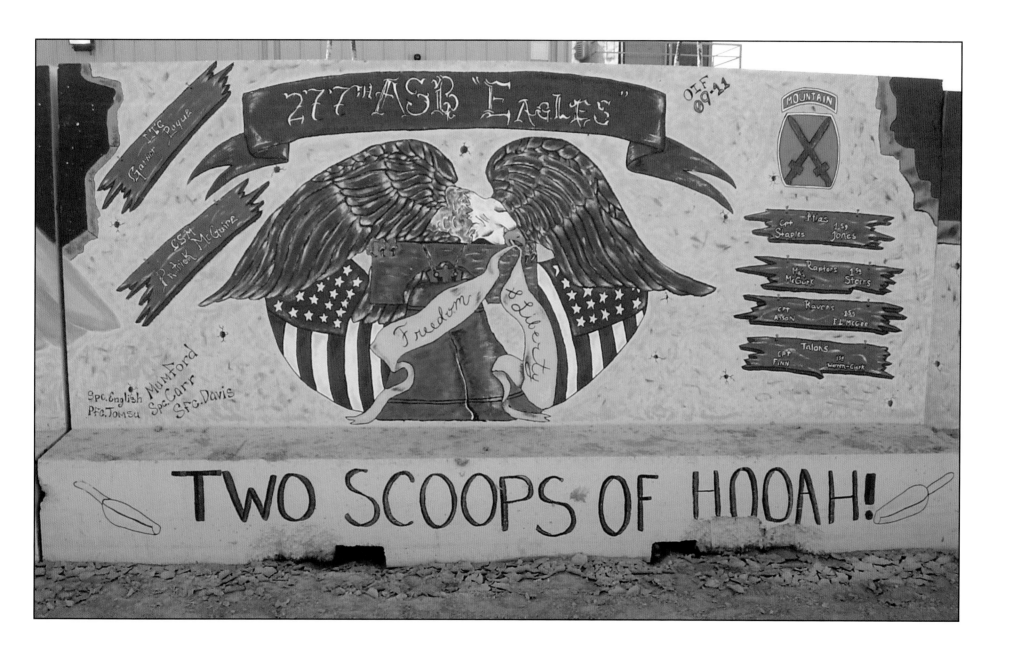

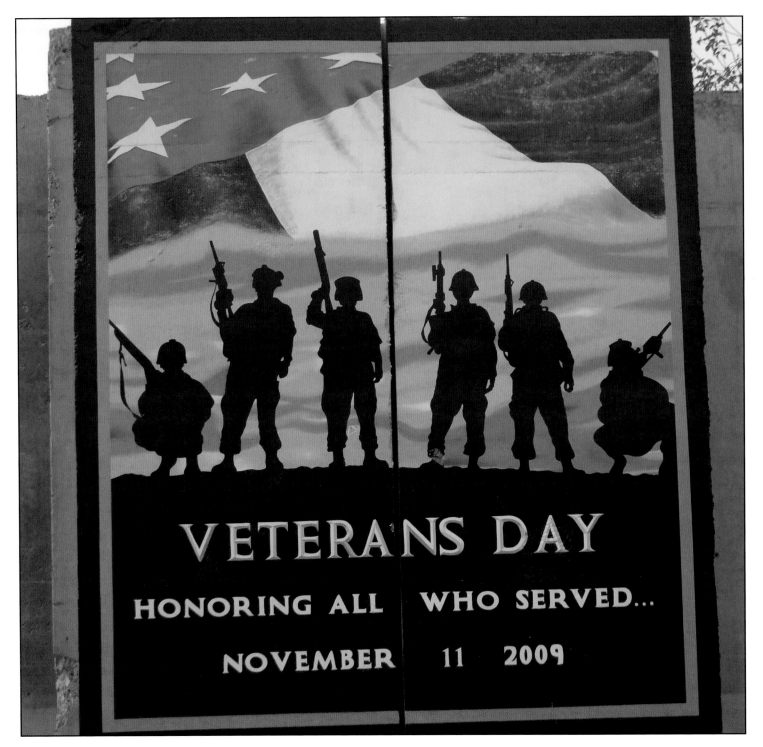

VETERANS DAY

HONORING ALL WHO SERVED...

NOVEMBER 11 2009

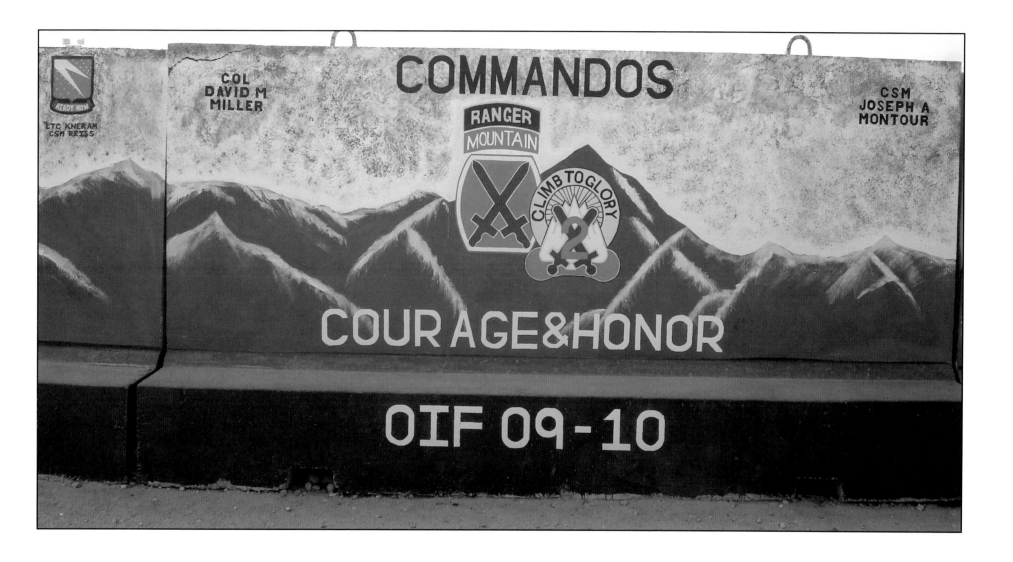

COMMANDOS

COURAGE&HONOR

OIF 09-10

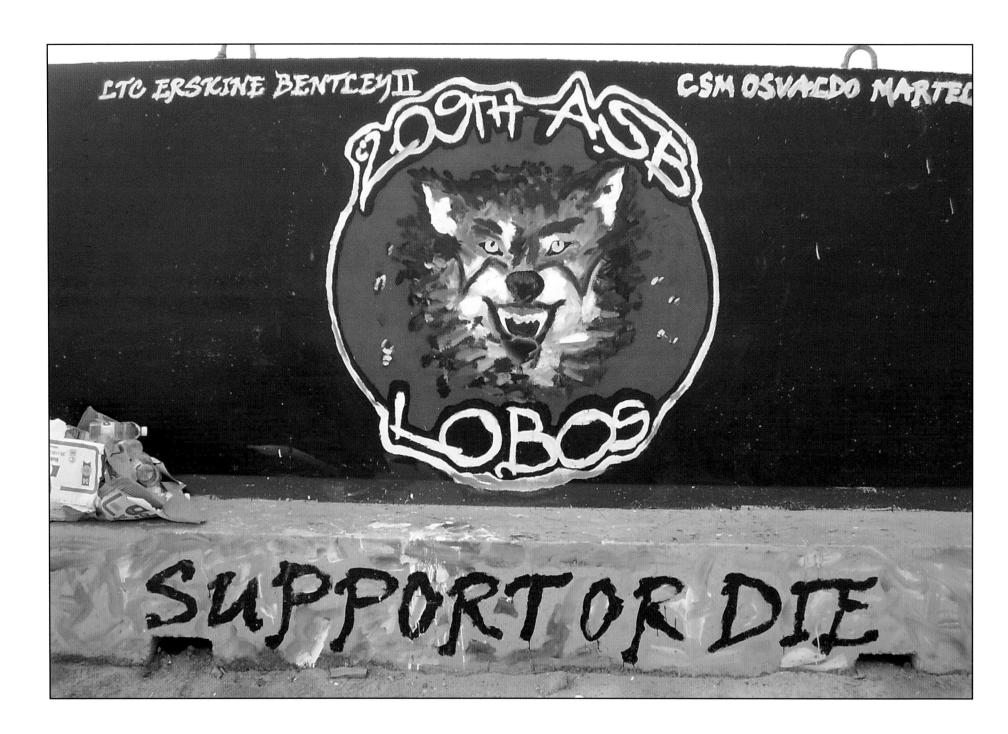

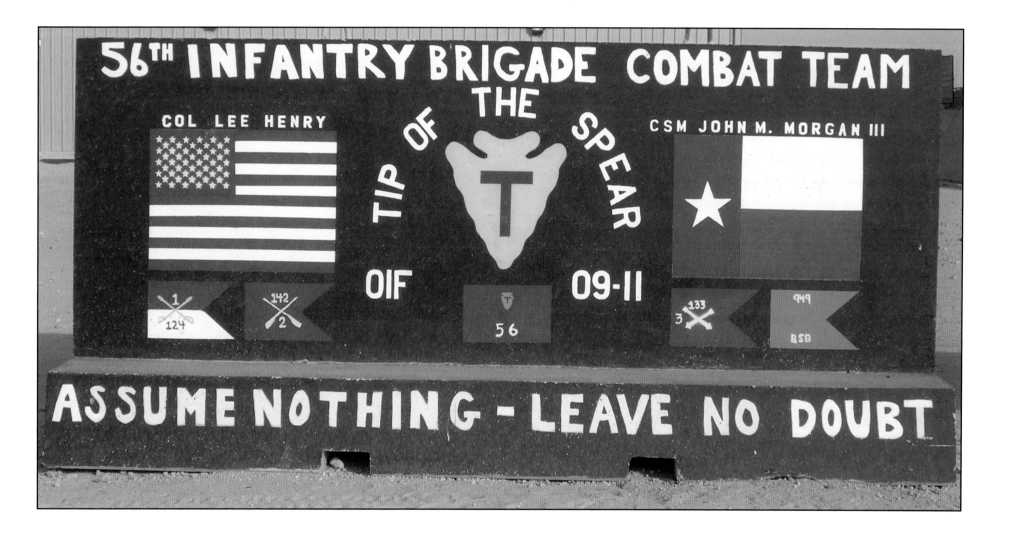

56TH INFANTRY BRIGADE COMBAT TEAM

THE

COL LEE HENRY

TIP OF

SPEAR

CSM JOHN M. MORGAN III

OIF

09-11

1
124

142
2

T
56

3 133

949

BSB

ASSUME NOTHING - LEAVE NO DOUBT

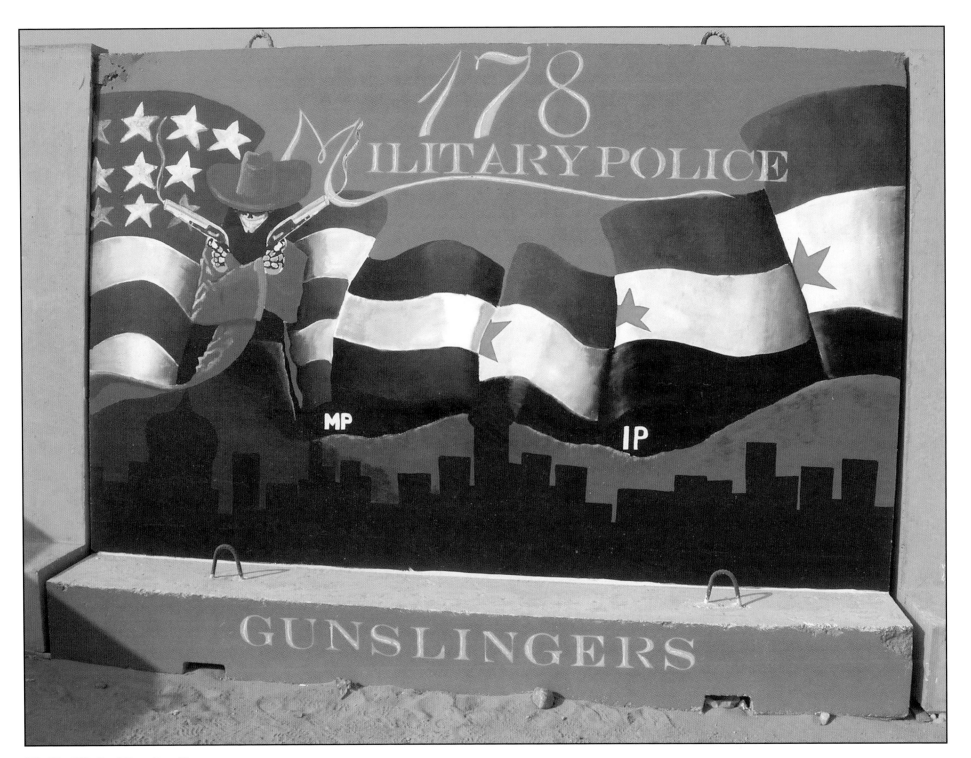

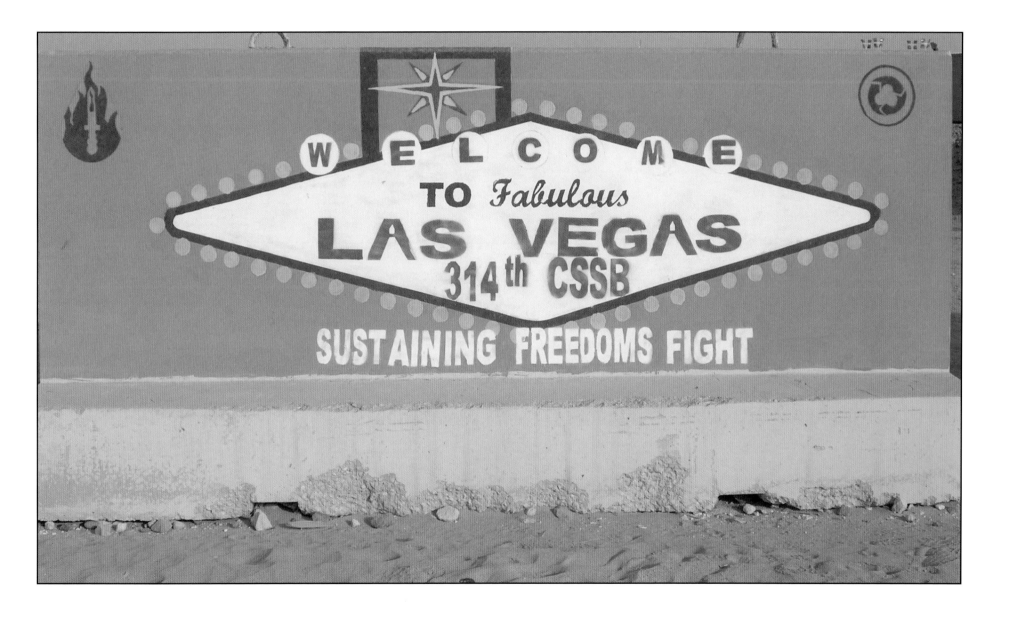

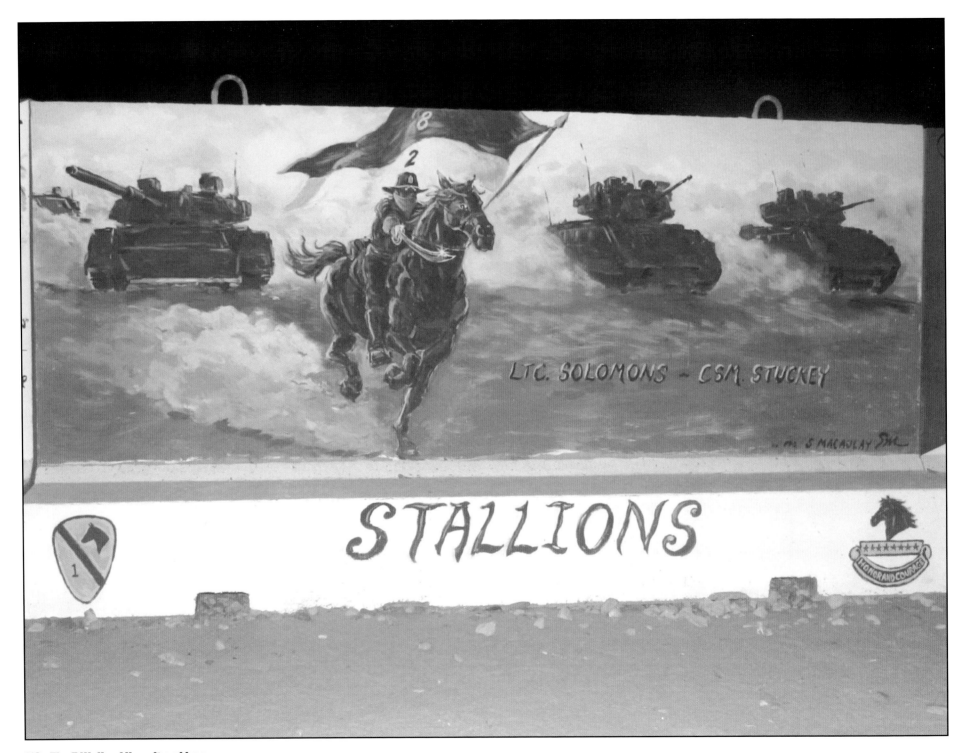

LTC. SOLOMONS – CSM STUCKEY

STALLIONS

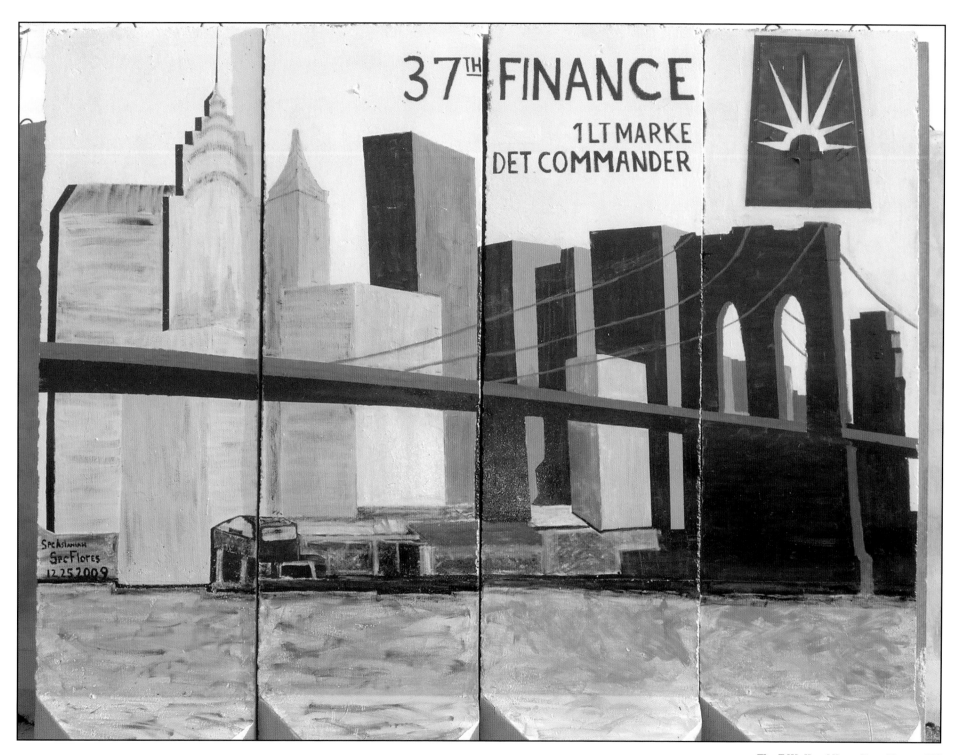

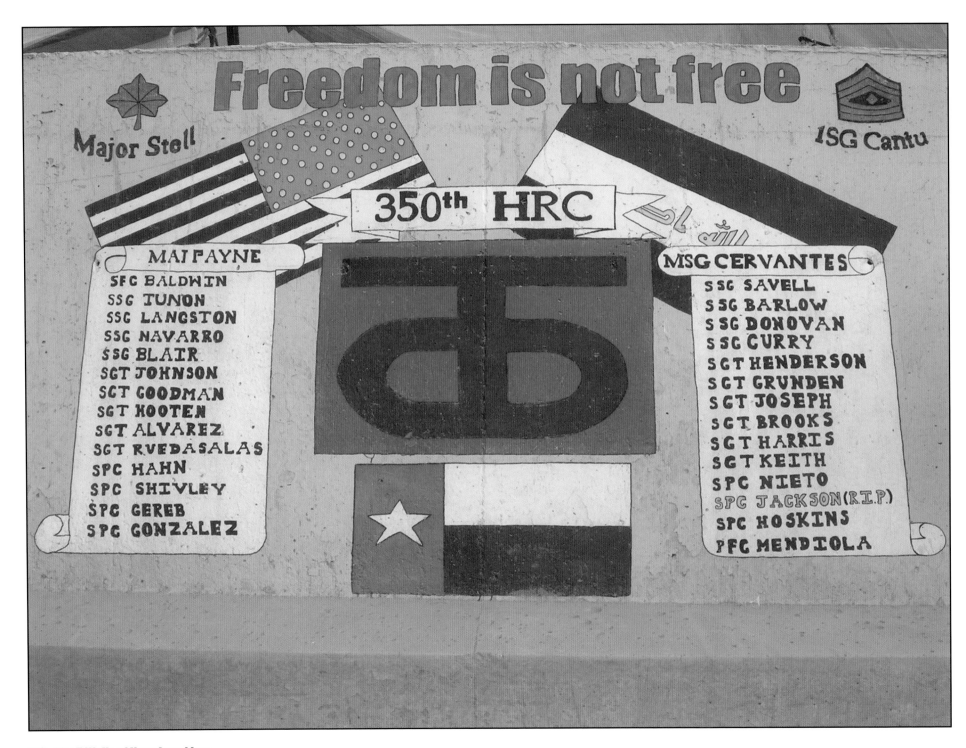

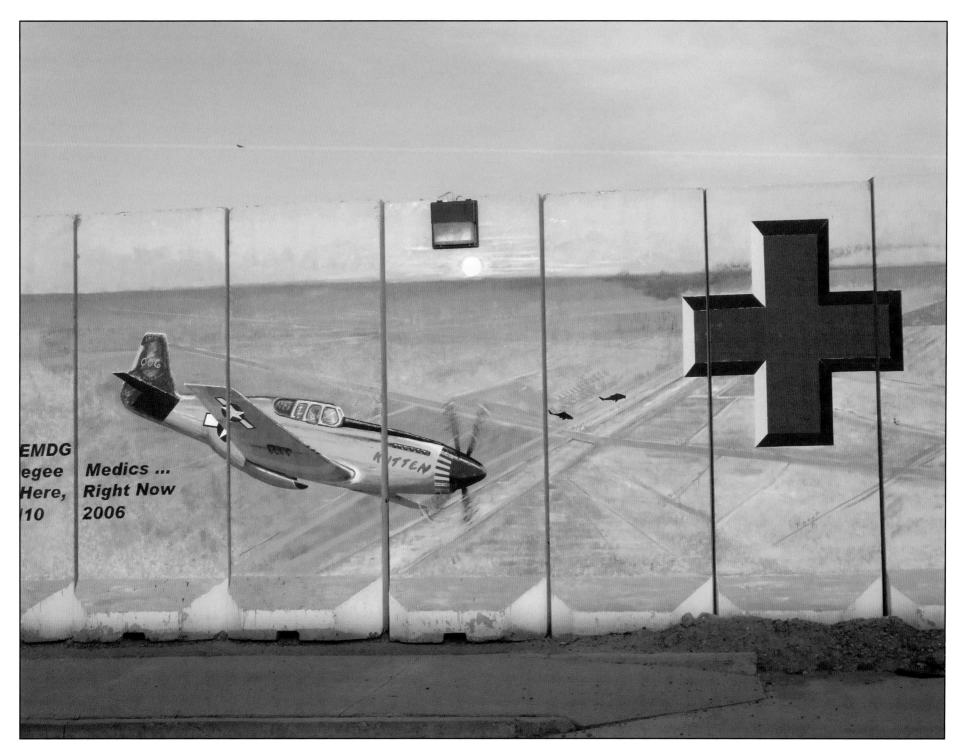

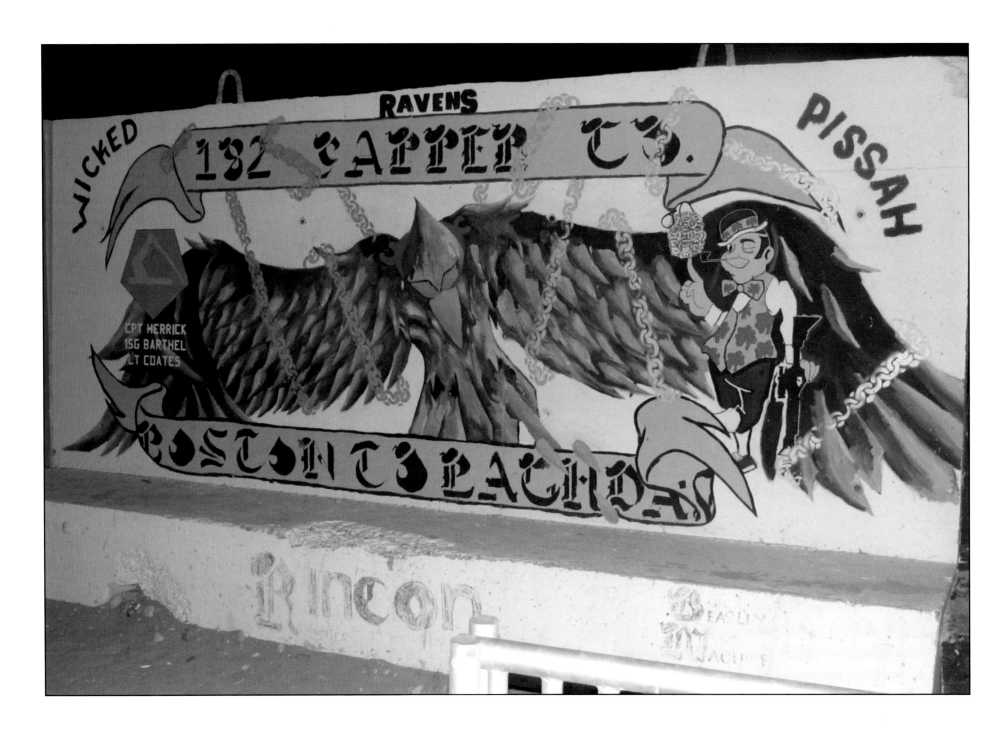

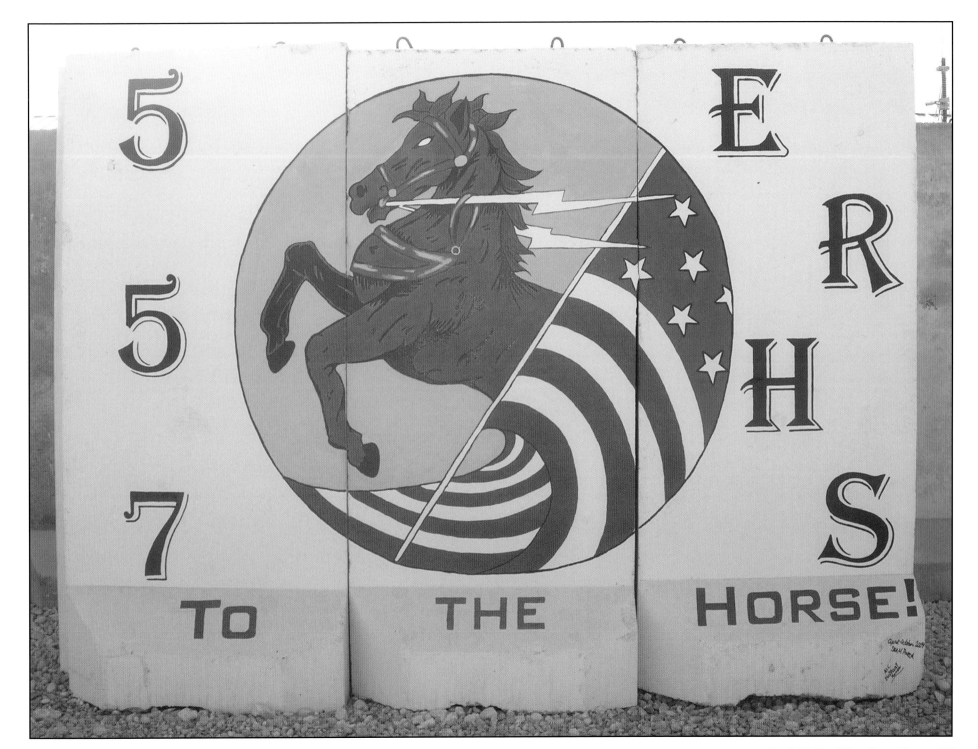

5557
TO
THE
ERS
H
S
HORSE!

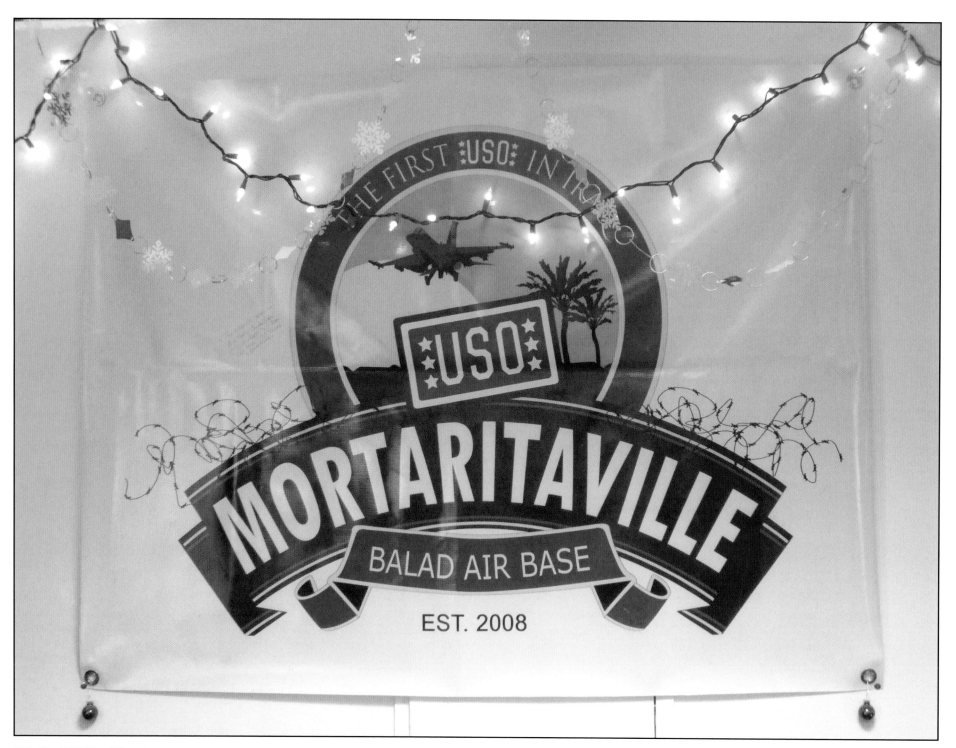

THE FIRST USO IN IRAQ

USO

MORTARITAVILLE

BALAD AIR BASE

EST. 2008

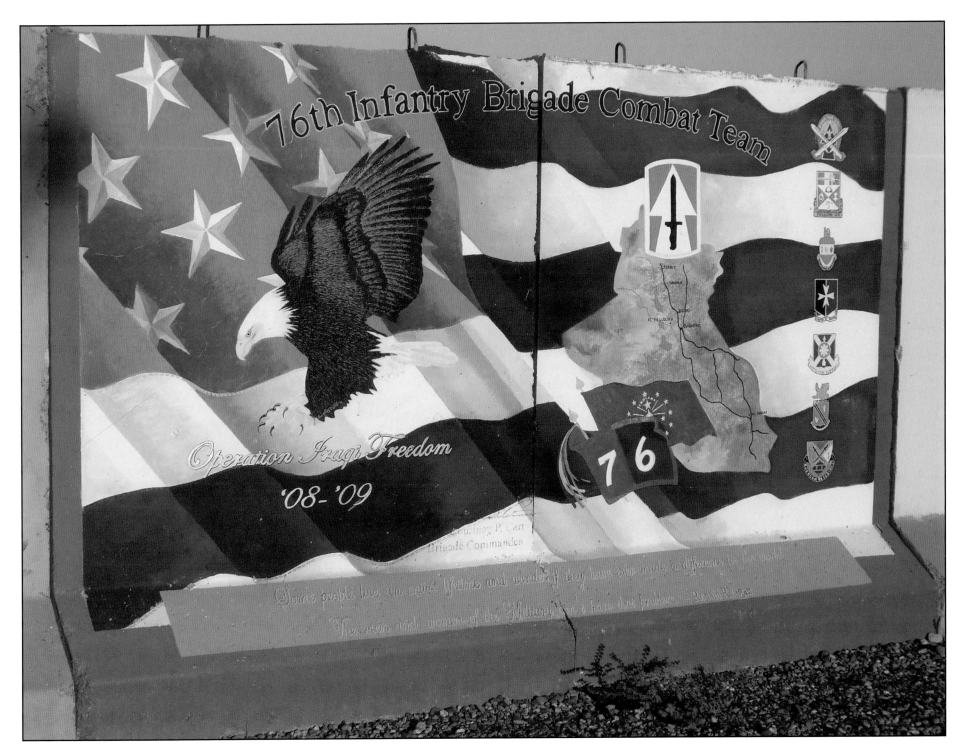

76th Infantry Brigade Combat Team

Operation Iraqi Freedom

'08- '09

Courtney P. Carr
Brigade Commander

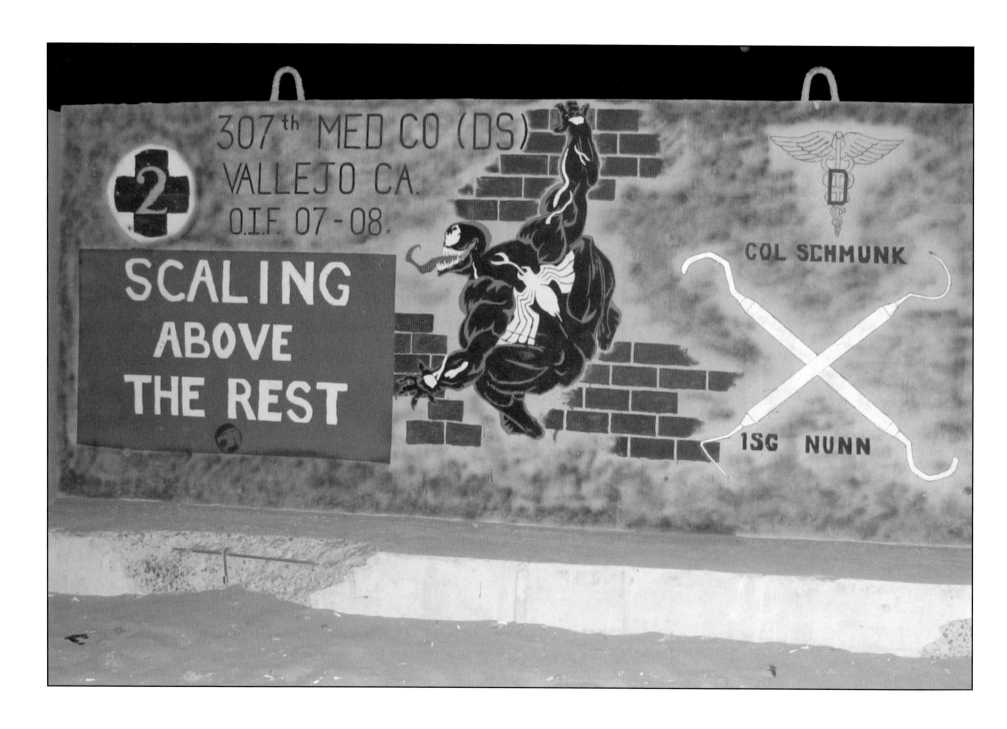

307th MED CO (DS)
VALLEJO CA.
O.I.F. 07-08.

SCALING ABOVE THE REST

COL SCHMUNK

1SG NUNN

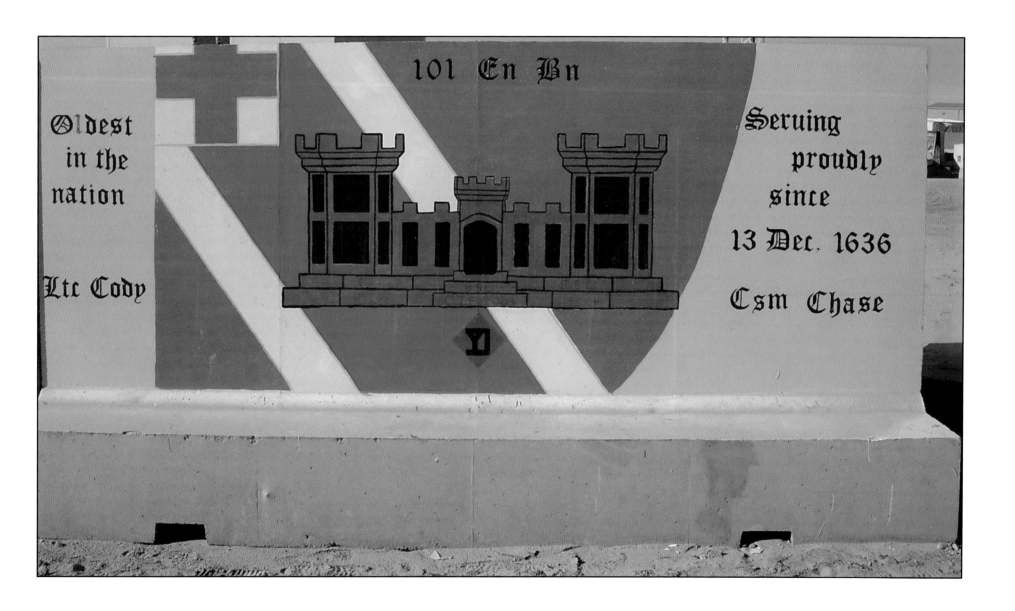

101 En Bn

Oldest
in the
nation

Ltc Cody

Serving
proudly
since
13 Dec. 1636

Csm Chase

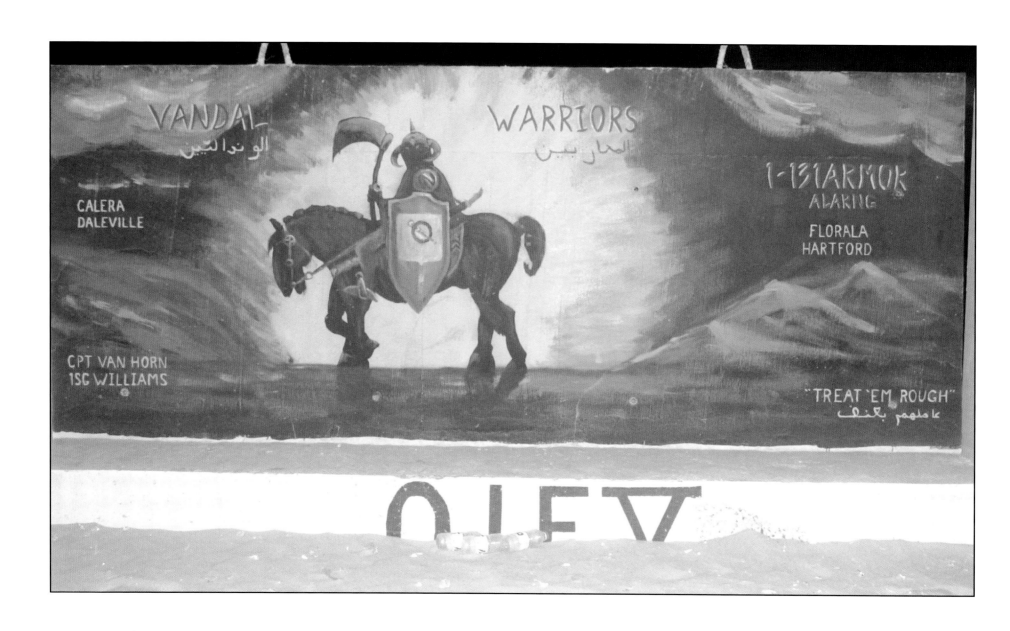

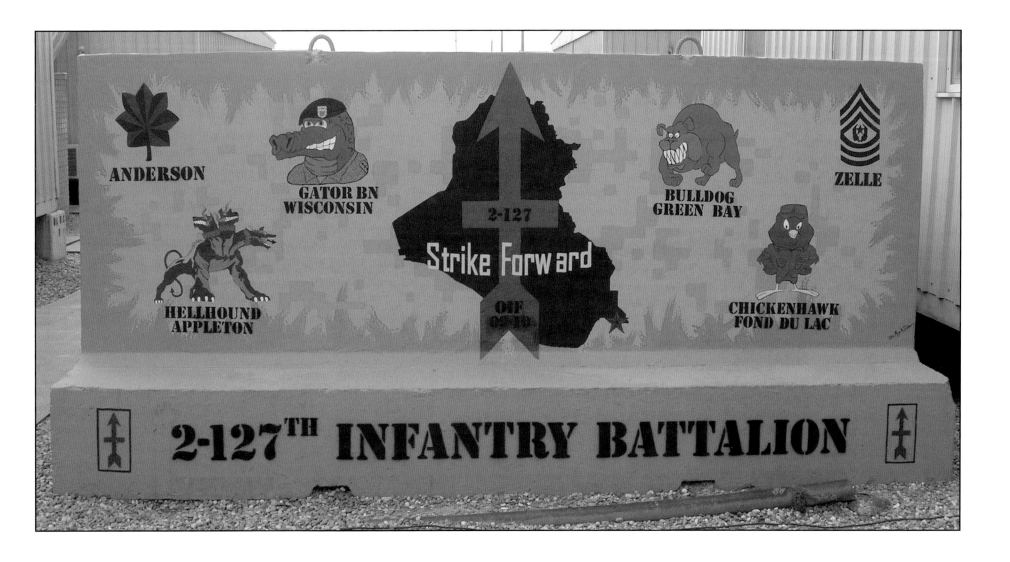

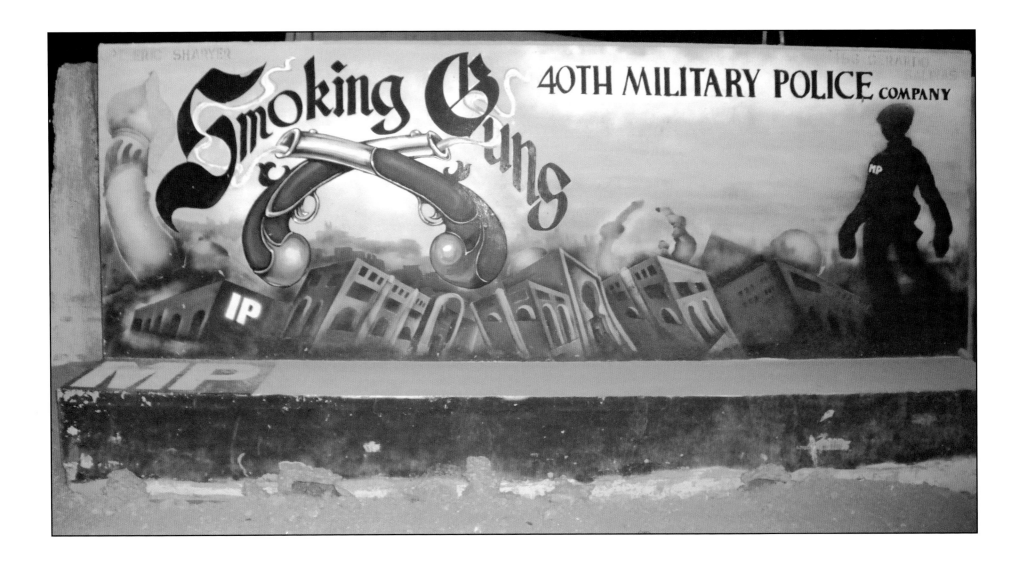

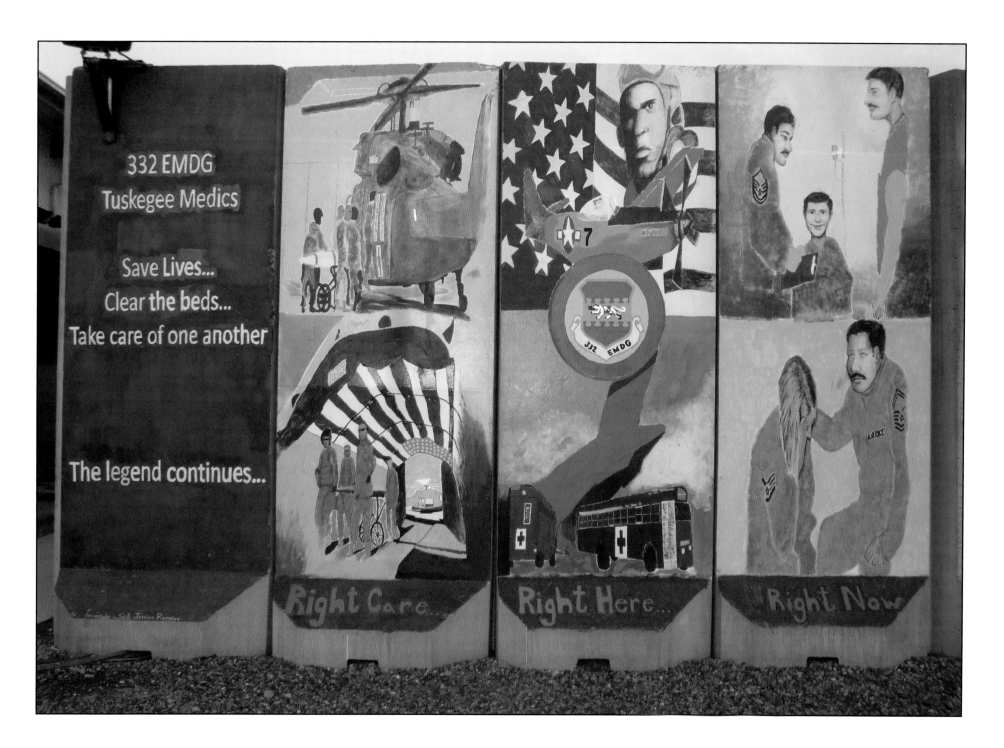

332 EMDG
Tuskegee Medics

Save Lives...
Clear the beds...
Take care of one another

The legend continues...

Right Care... Right Here... Right Now

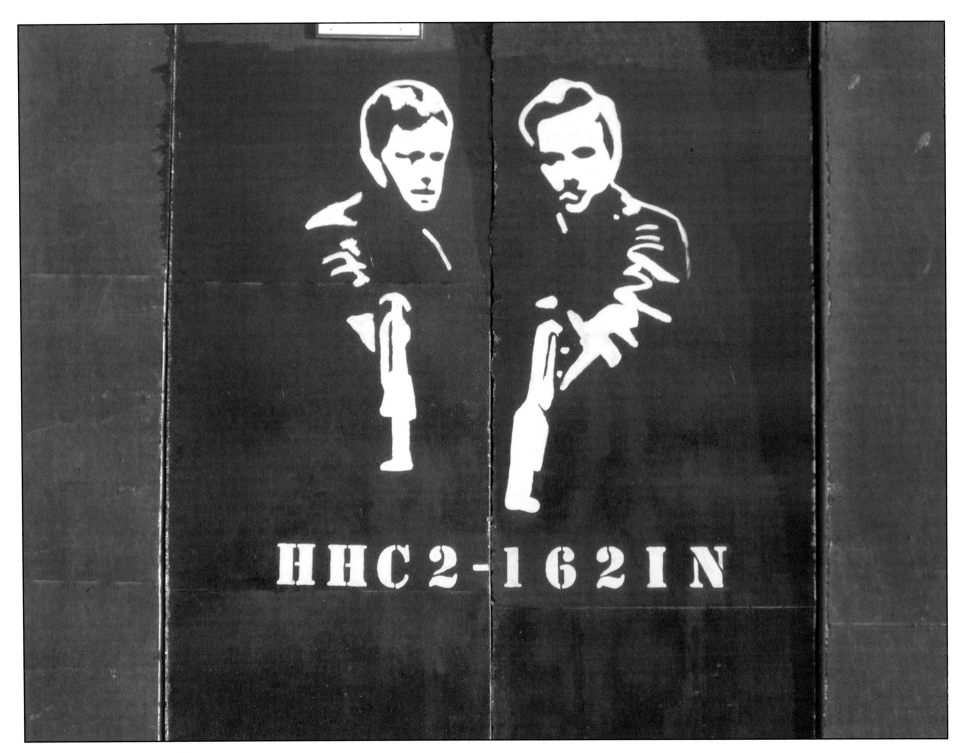

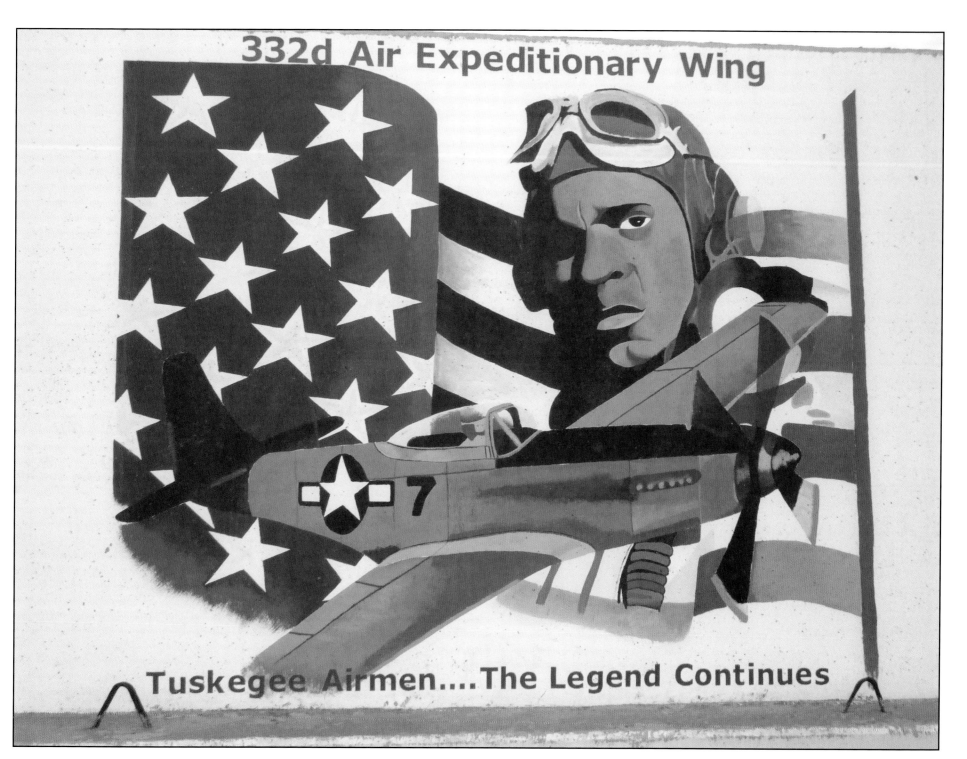

332d Air Expeditionary Wing

Tuskegee Airmen....The Legend Continues

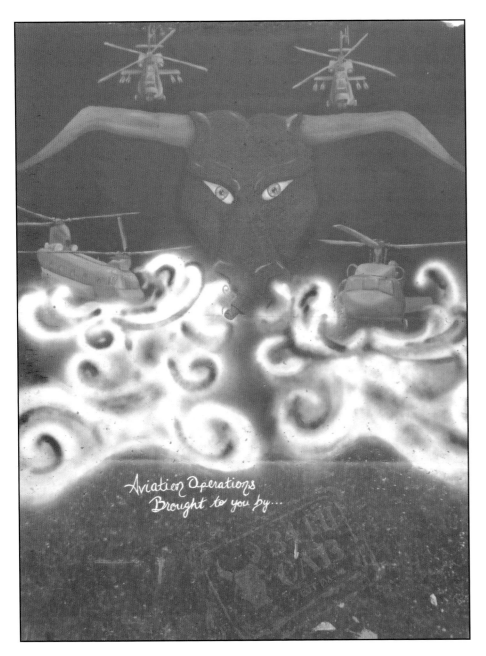

Aviation Operations
Brought to you by...

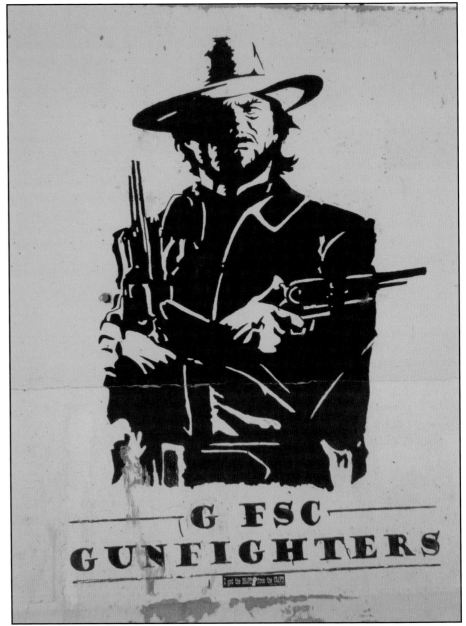

G FSC
GUNFIGHTERS

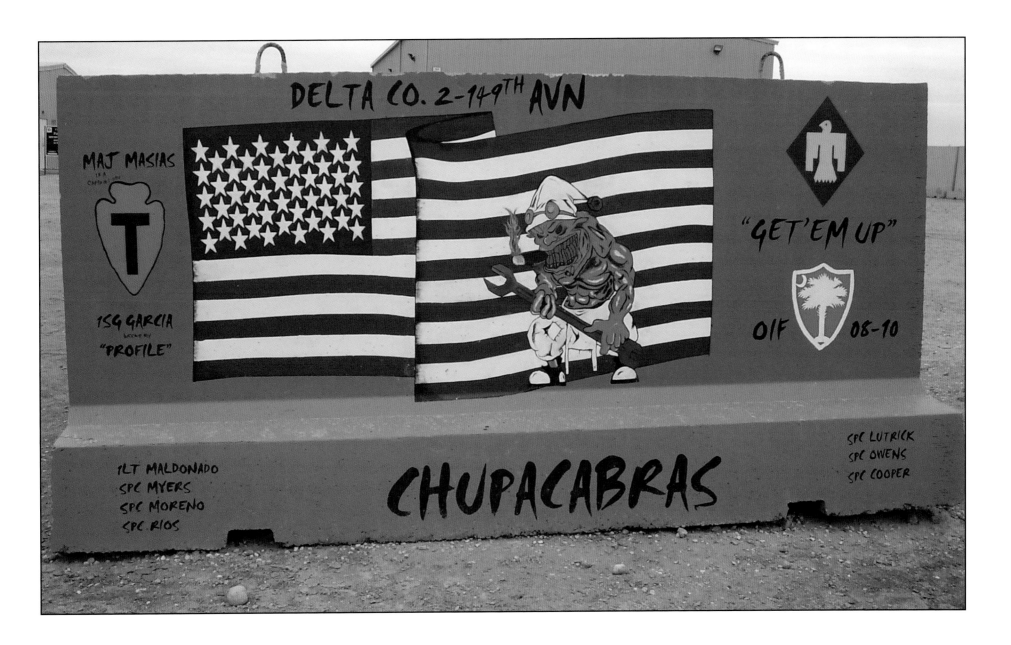

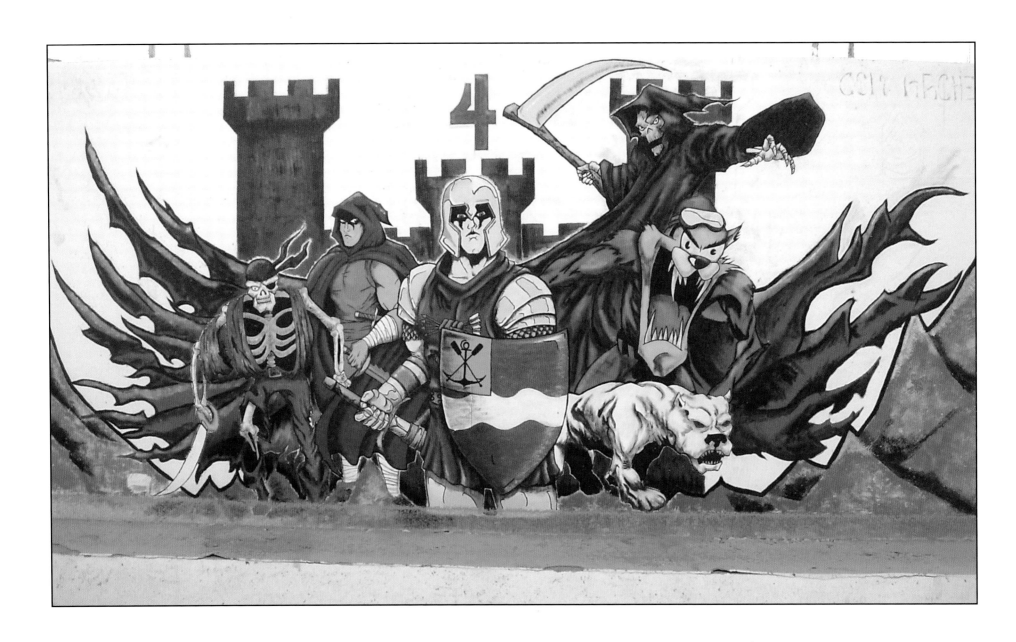

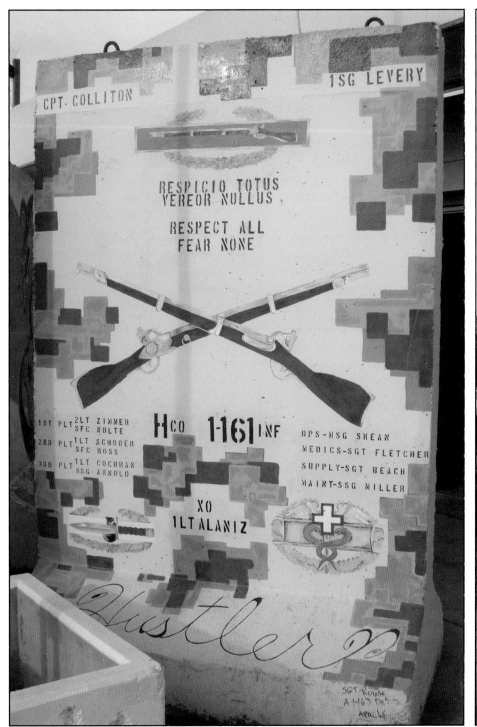

CPT. COLLITON   1SG LEVERY

RESPICIO TOTUS
VEREOR NULLUS

RESPECT ALL
FEAR NONE

1ST PLT 2LT ZIMMER
SFC NOLTE
2ND PLT 1LT SCHOBER
SFC ROSS
3RD PLT 1LT COCHRAN
SSG ARNOLD

H CO 1-161 INF

OPS-MSG SKEAN
MEDICS-SGT FLETCHER
SUPPLY-SGT BEACH
MAINT-SSG MILLER

XO
1LT ALANIZ

Hustler

SGT House
A 1-163 Det
Apache

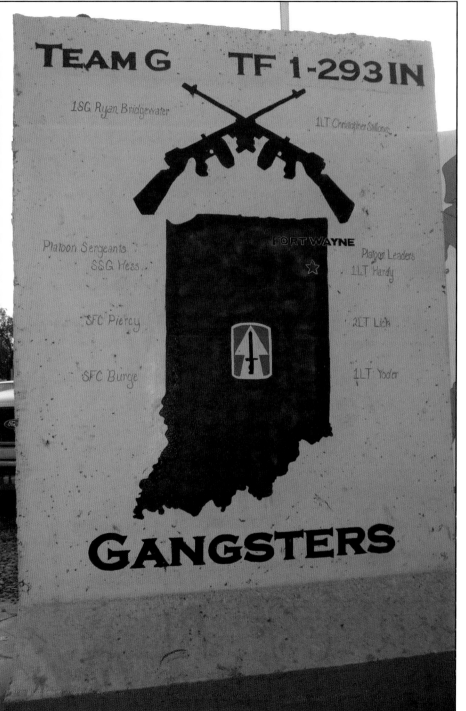

TEAM G   TF 1-293 IN

1SG Ryan Bridgewater   1LT Christopher Stilions

Platoon Sergeants
SSG Hess

FORT WAYNE

Platoon Leaders
1LT Hardy

SFC Piercy

2LT Lich

SFC Burge

1LT Yoder

GANGSTERS

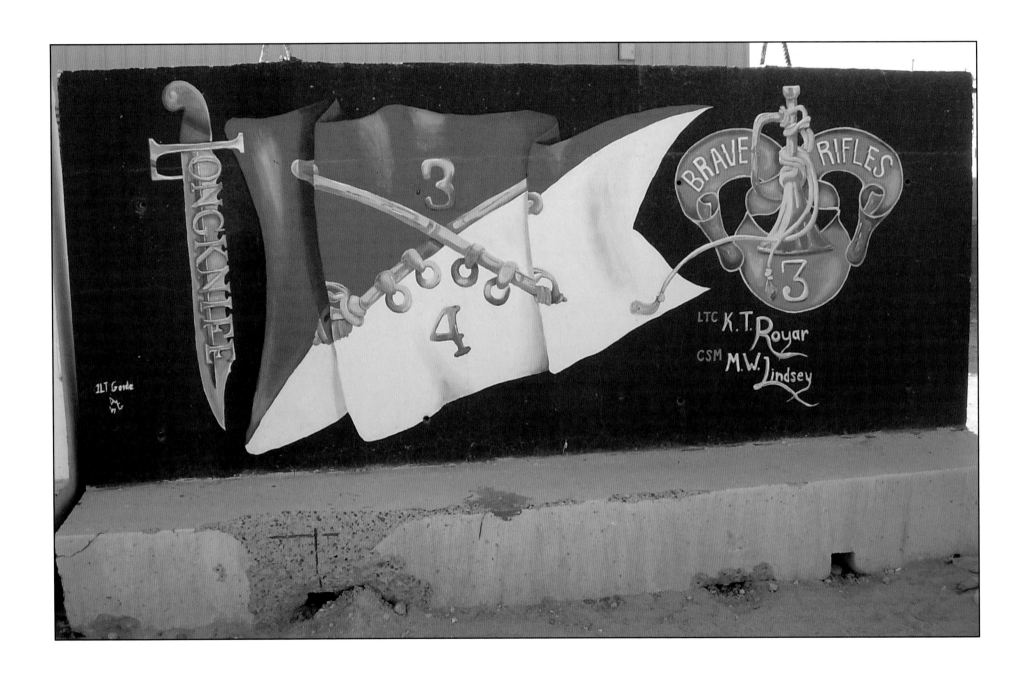

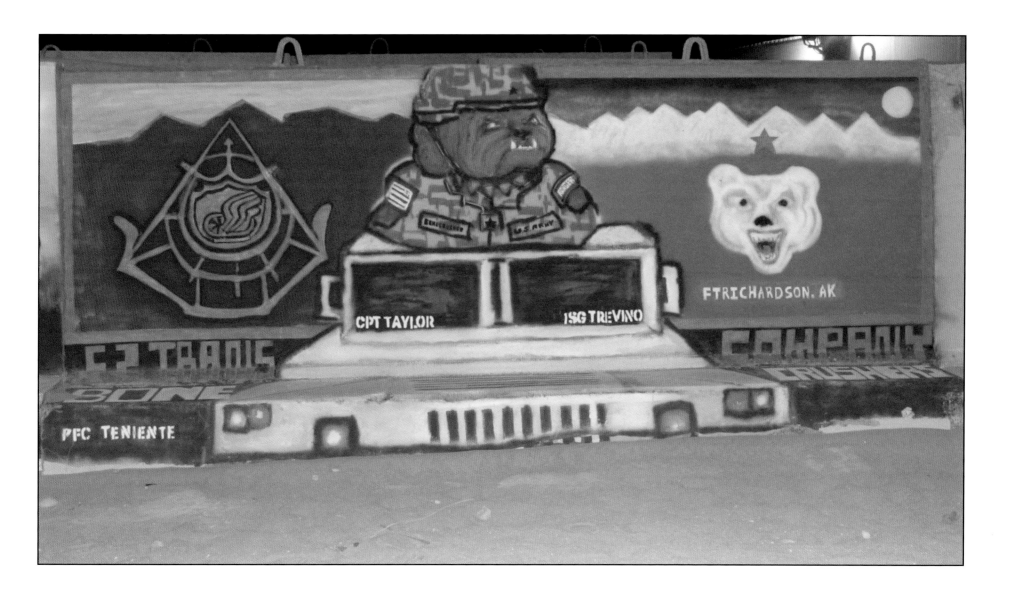

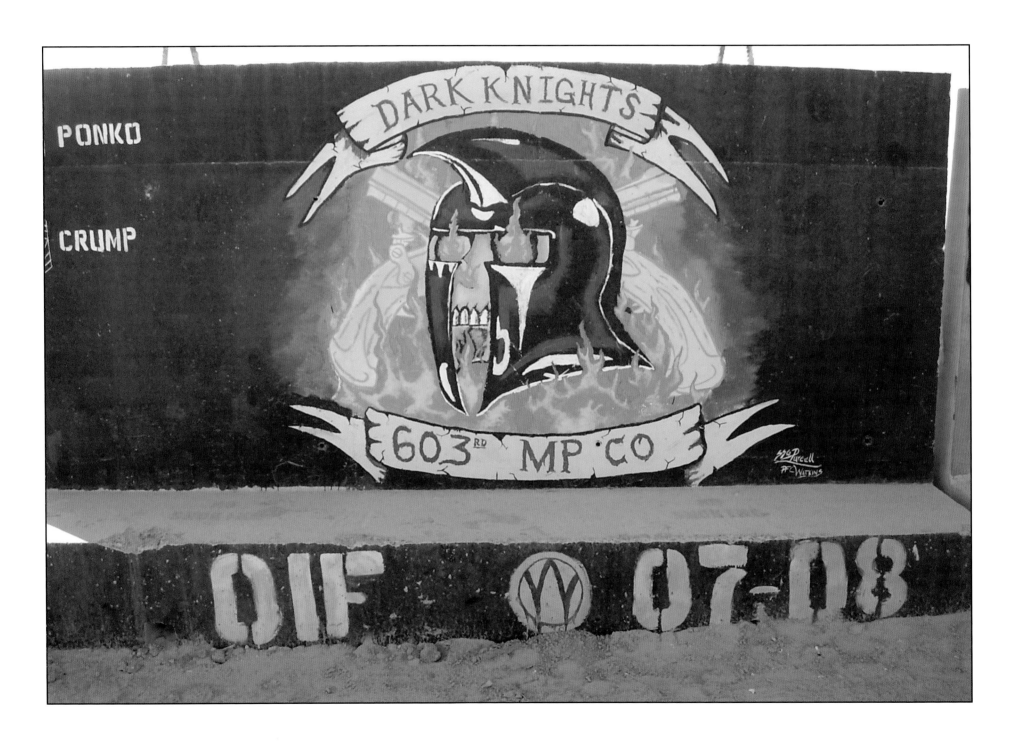

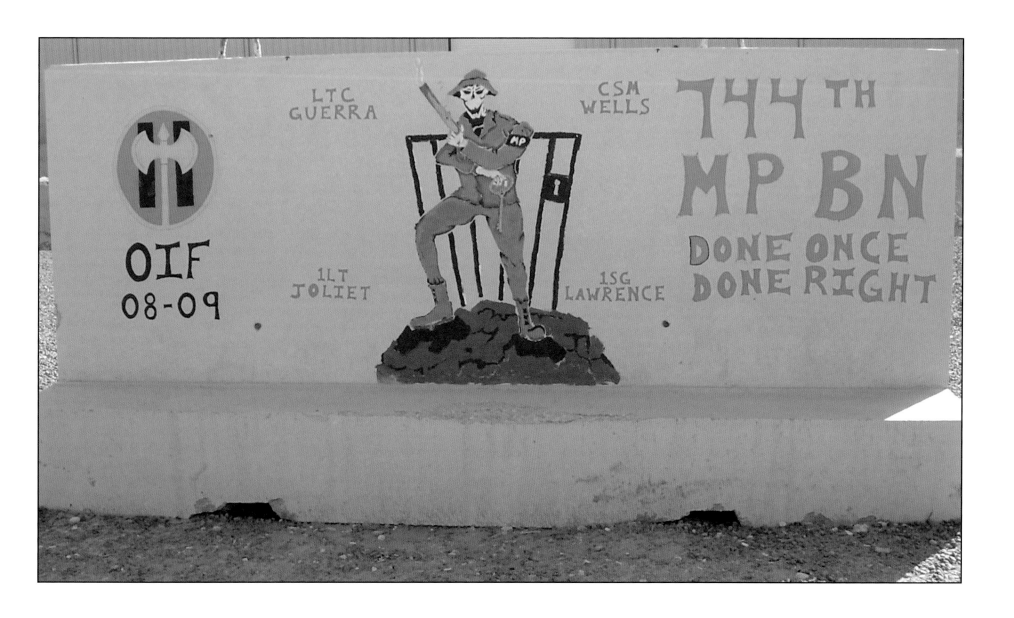

LTC
GUERRA

CSM
WELLS

744TH
MP BN

OIF
08-09

1LT
JOLIET

1SG
LAWRENCE

DONE ONCE
DONE RIGHT

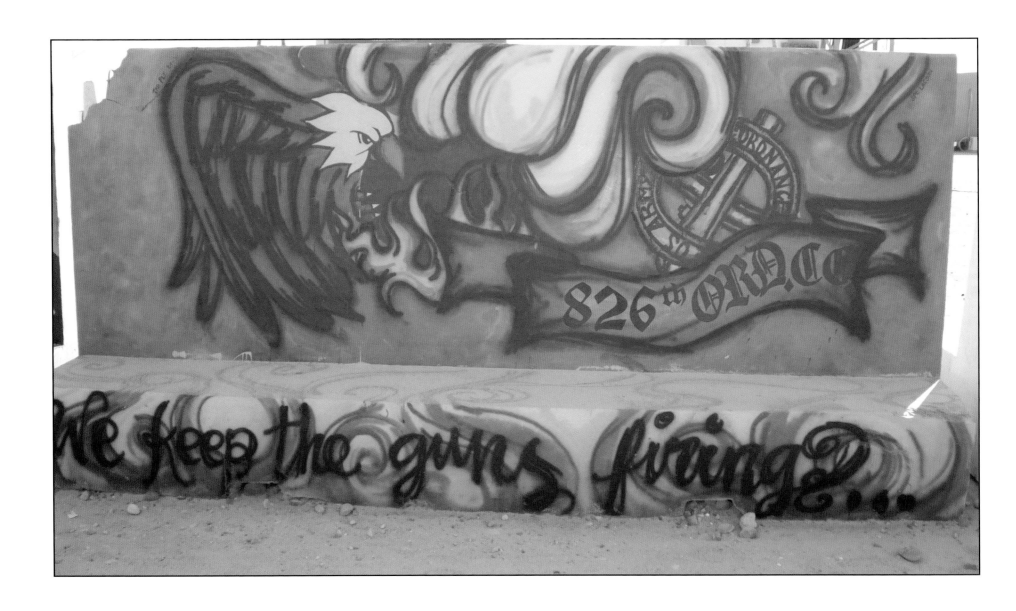

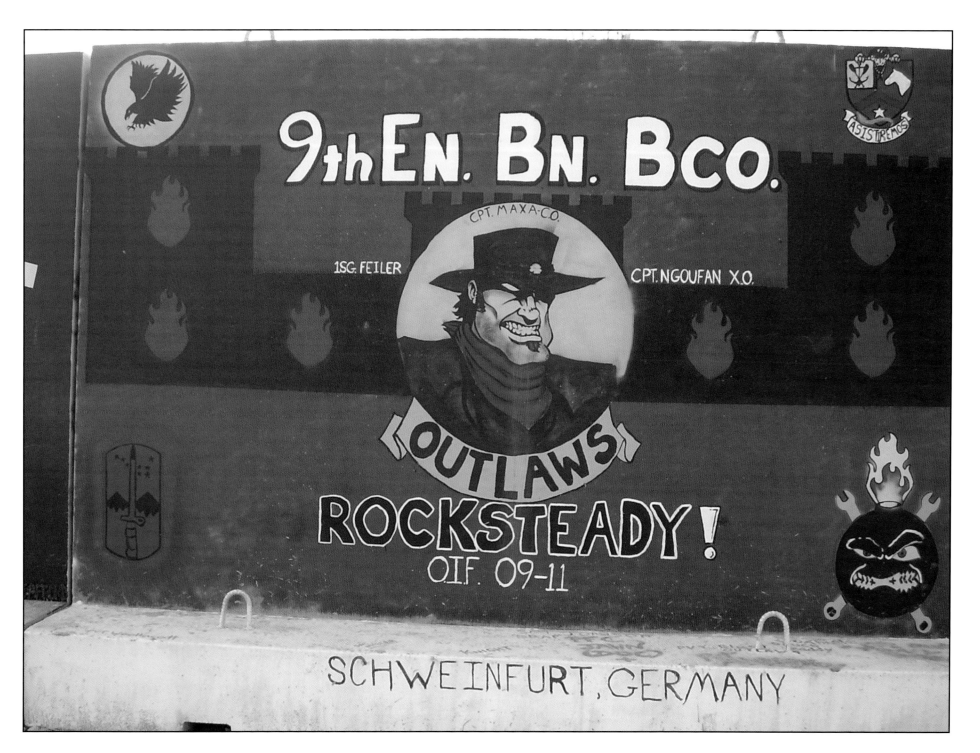

9th EN. BN. B CO.

CPT. MAXA - C.O.

1SG. FEILER   CPT. NGOUFAN X.O.

OUTLAWS

ROCKSTEADY!
O.I.F. 09-11

SCHWEINFURT, GERMANY

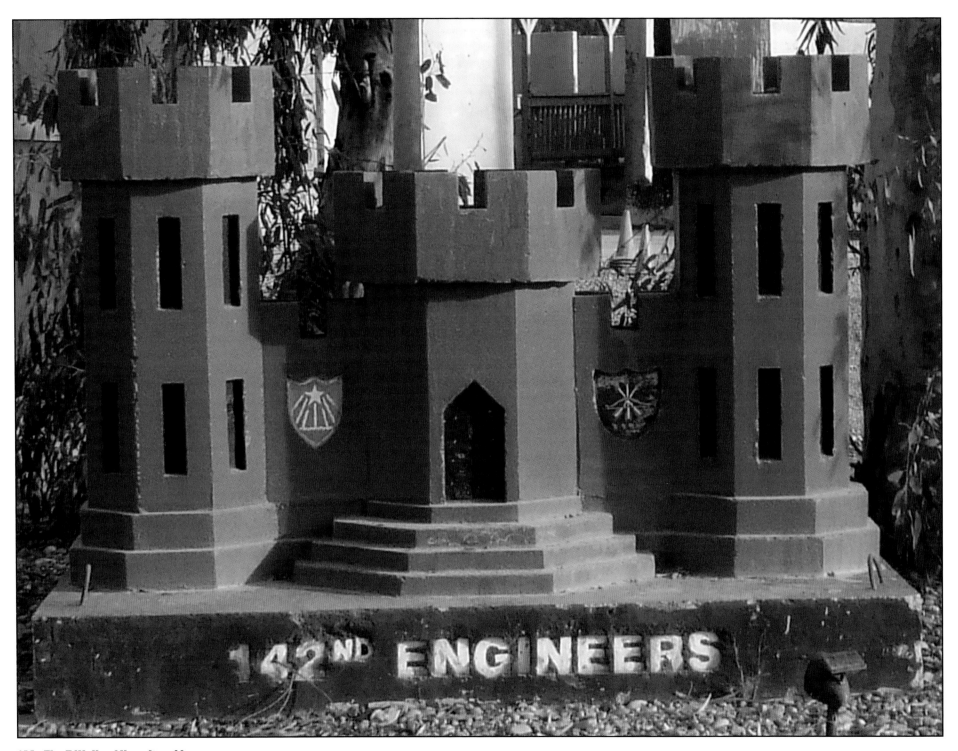

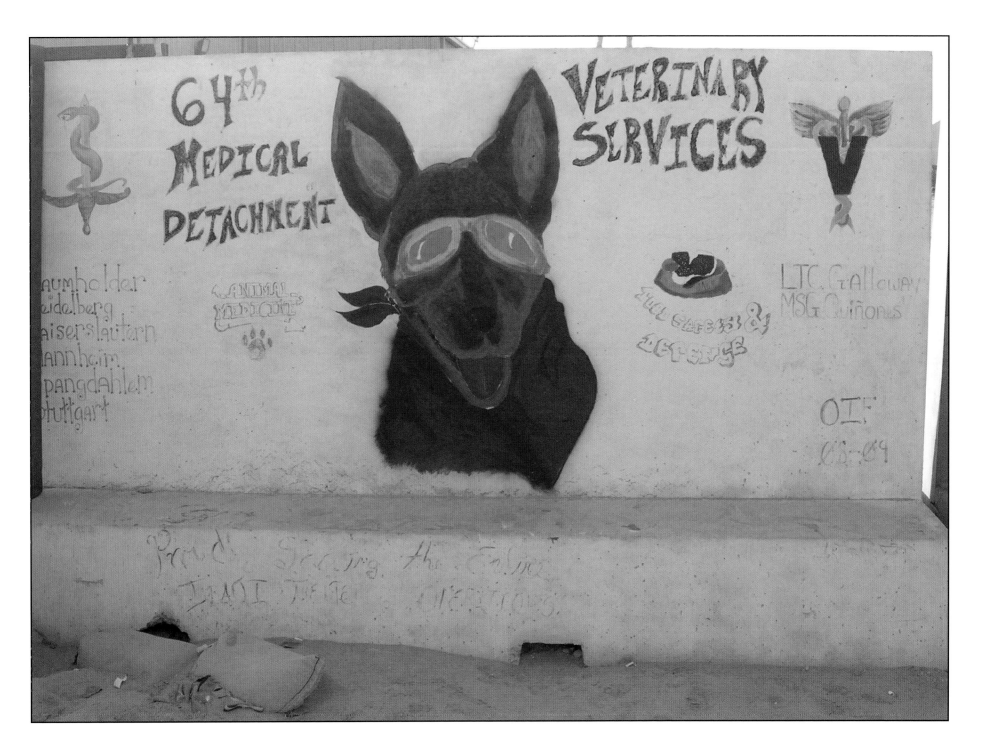

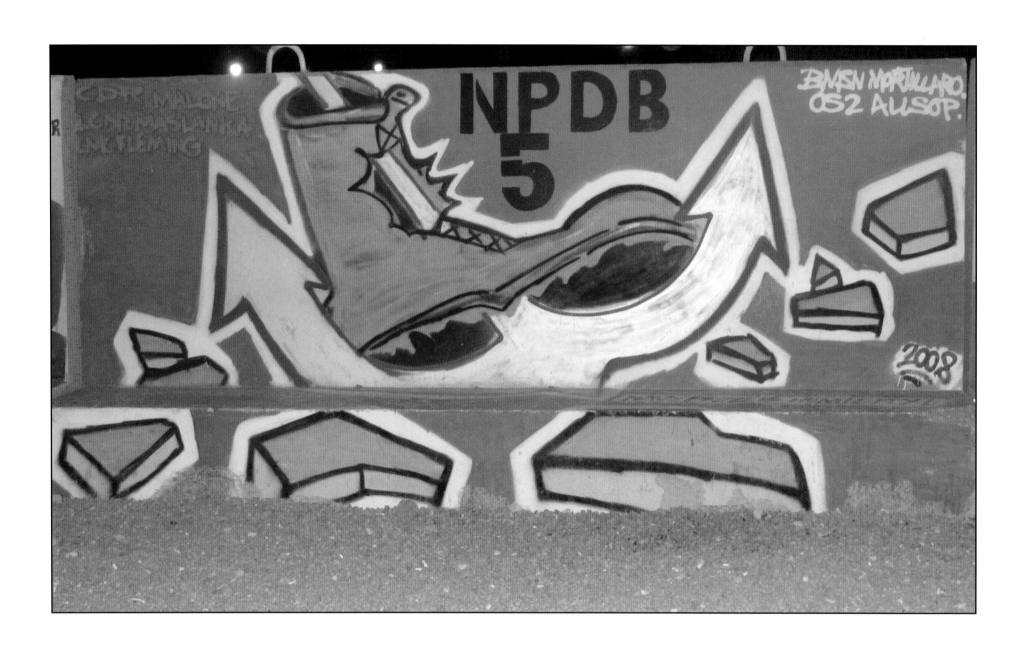

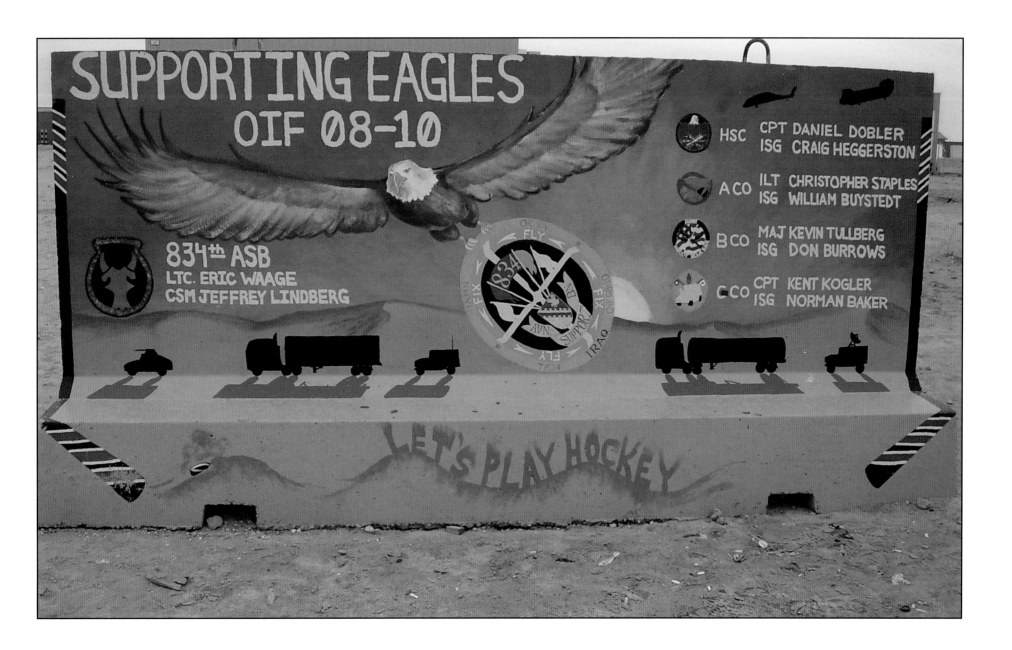

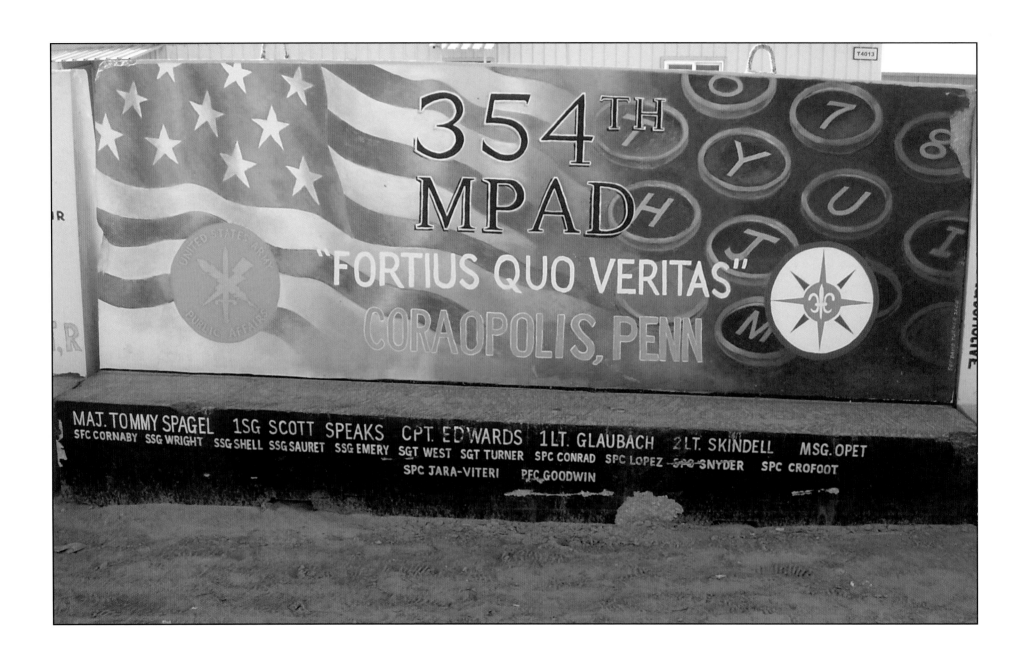

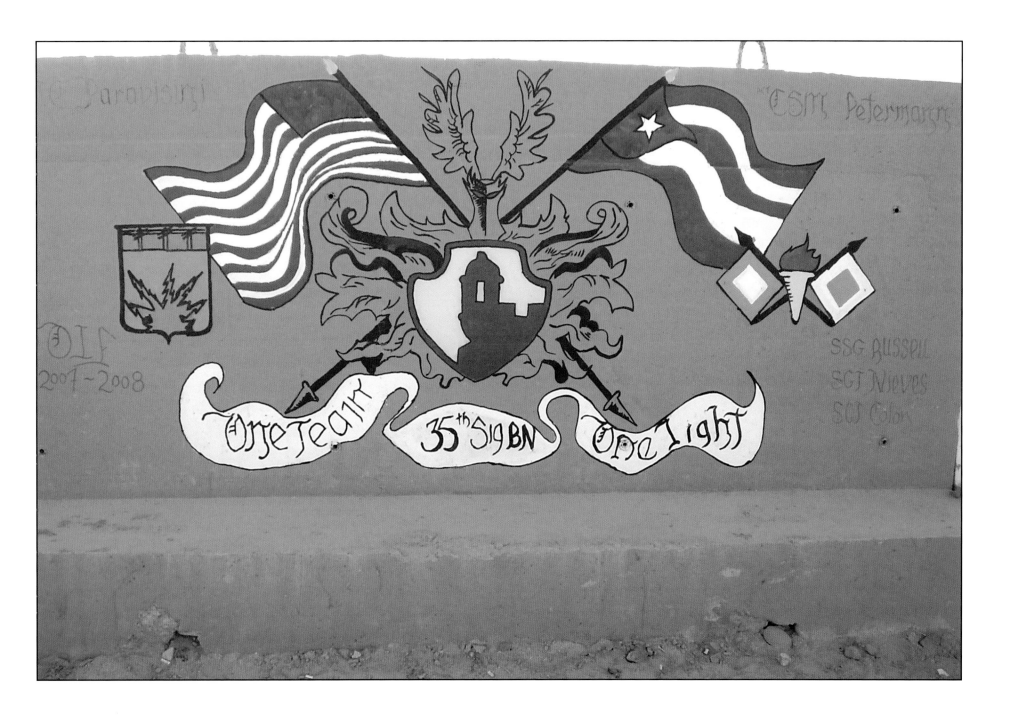

NATIONAL GUARD UNITS

ALABAMA	KANSAS	NEW YORK
ALASKA	KANSAS CITY, KANSAS	NORTH CAROLINA
ARIZONA	KENTUCKY	NORTH DAKOTA
ARKANSAS	MARYLAND	OKLAHOMA
CHICAGO	MICHIGAN	OHIO
CONNECTICUT	MINNESOTA	OREGON
COLORADO	MISSOURI	PENNSYLVANIA
DELAWARE	MISSISSIPPI	PUERTO RICO
HAWAII	NEW HAMPSHIRE	SOUTH CAROLINA
ILLINOIS	NEW JERSEY	TENNESSEE
INDIANA	NEW MEXICO	WASHINGTON
IOWA	NEW ORLEANS	WISCONSIN

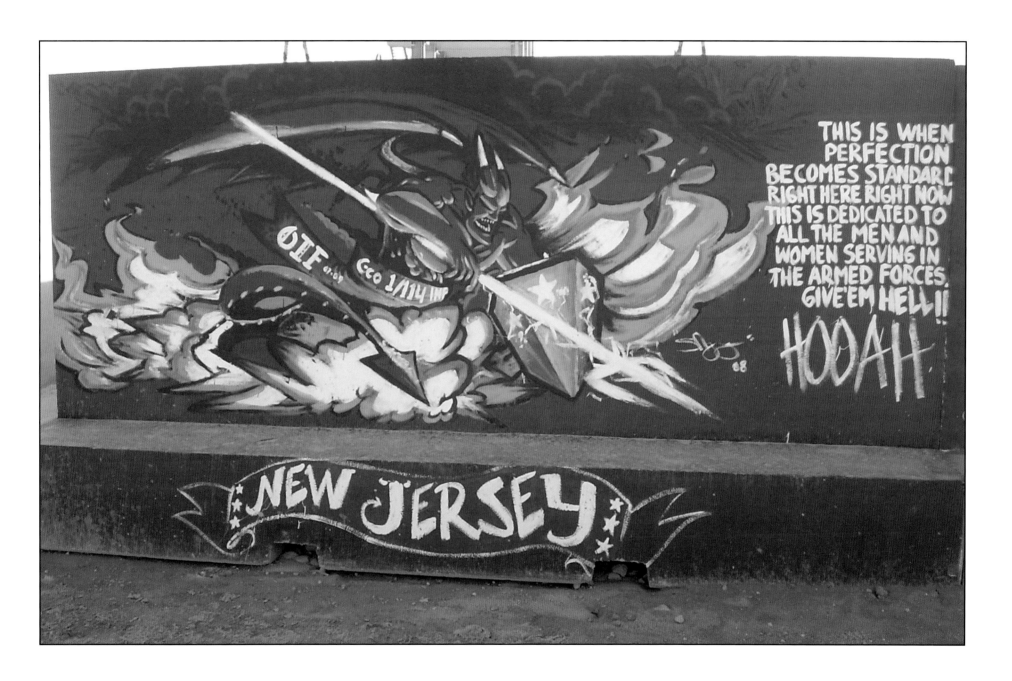

THIS IS WHEN PERFECTION BECOMES STANDARD RIGHT HERE RIGHT NOW THIS IS DEDICATED TO ALL THE MEN AND WOMEN SERVING IN THE ARMED FORCES. GIVE'EM HELL !! HOOAH

OIF 07-09 Cco 1/114 INF

NEW JERSEY

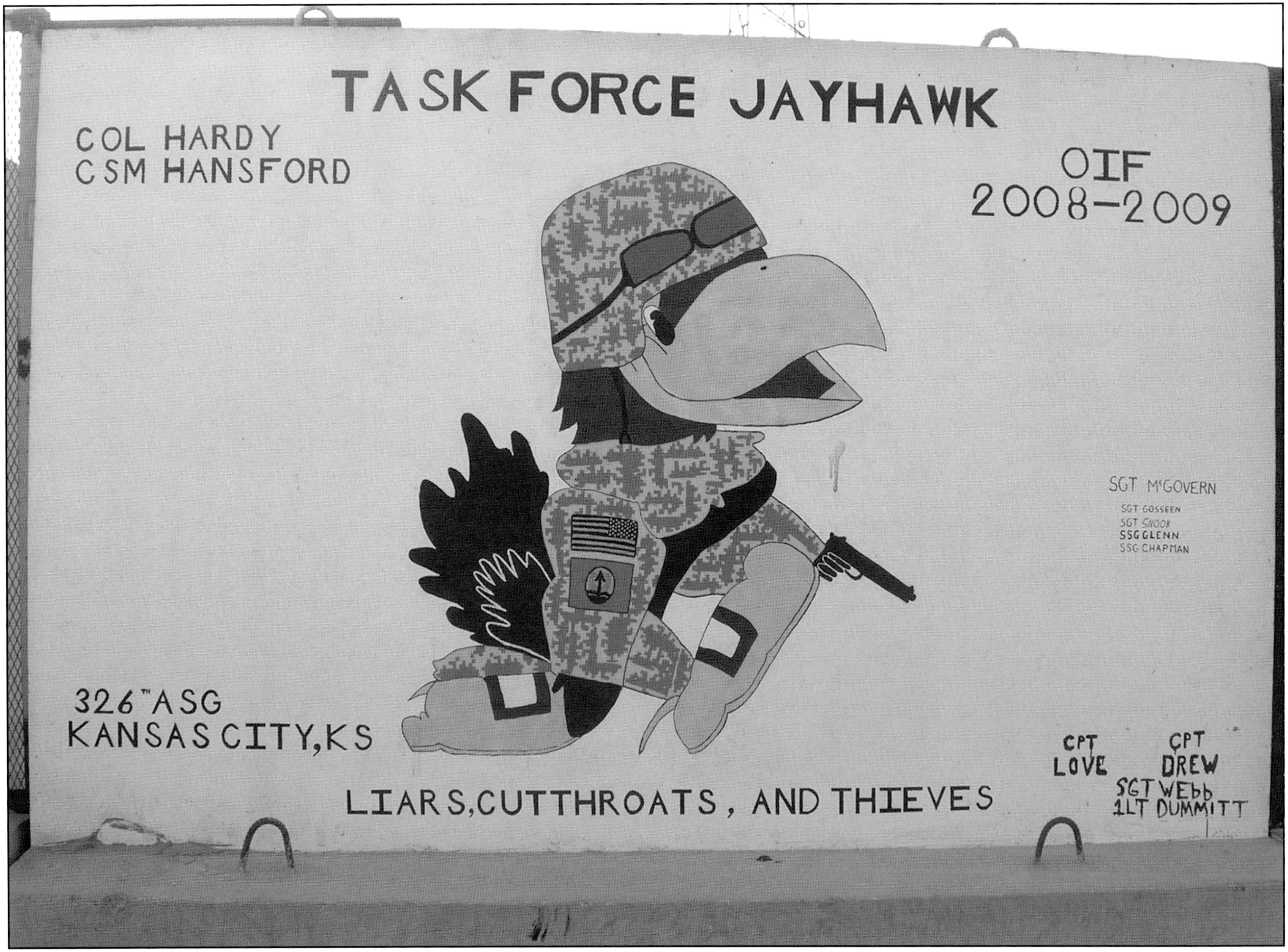

TASK FORCE JAYHAWK

COL HARDY
CSM HANSFORD

OIF
2008-2009

SGT McGOVERN

SGT GOSSEEN
SGT SNOOK
SSG GLENN
SSG CHAPMAN

326ᵀᴴ ASG
KANSAS CITY, KS

CPT
LOVE

CPT
DREW
SGT WEBB
1LT DUMMITT

LIARS, CUTTHROATS, AND THIEVES

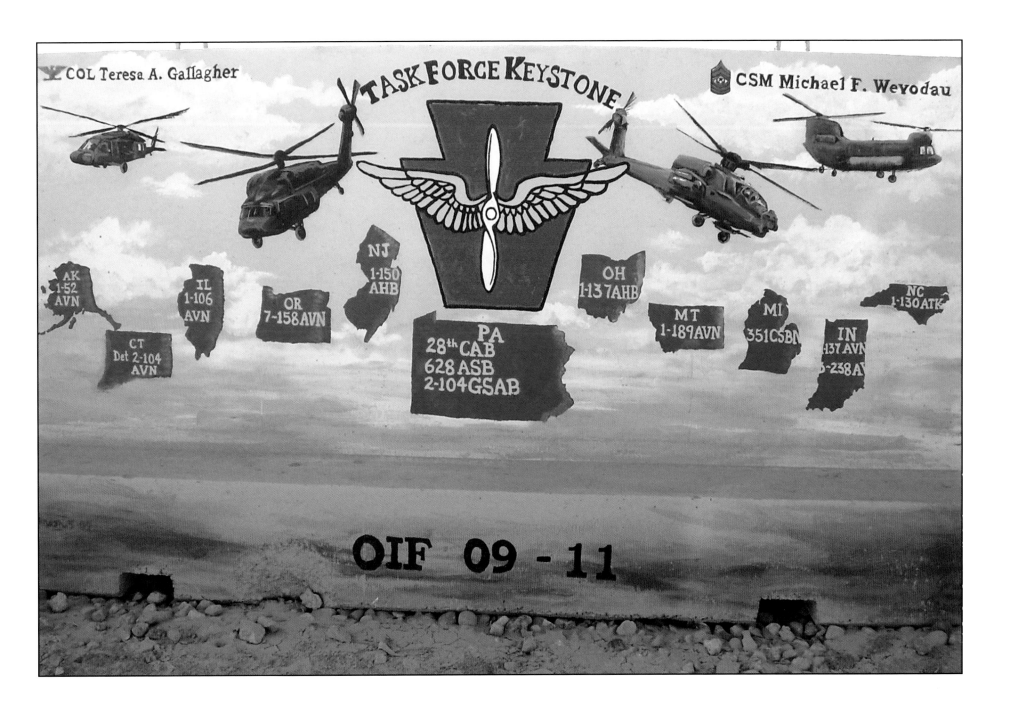

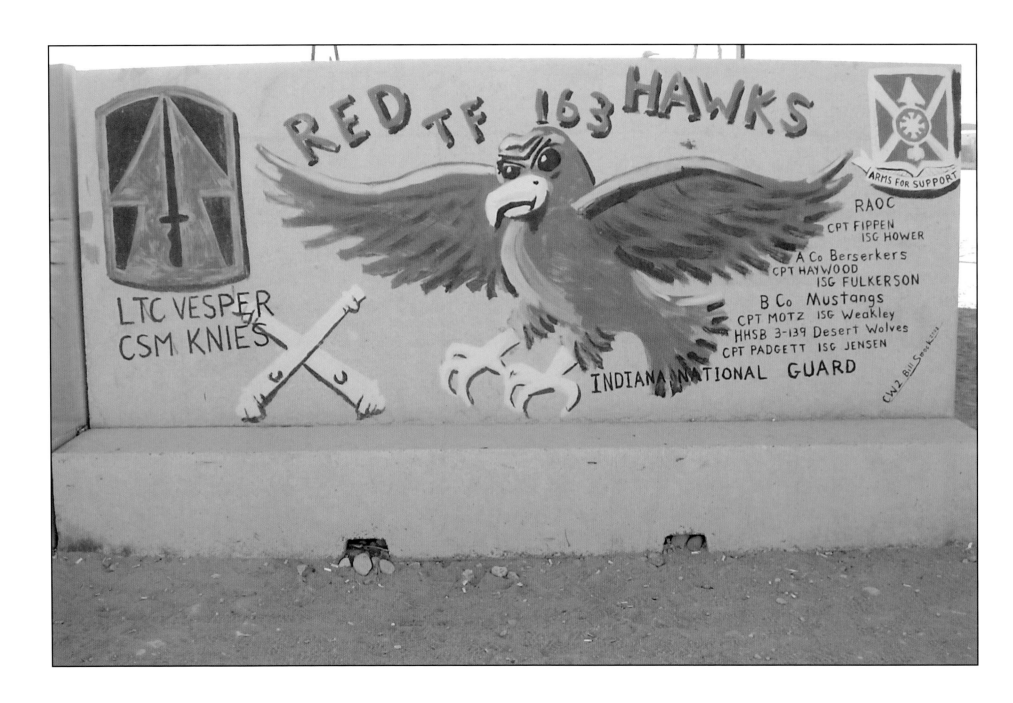

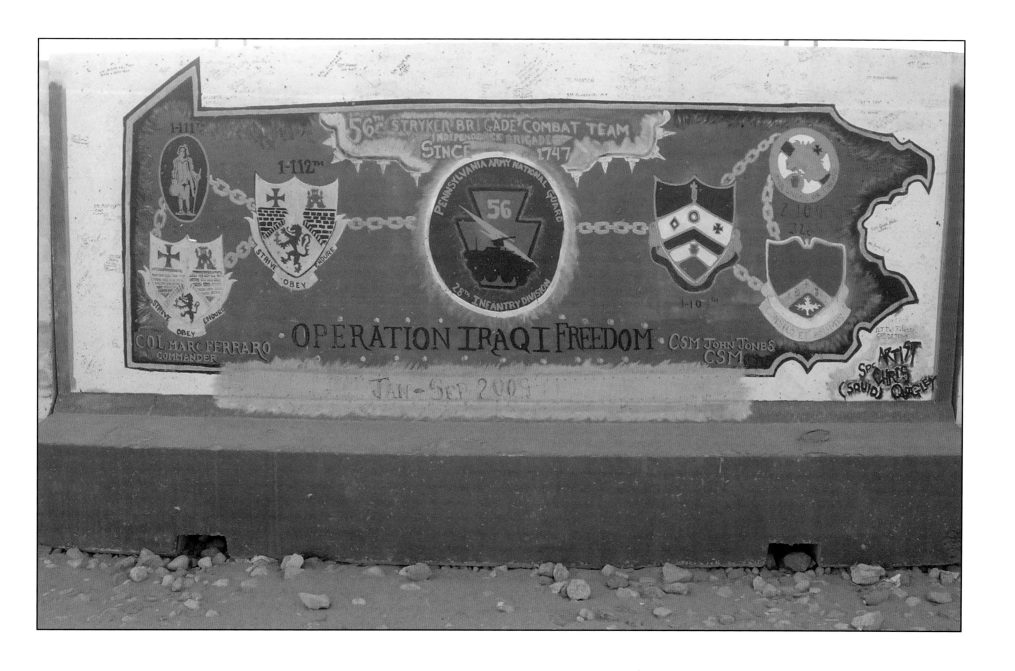

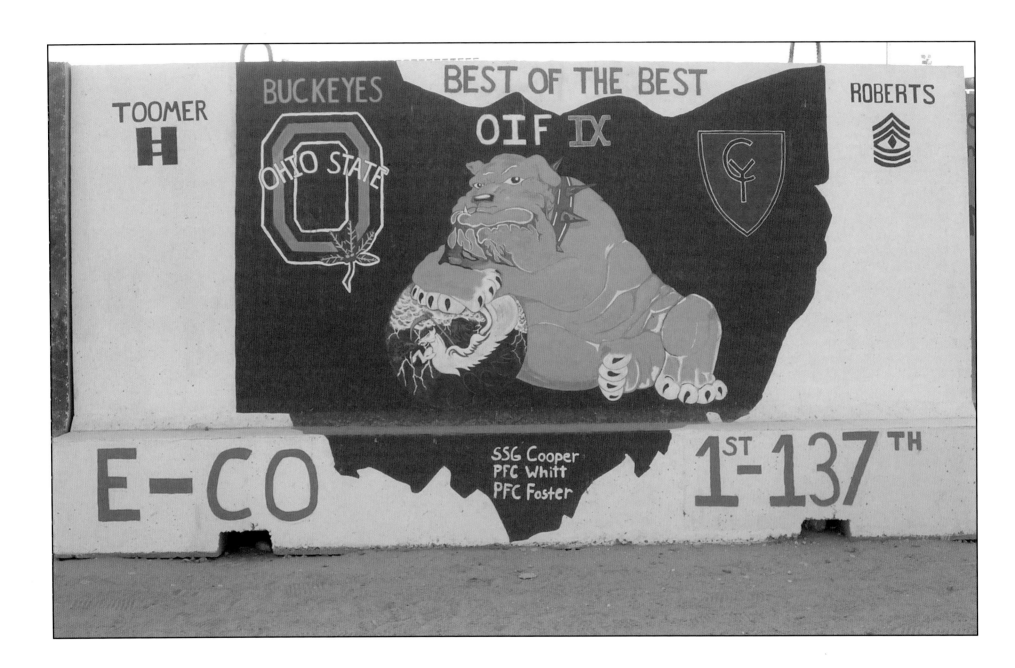

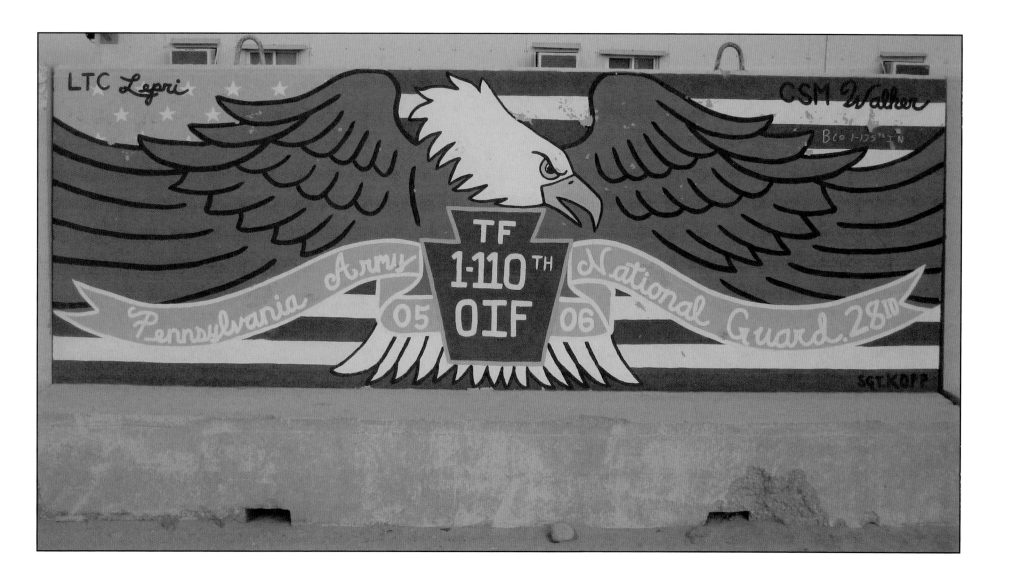

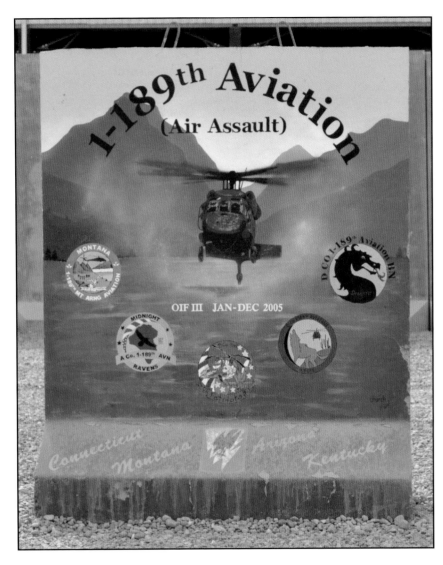

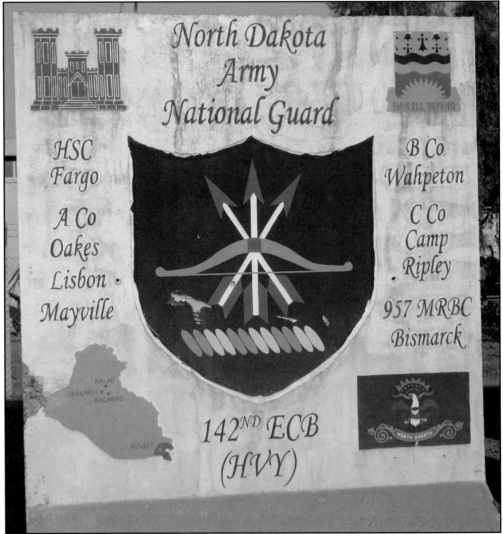

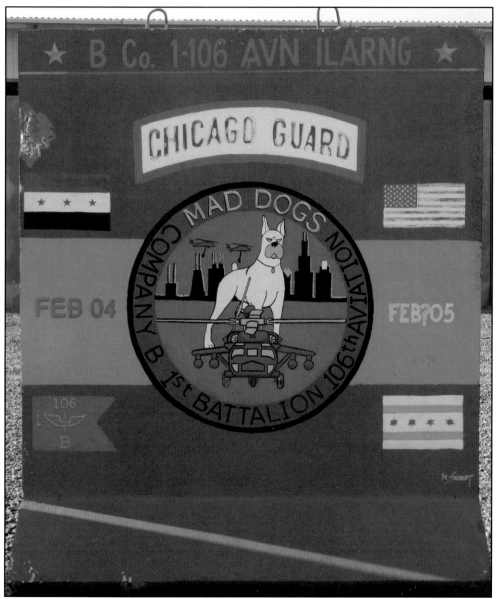

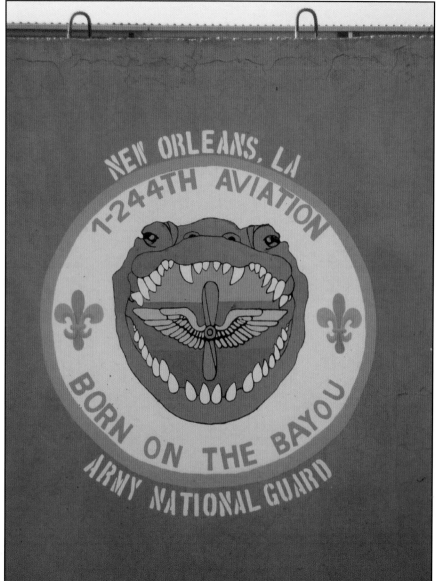

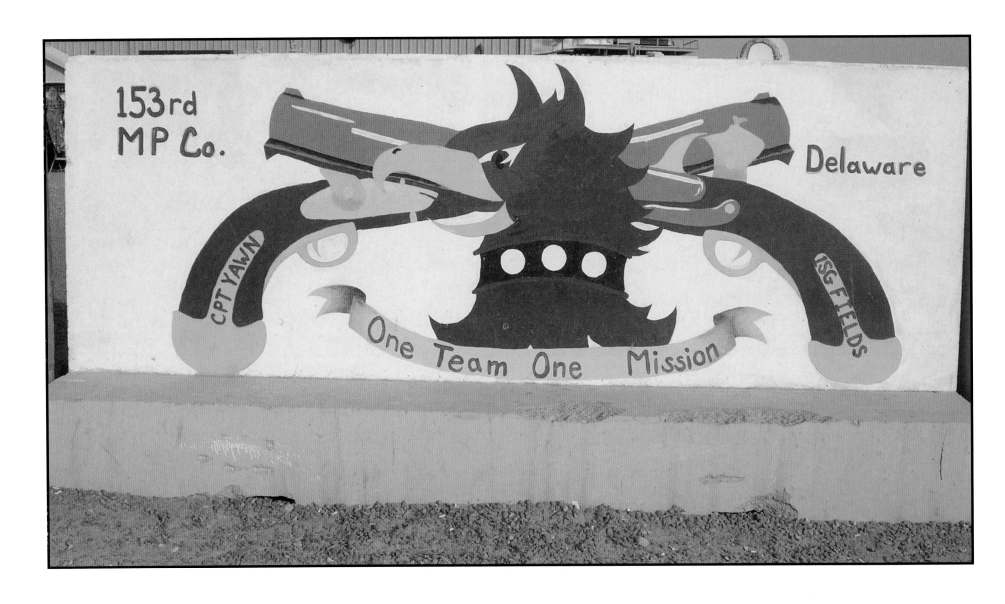

153rd MP Co.

Delaware

CPT YAWN

1SG FIELDS

One Team One Mission

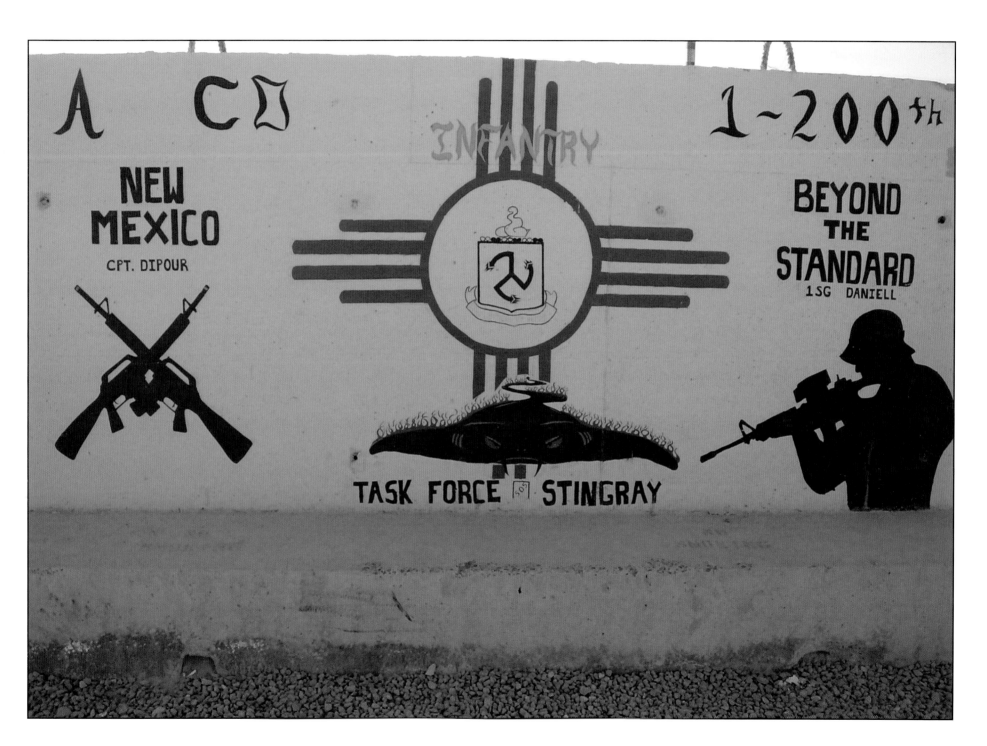

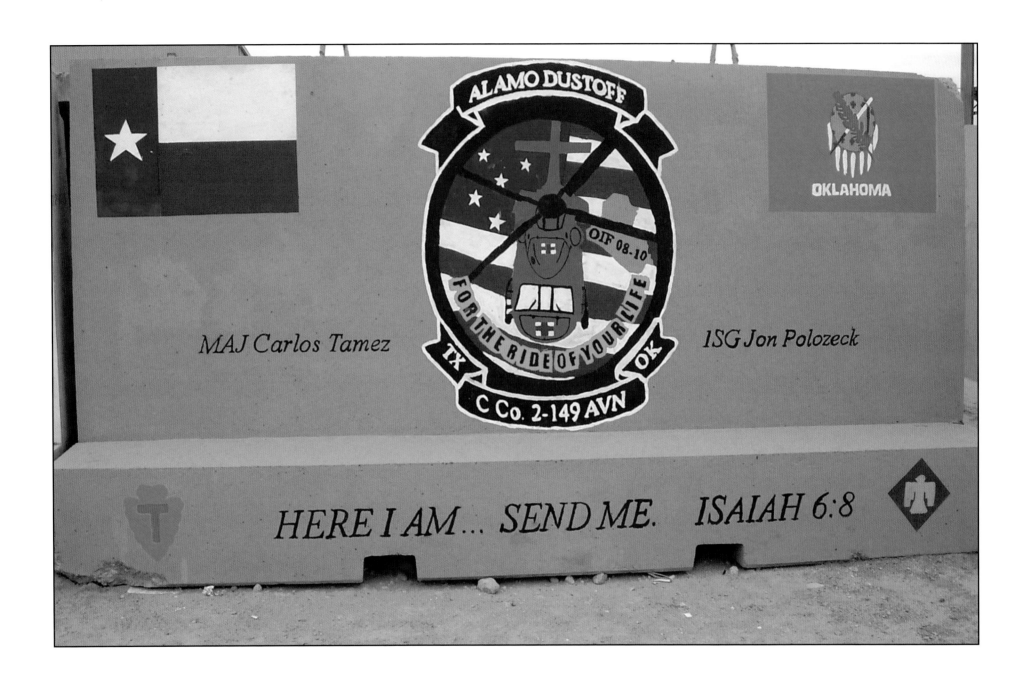

ALAMO DUSTOFF

OIF 08-10

FOR THE RIDE OF YOUR LIFE

TX   OK

C Co. 2-149 AVN

OKLAHOMA

MAJ Carlos Tamez

1SG Jon Polozeck

HERE I AM... SEND ME.   ISAIAH 6:8

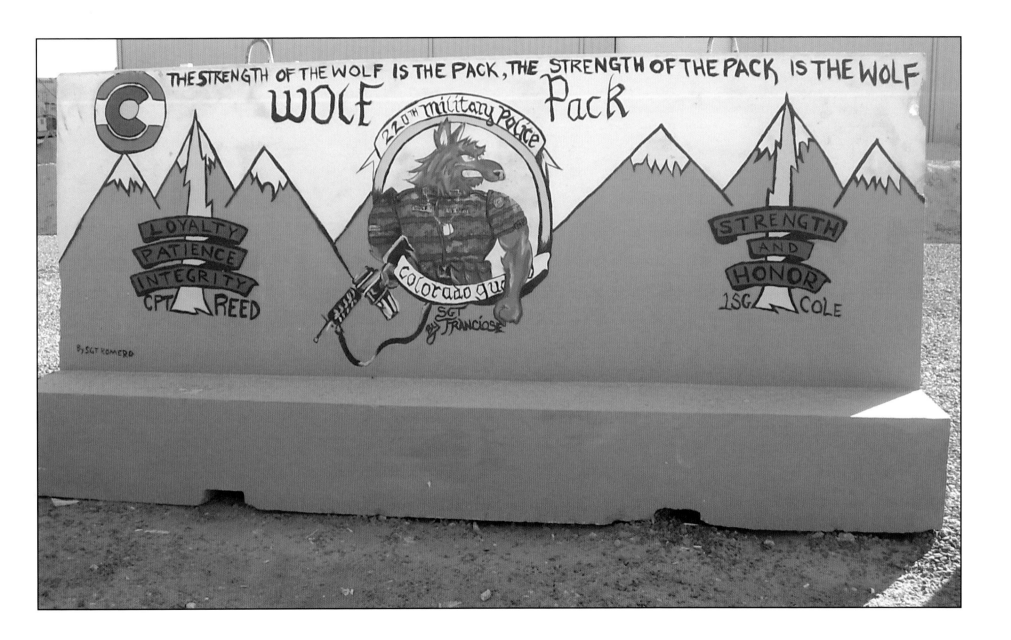

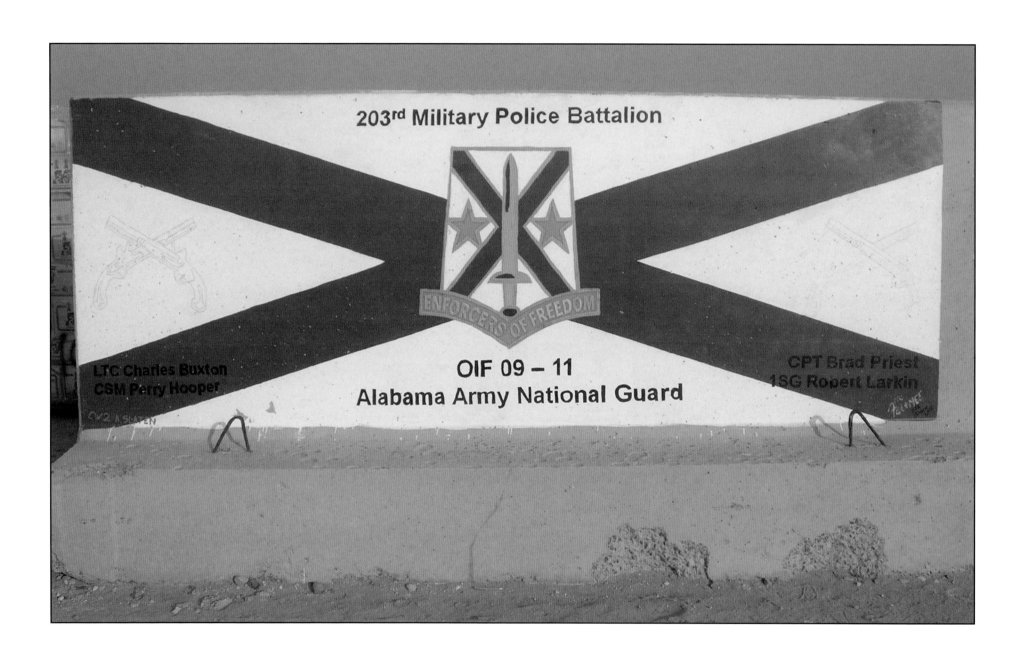

203rd Military Police Battalion

ENFORCERS OF FREEDOM

OIF 09 – 11
Alabama Army National Guard

LTC Charles Buxton
CSM Perry Hooper

CPT Brad Priest
1SG Robert Larkin

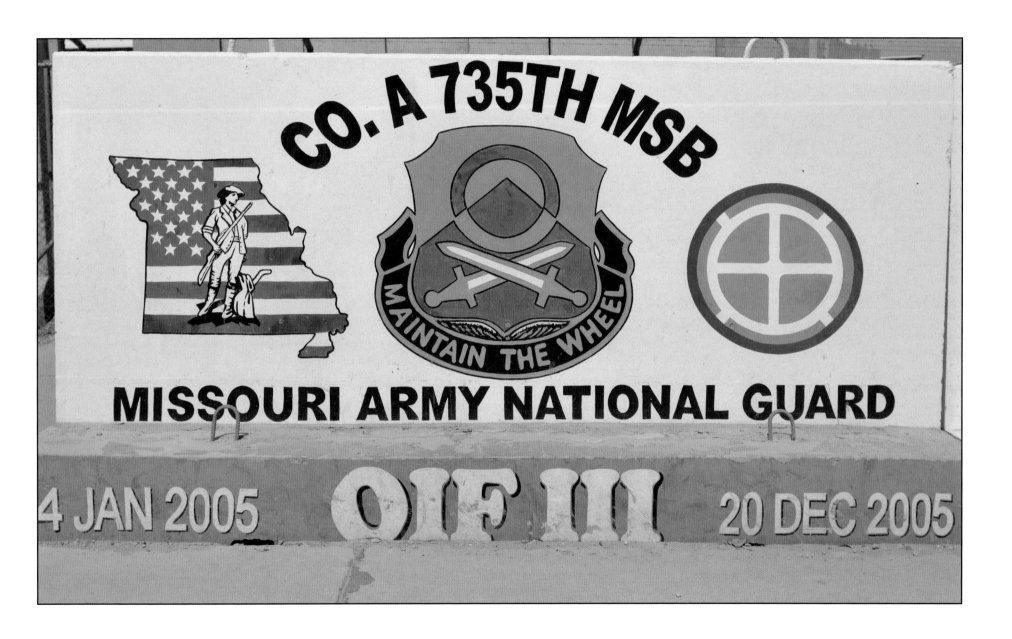

CO. A 735TH MSB

MAINTAIN THE WHEEL

MISSOURI ARMY NATIONAL GUARD

4 JAN 2005   OIF III   20 DEC 2005

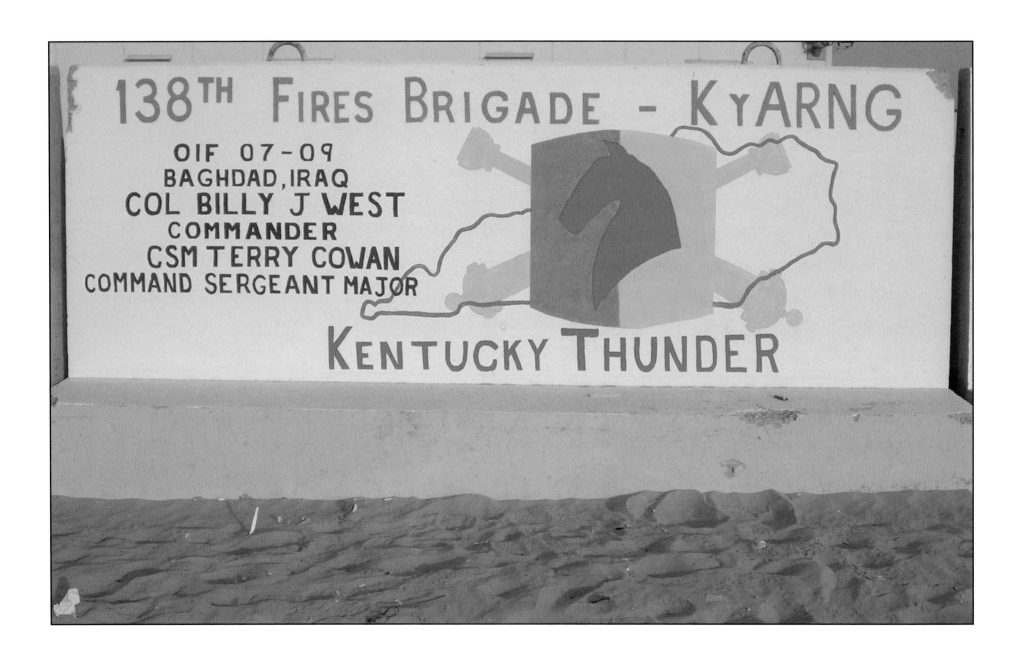

138TH FIRES BRIGADE - KYARNG

OIF 07-09
BAGHDAD, IRAQ
COL BILLY J WEST
COMMANDER
CSM TERRY COWAN
COMMAND SERGEANT MAJOR

KENTUCKY THUNDER

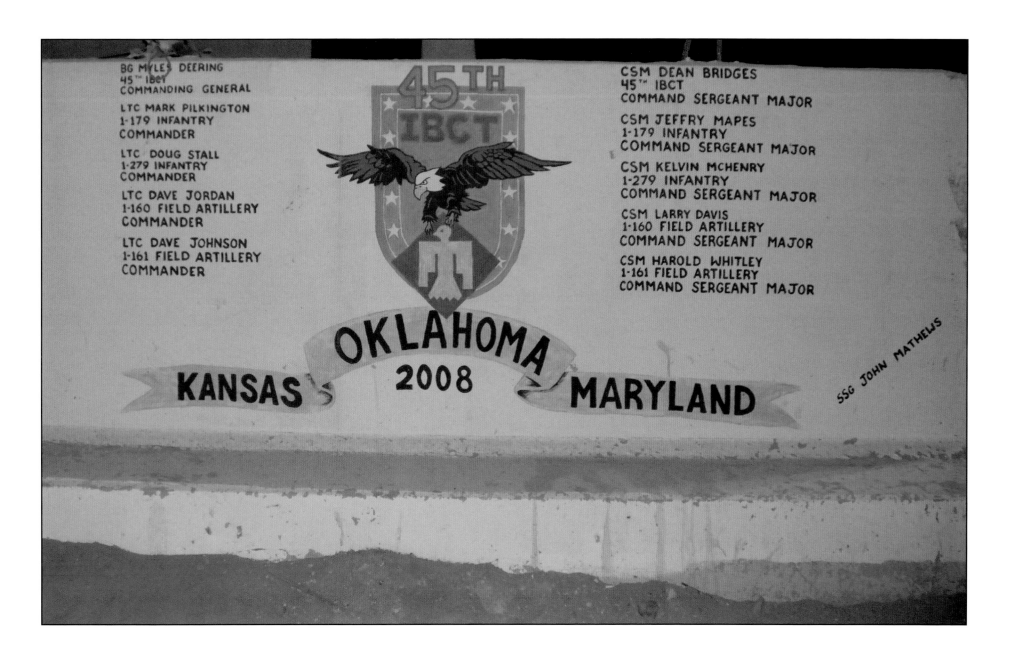

BG MYLES DEERING
45TH IBCT
COMMANDING GENERAL

LTC MARK PILKINGTON
1-179 INFANTRY
COMMANDER

LTC DOUG STALL
1-279 INFANTRY
COMMANDER

LTC DAVE JORDAN
1-160 FIELD ARTILLERY
COMMANDER

LTC DAVE JOHNSON
1-161 FIELD ARTILLERY
COMMANDER

45TH IBCT

CSM DEAN BRIDGES
45TH IBCT
COMMAND SERGEANT MAJOR

CSM JEFFRY MAPES
1-179 INFANTRY
COMMAND SERGEANT MAJOR

CSM KELVIN MCHENRY
1-279 INFANTRY
COMMAND SERGEANT MAJOR

CSM LARRY DAVIS
1-160 FIELD ARTILLERY
COMMAND SERGEANT MAJOR

CSM HAROLD WHITLEY
1-161 FIELD ARTILLERY
COMMAND SERGEANT MAJOR

OKLAHOMA
2008
KANSAS   MARYLAND

SSG JOHN MATHEWS

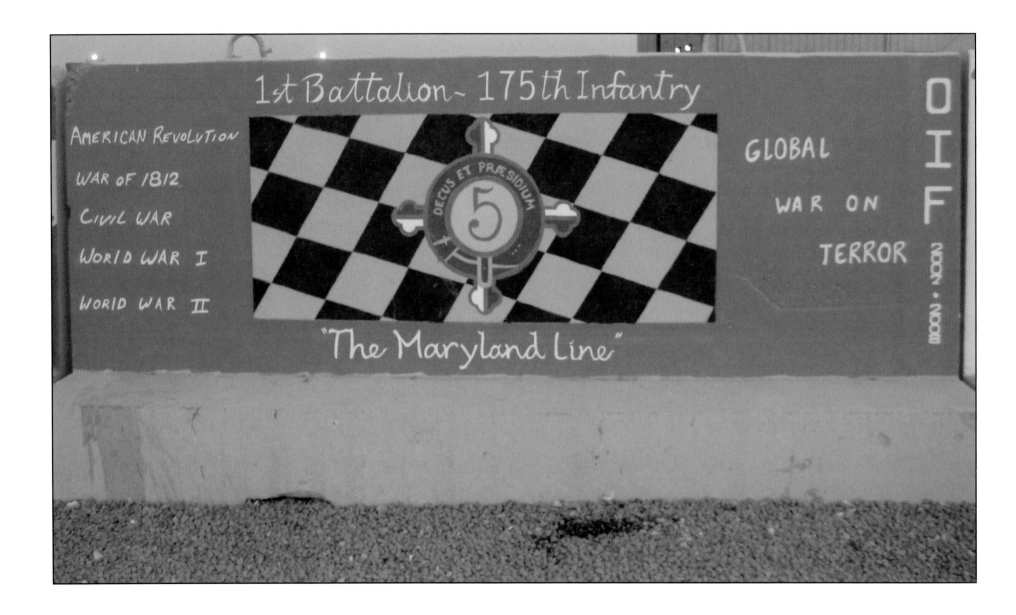

1st Battalion ~ 175th Infantry

AMERICAN REVOLUTION

WAR OF 1812

CIVIL WAR

WORLD WAR I

WORLD WAR II

DECUS ET PRÆSIDIUM
5

GLOBAL

WAR ON

TERROR

OIF
2003 • 2004

"The Maryland Line"

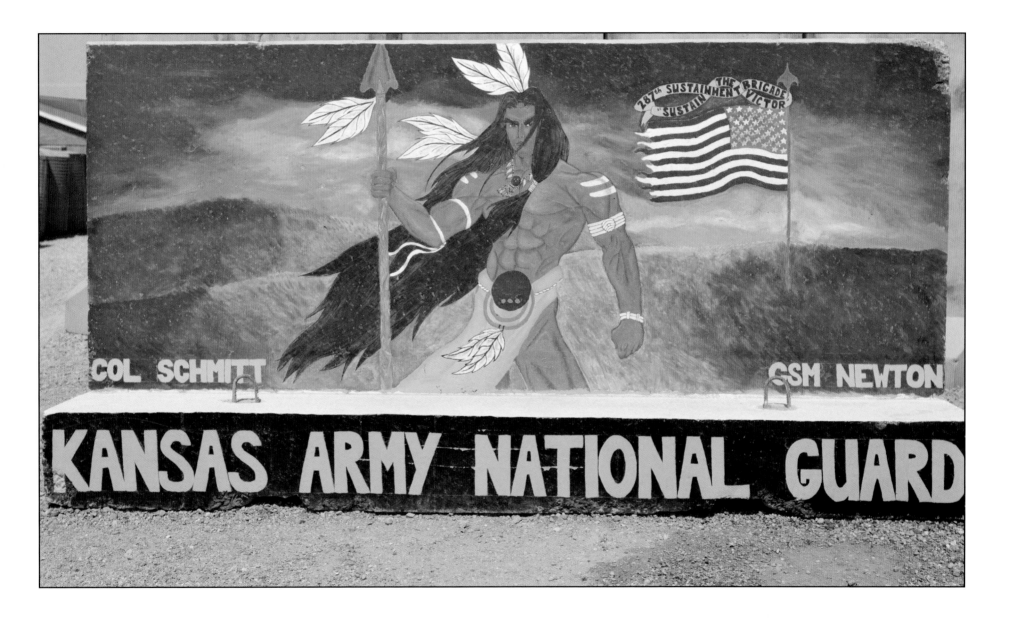

COL SCHMITT

CSM NEWTON

287th SUSTAINMENT BRIGADE
"SUSTAIN THE VICTOR"

KANSAS ARMY NATIONAL GUARD

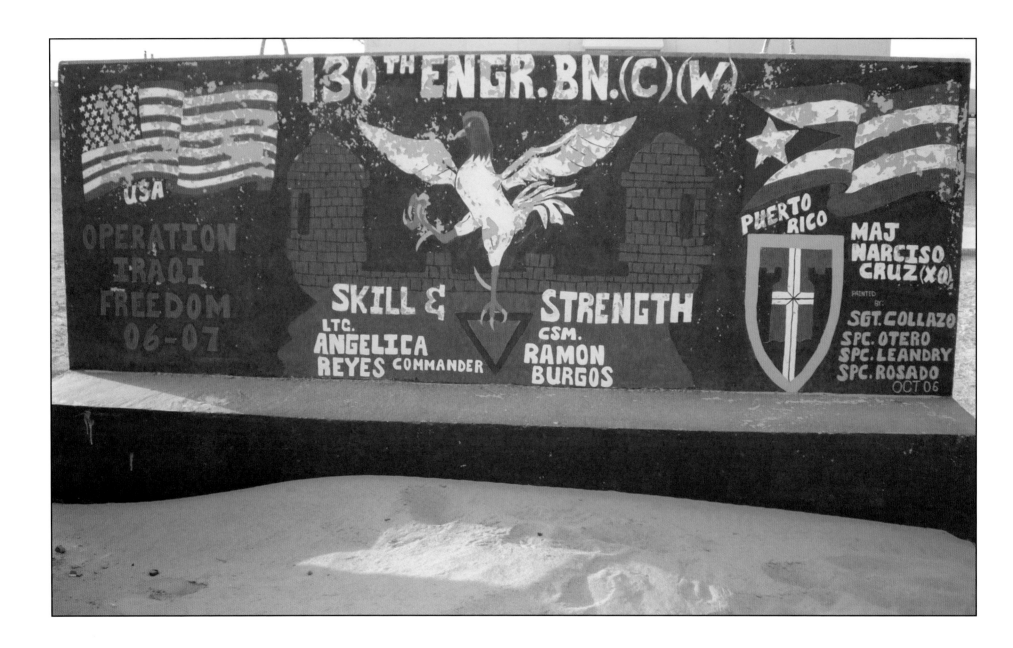

130TH ENGR. BN. (C) (W)

USA

OPERATION
IRAQI
FREEDOM
06-07

SKILL &

LTC.
ANGELICA
REYES COMMANDER

STRENGTH

CSM.
RAMON
BURGOS

PUERTO
RICO

MAJ
NARCISO
CRUZ (XO)

PAINTED
BY:
SGT. COLLAZO
SPC. OTERO
SPC. LEANDRY
SPC. ROSADO
OCT 06

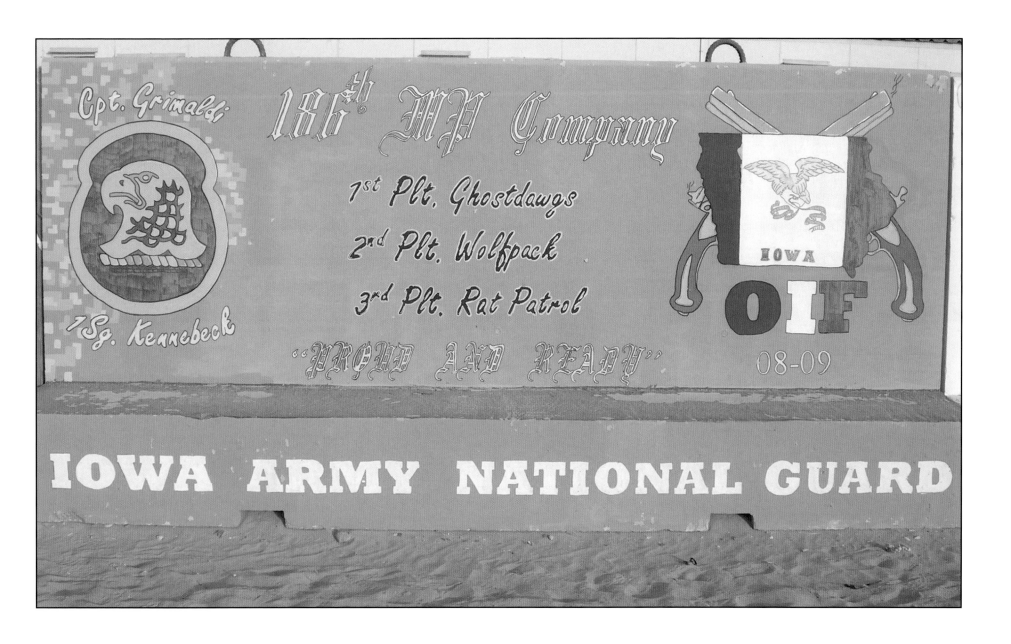

Cpt. Grimaldi

1Sg. Kennebeck

186th MP Company

1st Plt. Ghostdawgs
2nd Plt. Wolfpack
3rd Plt. Rat Patrol

"PROUD AND READY"

IOWA

OIF

08-09

IOWA ARMY NATIONAL GUARD

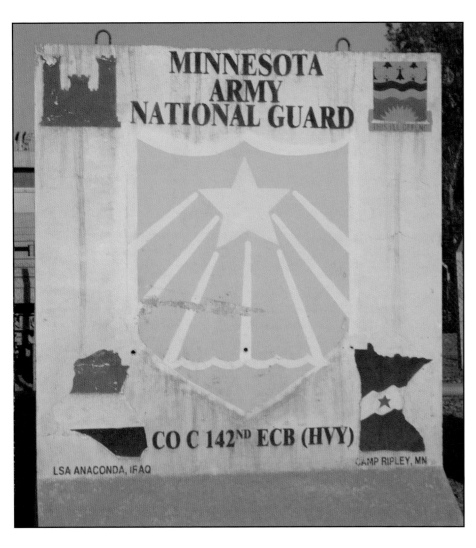

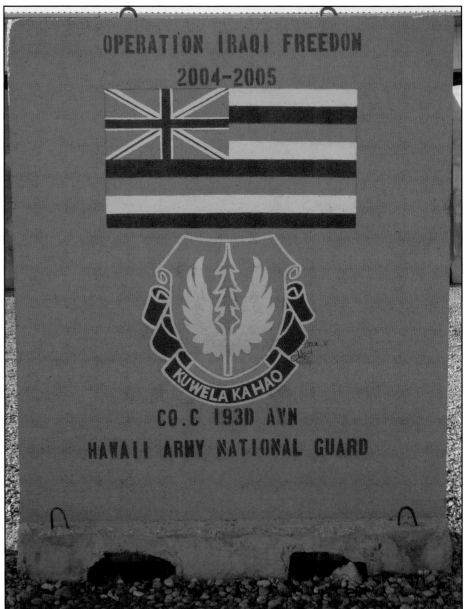

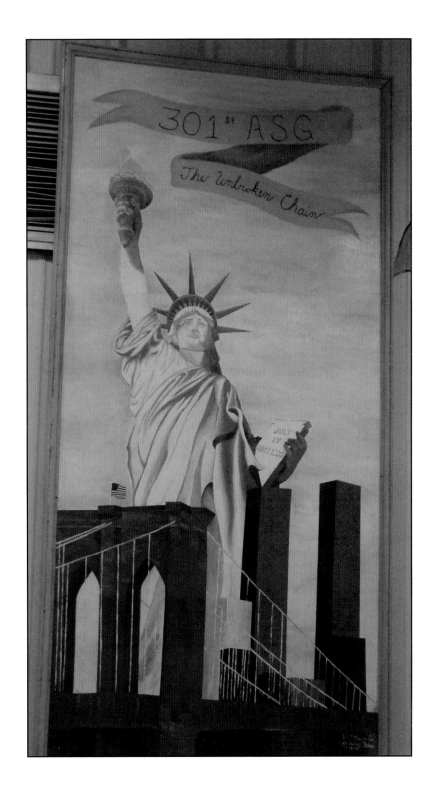

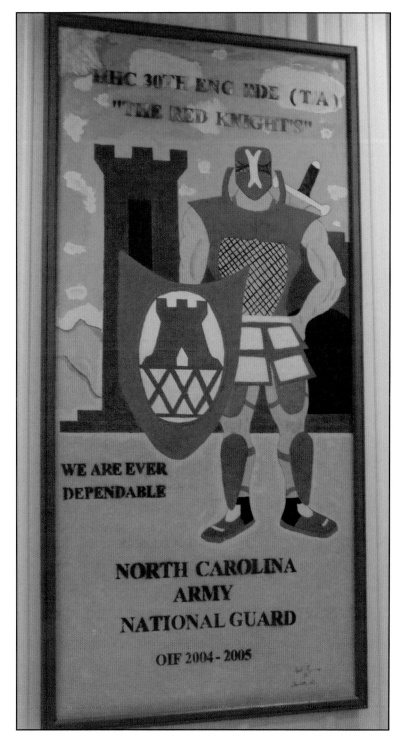

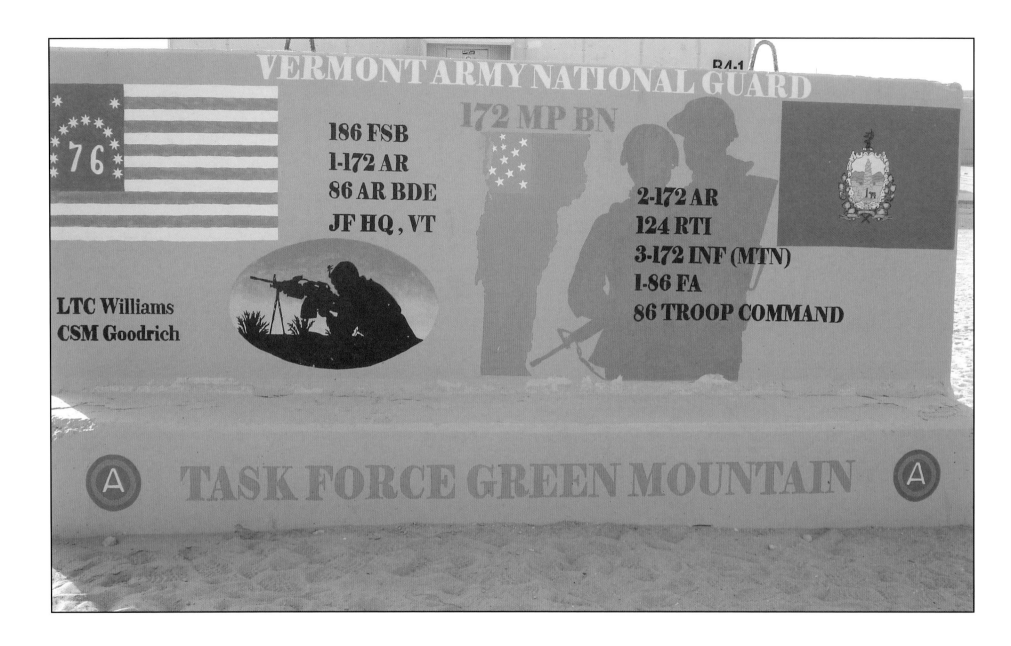

VERMONT ARMY NATIONAL GUARD

172 MP BN

186 FSB
1-172 AR
86 AR BDE
JF HQ , VT

2-172 AR
124 RTI
3-172 INF (MTN)
1-86 FA
86 TROOP COMMAND

LTC Williams
CSM Goodrich

TASK FORCE GREEN MOUNTAIN

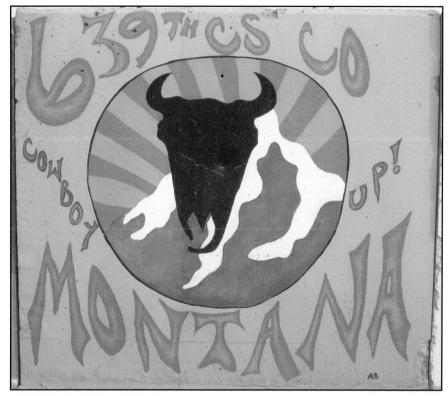

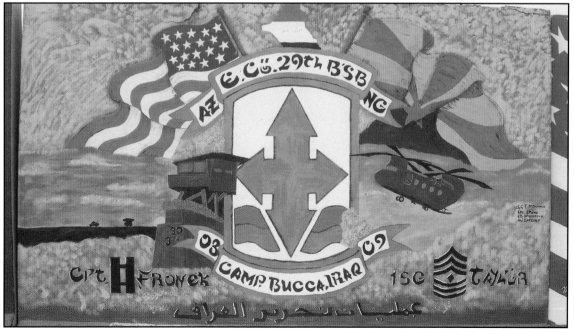

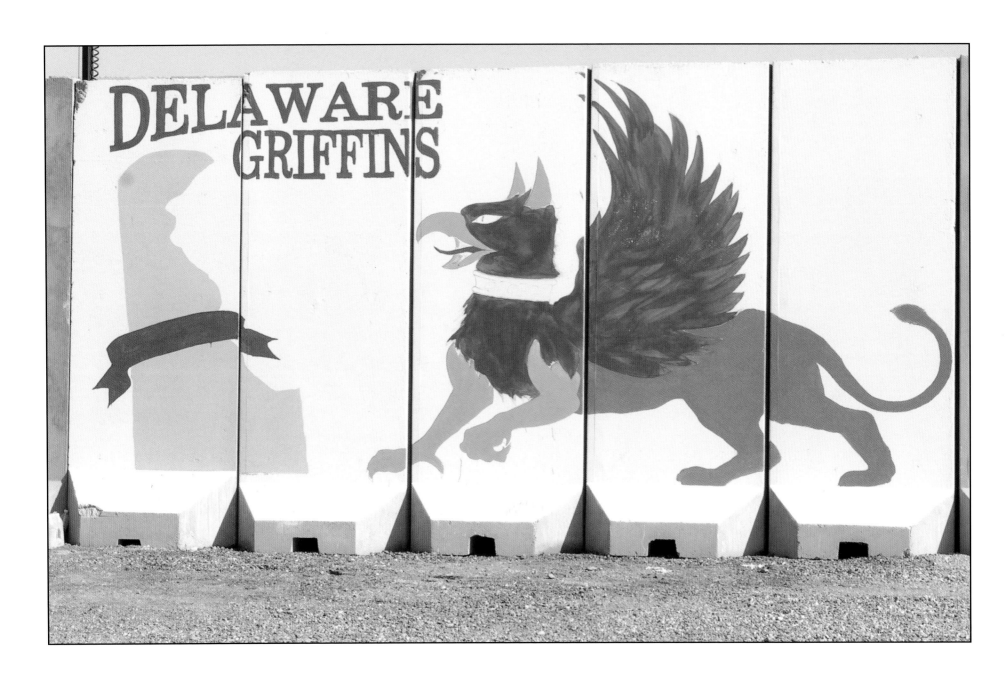

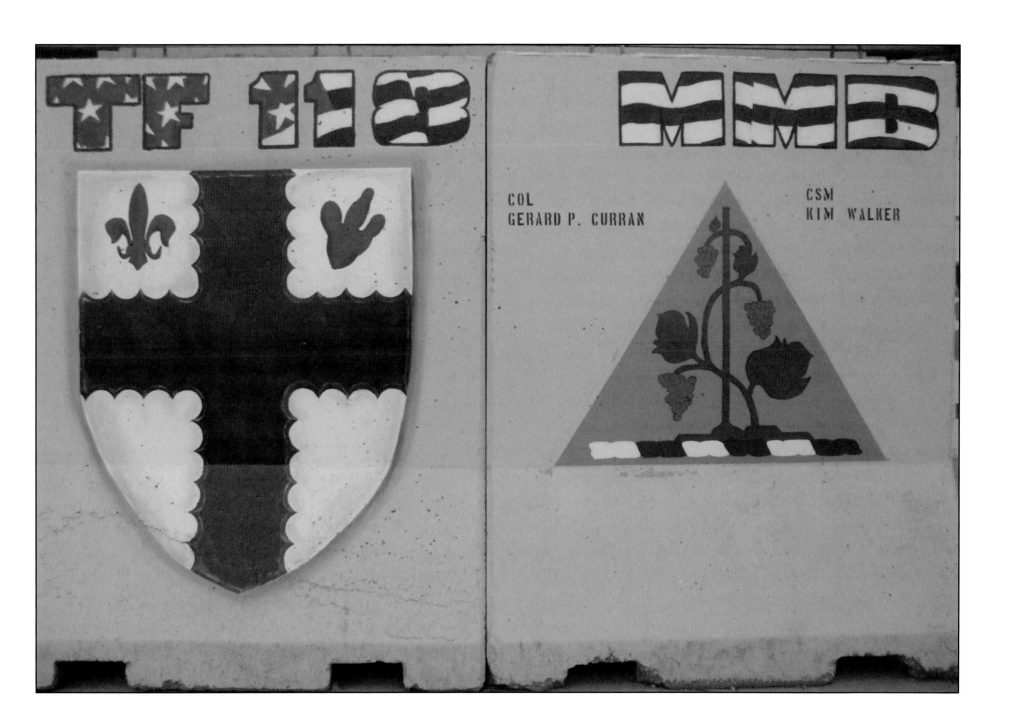

COL
GERARD P. CURRAN

CSM
KIM WALKER

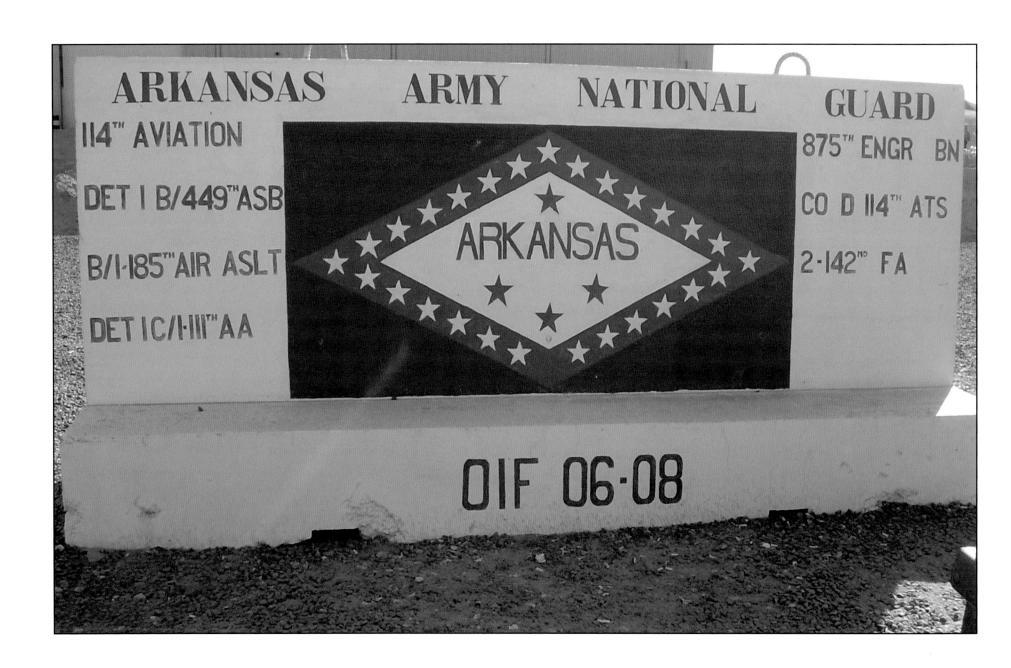

ARKANSAS ARMY NATIONAL GUARD

114TH AVIATION

DET I B/449TH ASB

B/1-185TH AIR ASLT

DET 1C/1-111TH AA

875TH ENGR BN

CO D 114TH ATS

2-142ND FA

ARKANSAS

OIF 06-08

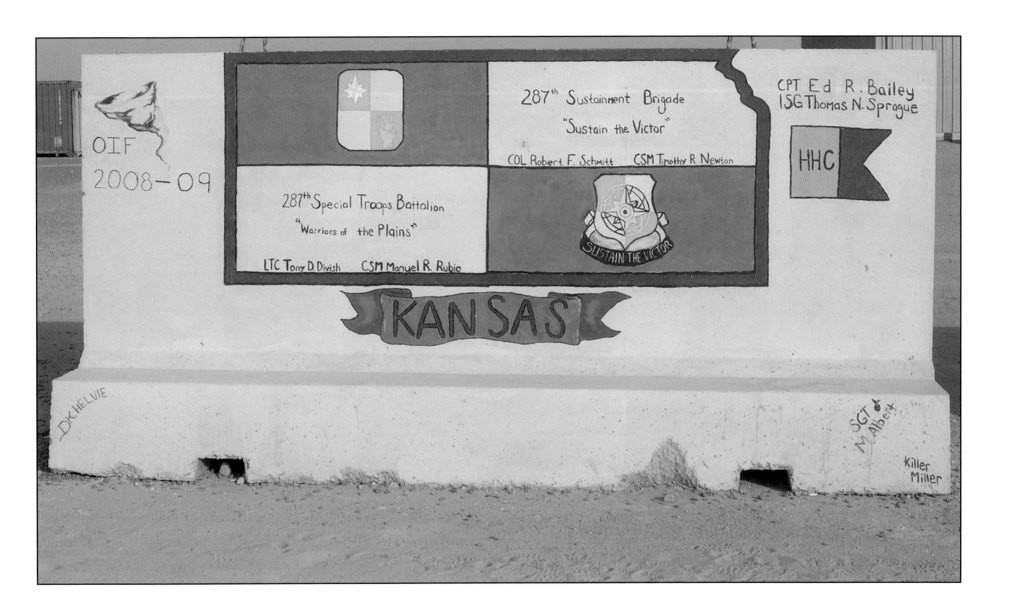

OIF 2008-09

287th Special Troops Battalion
"Warriors of the Plains"

LTC Tony D. Divish   CSM Manuel R. Rubio

287th Sustainment Brigade
"Sustain the Victor"

COL Robert F. Schmitt   CSM Timothy R. Newton

SUSTAIN THE VICTOR

CPT Ed R. Bailey
1SG Thomas N. Sprague

HHC

KANSAS

DK HELVIE

SGT M. Albert

Killer Miller

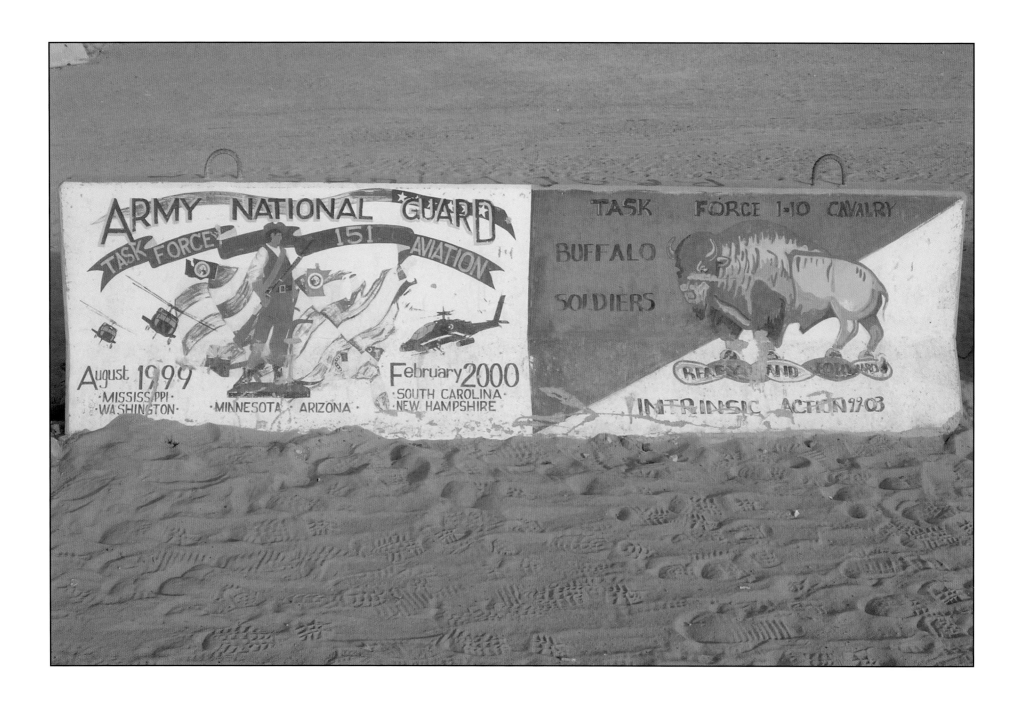

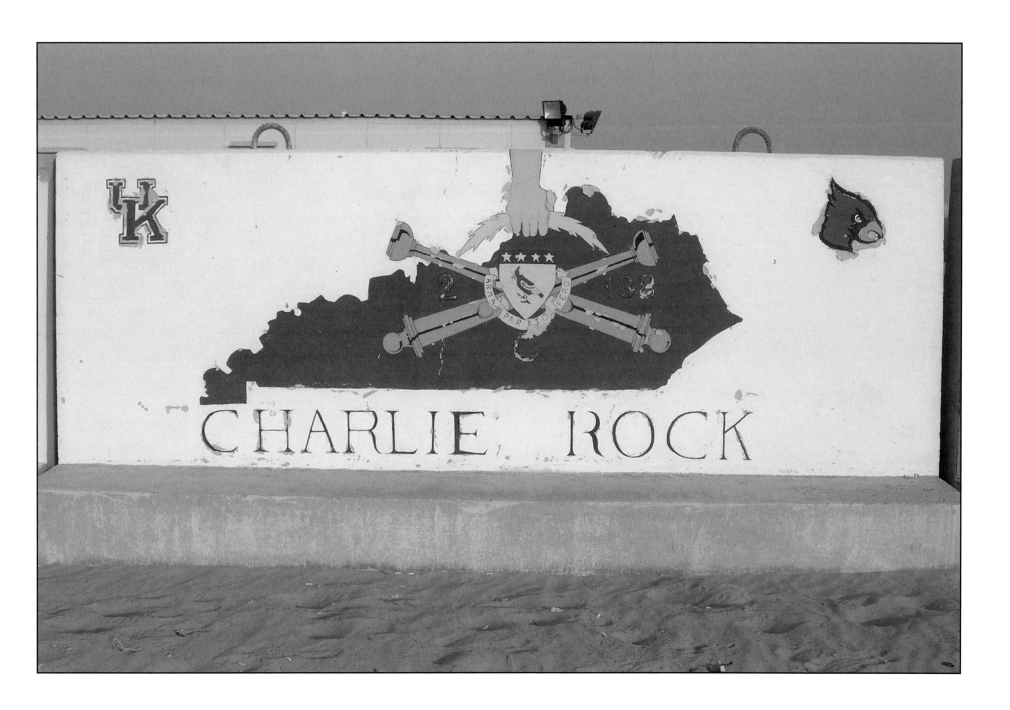

194th ENGINEER BRIGADE
TENNESSEE ARMY NATIONAL GUARD

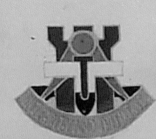

TASK FORCE
TITAN

BG ROBERT HARRIS
CSM CHARLES HUDSON

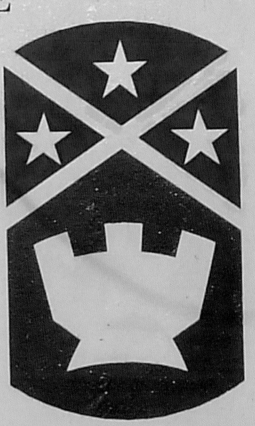

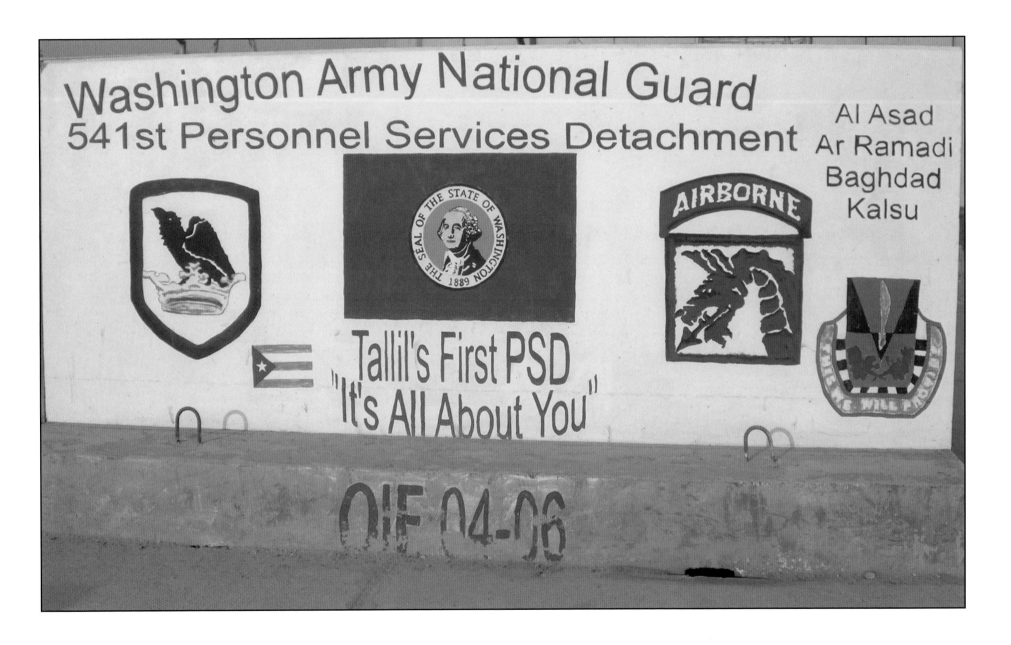

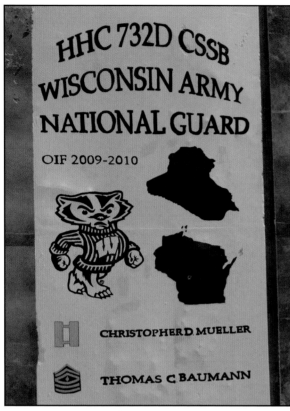

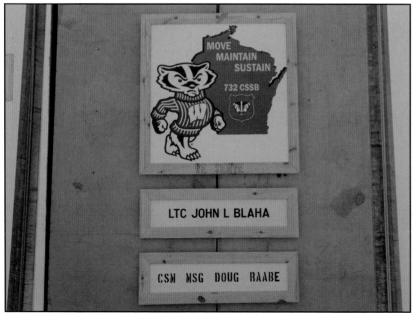

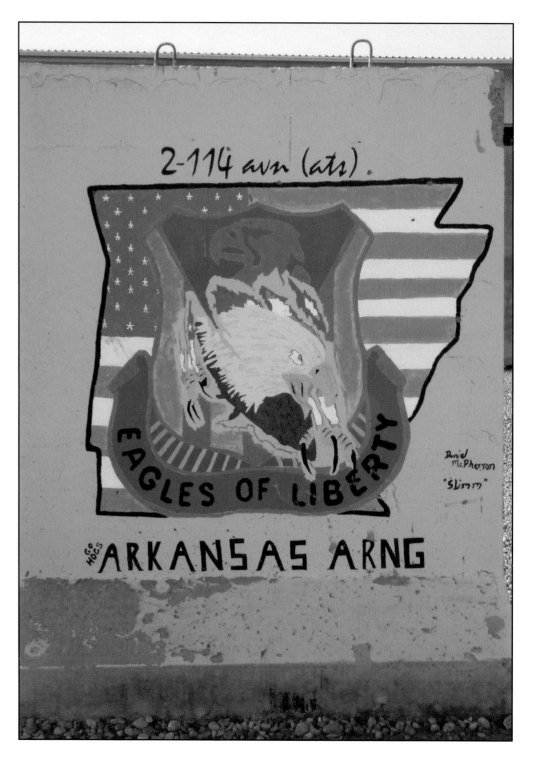

COALITION WALLS

AUSTRALIA

CZECH REPUBLIC

FRANCE

ITALY

NEW ZEALAND

ROMANIA

UNITED KINGDOM

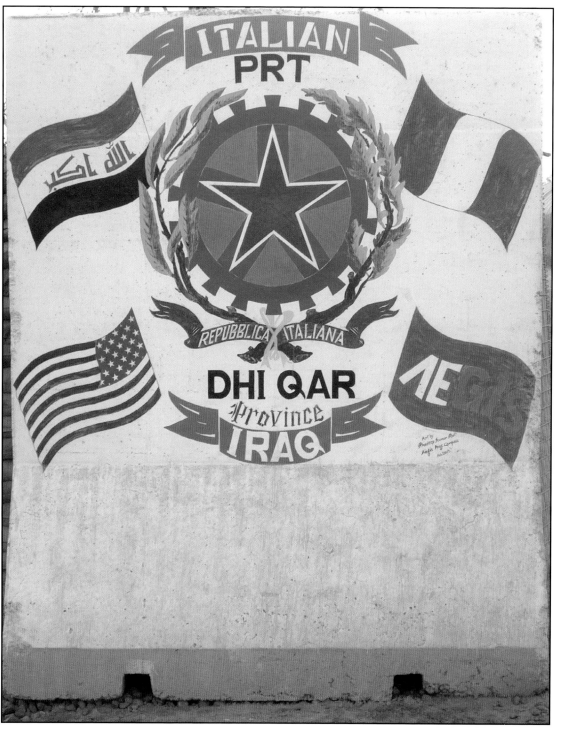

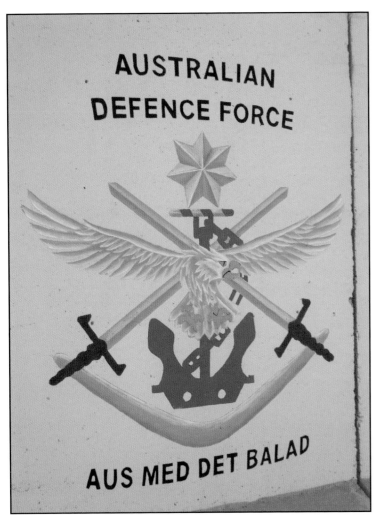

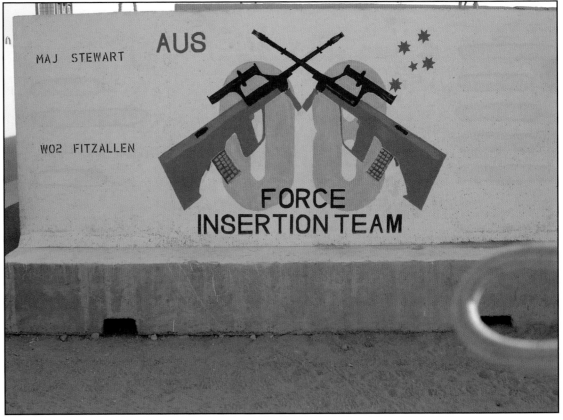

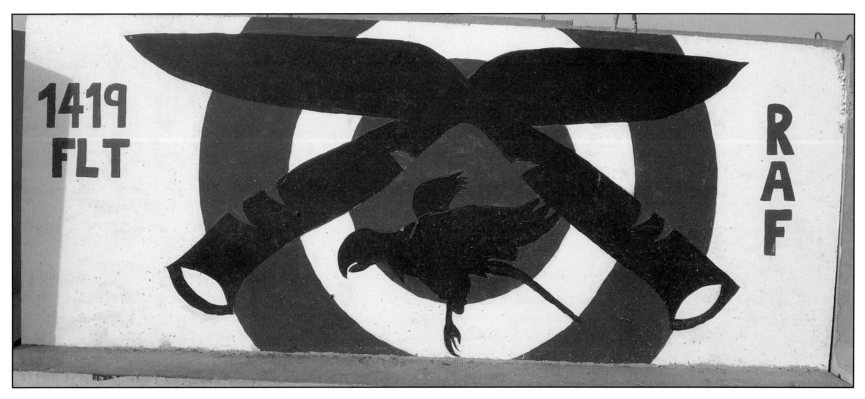

1419 FLT

RAF

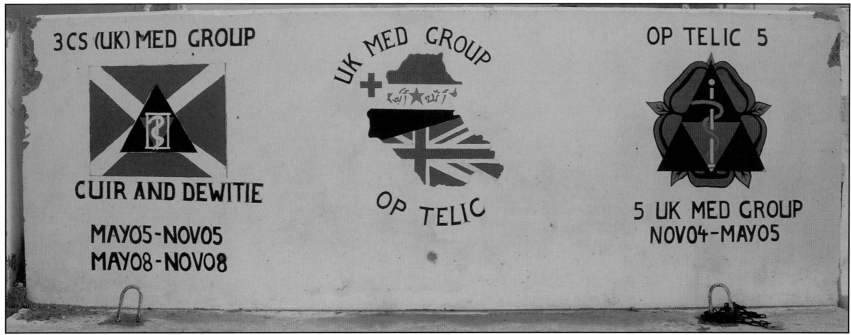

3CS (UK) MED GROUP

UK MED GROUP
+
OP TELIC

OP TELIC 5

CUIR AND DEWITIE

MAY05-NOV05
MAY08-NOV08

5 UK MED GROUP
NOV04-MAY05

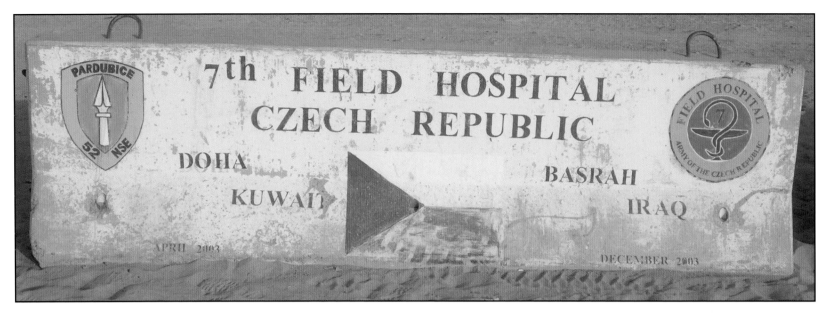

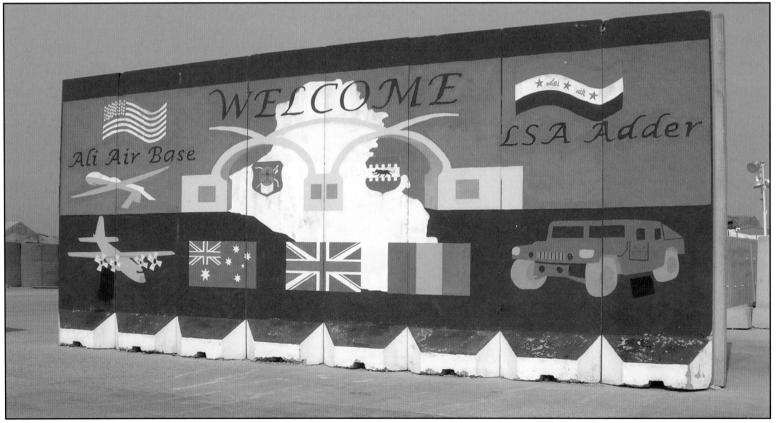

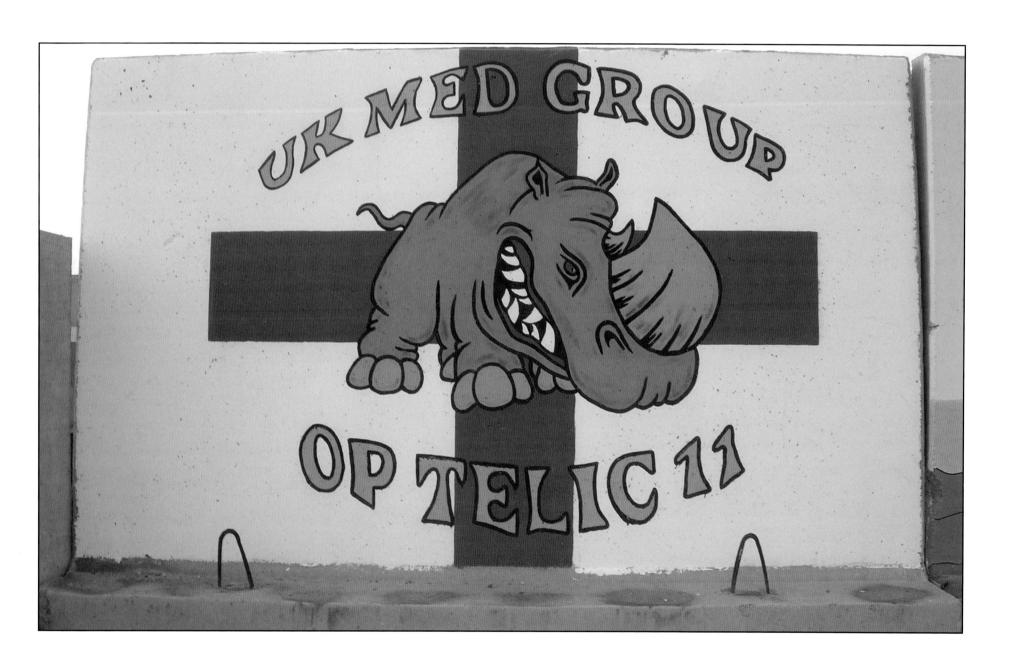

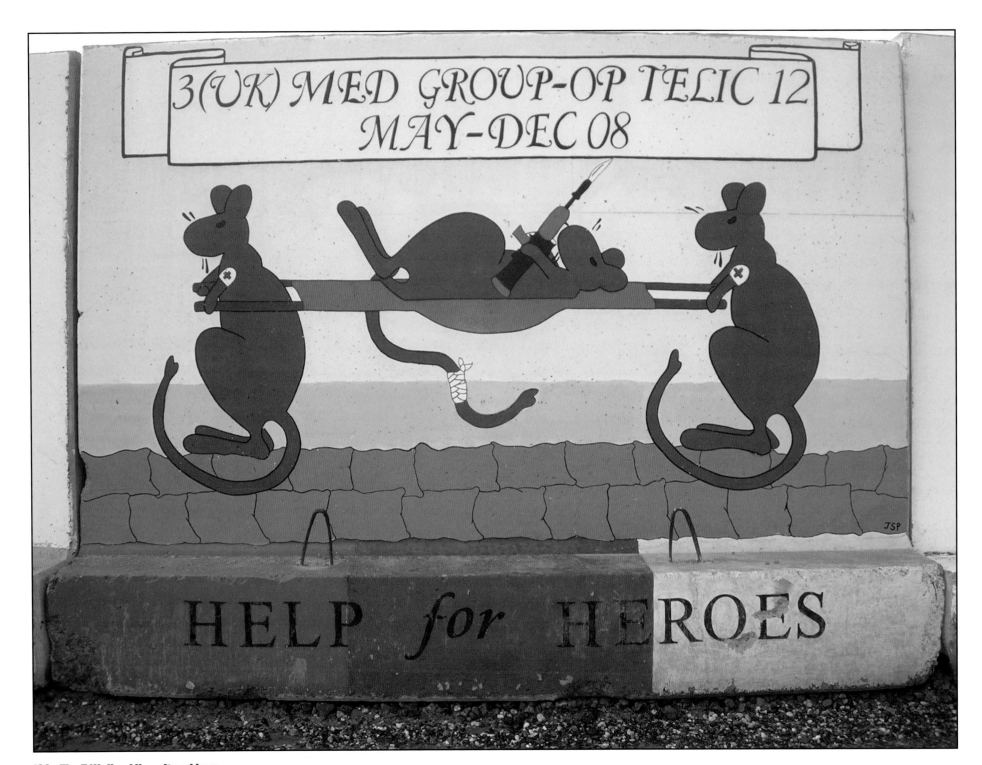

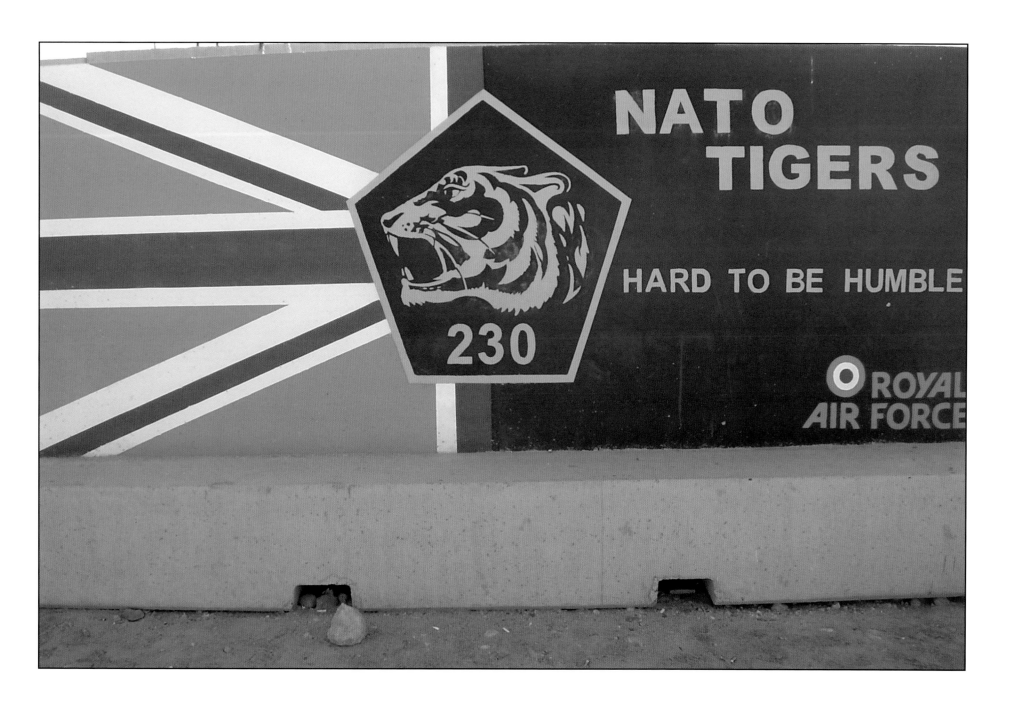

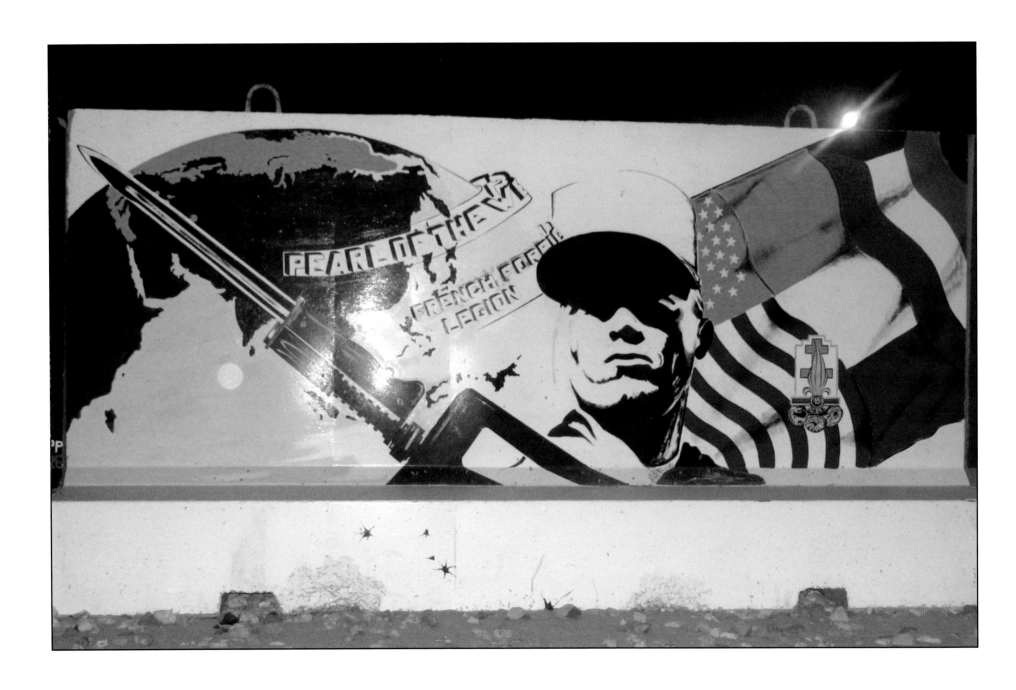

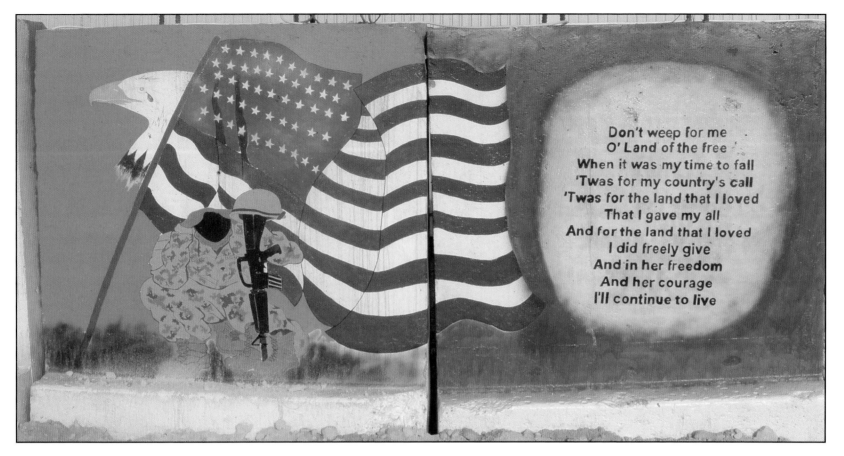

Don't weep for me
O' Land of the free
When it was my time to fall
'Twas for my country's call
'Twas for the land that I loved
That I gave my all
And for the land that I loved
I did freely give
And in her freedom
And her courage
I'll continue to live

MEMORIAL WALLS

TUSKEGEE AIRMEN-407 AEG 49
CAMP ADDER MEMORIAL 88

MAJOR STUART M. ANDERSON
SGT DANIEL J. BEARD
FRED BRYANT
PFC TROY COOPER
SGT JESSICA CAWVEY
SGT GERMAINE DEBRO
SPC DARYL DENT

CW2 BARRY EDWARDS
SPC RAYMOND J FAULSTICH
VERNON GASTON
SPC GREGORY GOODRICH
PFC ISAIAH HUNT
SPC KENNETH HAINES
DUSTIN JACKSON
DR. MARTIN LUTHER KING
SGT ELMER KRAUSE
SPC CHARLES LAMB

SPC VINCENT MADURO
PV 2 BARRY MAYO
SGT SHAWNA MORRISON
SGT JOSEPH NURRE
SGT IVORY PHIPPS
SGT ROCKY PAYNE
SPC JEREMY RIDLEN
SGT ERICH SMALLWOOD
SGT BRAD WENTZ

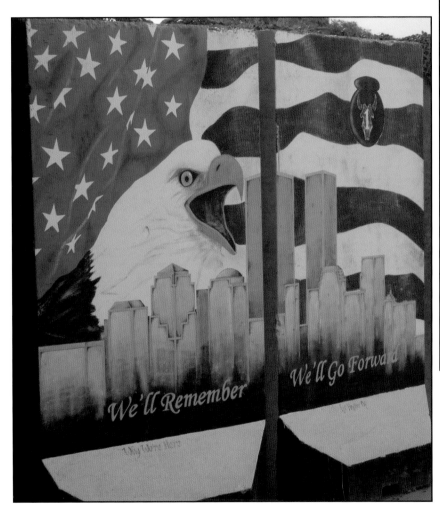

We'll Remember   We'll Go Forward

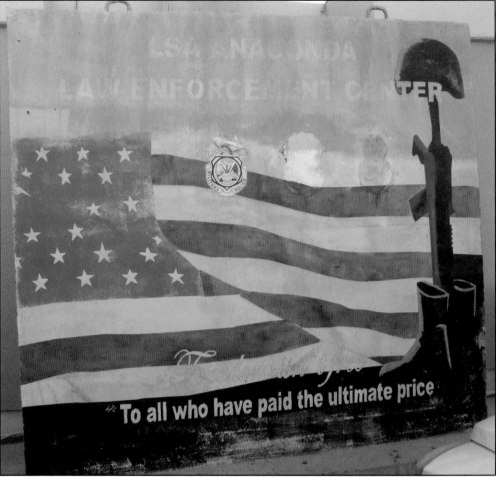

To all who have paid the ultimate price

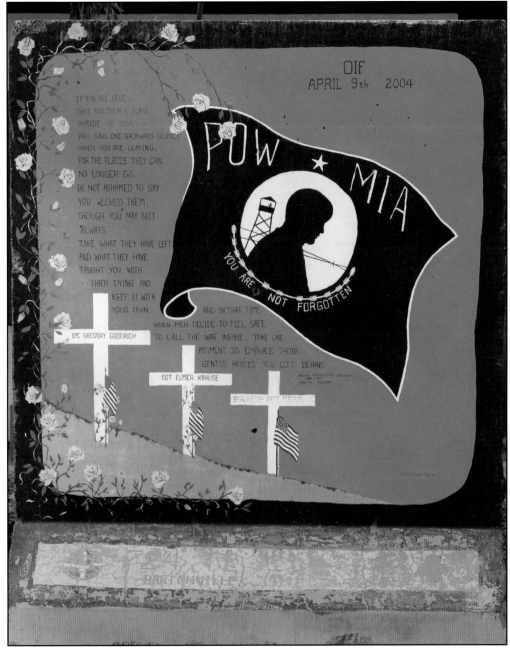

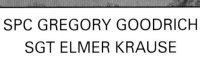

SPC GREGORY GOODRICH
SGT ELMER KRAUSE

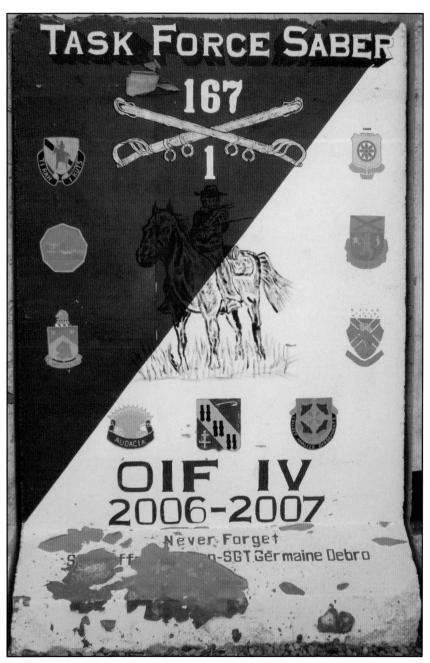

SGT GERMAINE DEBRO

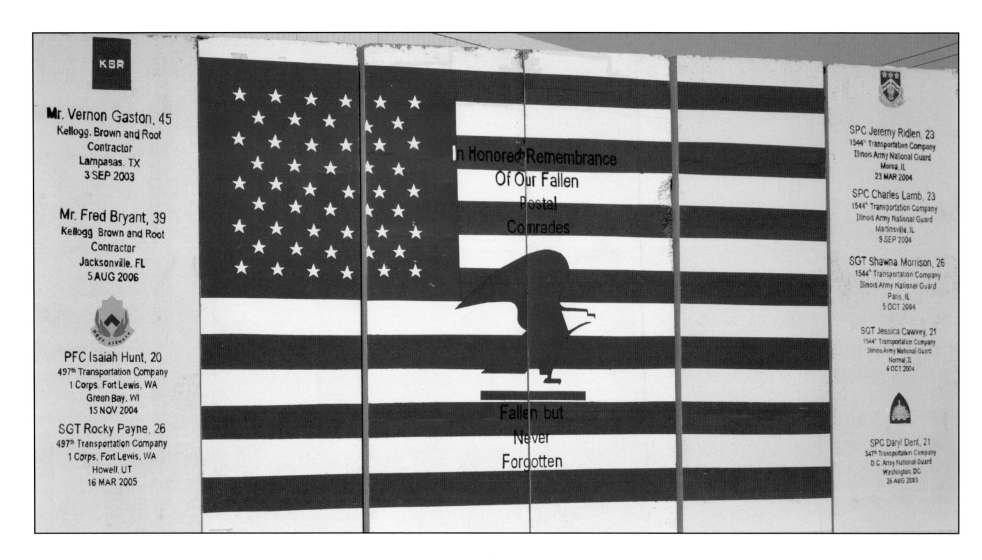

In Honored Remembrance
Of Our Fallen
Postal
Comrades

Fallen but
Never
Forgotten

KBR

Mr. Vernon Gaston, 45
Kellogg, Brown and Root
Contractor
Lampasas, TX
3 SEP 2003

Mr. Fred Bryant, 39
Kellogg Brown and Root
Contractor
Jacksonville, FL
5 AUG 2006

PFC Isaiah Hunt, 20
497th Transportation Company
1 Corps, Fort Lewis, WA
Green Bay, WI
15 NOV 2004

SGT Rocky Payne, 26
497th Transportation Company
1 Corps, Fort Lewis, WA
Howell, UT
16 MAR 2005

SPC Jeremy Ridlen, 23
1544th Transportation Company
Illinois Army National Guard
Moroa, IL
23 MAR 2004

SPC Charles Lamb, 23
1544th Transportation Company
Illinois Army National Guard
Martinsville, IL
9 SEP 2004

SGT Shawna Morrison, 26
1544th Transportation Company
Illinois Army National Guard
Paris, IL
5 OCT 2004

SGT Jessica Cawvey, 21
1544th Transportation Company
Illinois Army National Guard
Normal, IL
6 OCT 2004

SPC Daryl Dent, 21
547th Transportation Company
D.C. Army National Guard
Washington, DC
26 AUG 2003

VERNON GASTON - Lampasas, TX

FRED BRYANT - Jacksonville, FL

PFC ISAIAH HUNT - Green Bay, WI
497TH TRANS. CO. - FT. LEWIS, WA

SGT ROCKY PAYNE - Howell, UT
497TH TRANS. CO. - FT. LEWIS, WA

SPC JEREMY RIDLEN - Moroa, IL
1544TH TRANS. CO. - IL ARMY N.G.

SPC CHARLES LAMB - Martinsville, IL
1544TH TRANS. CO. - IL ARMY N.G.

SGT SHAWNA MORRISON - Paris, IL
1544TH TRANS. CO. - IL ARMY N.G.

SGT JESSICA CAWVEY - Normal, IL
1544TH TRANS. CO. - IL ARMY N.G.

SPC DARYL DENT - Washington, DC
547TH TRANS. CO. - DC ARMY N.G.

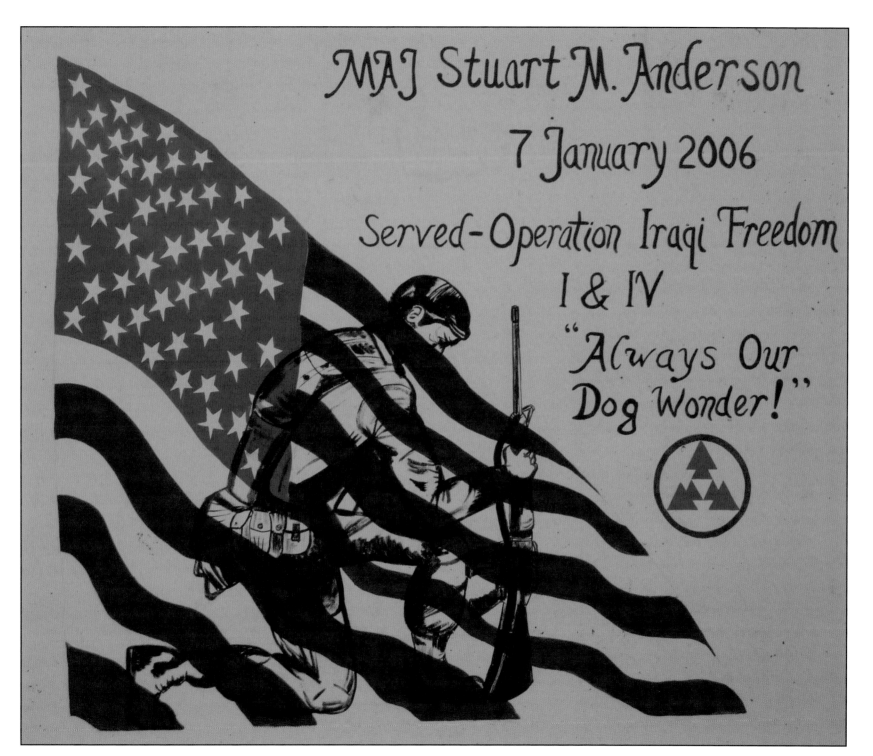

MAJ Stuart M. Anderson
7 January 2006
Served-Operation Iraqi Freedom
I & IV
"Always Our Dog Wonder!"

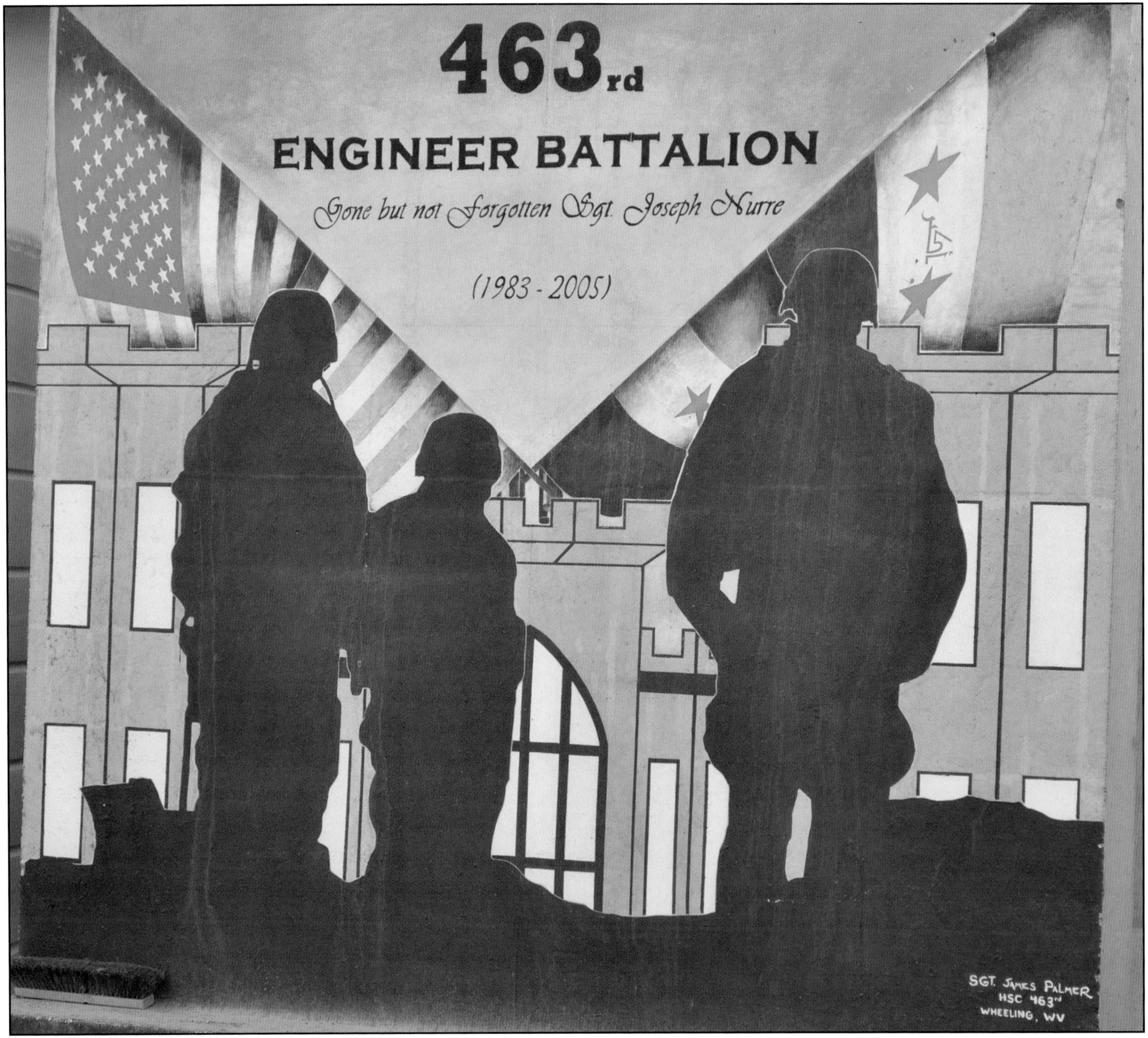
463rd
ENGINEER BATTALION
Gone but not Forgotten Sgt. Joseph Nurre
(1983 - 2005)
SGT. JAMES PALMER
HSC 463rd
WHEELING, WV

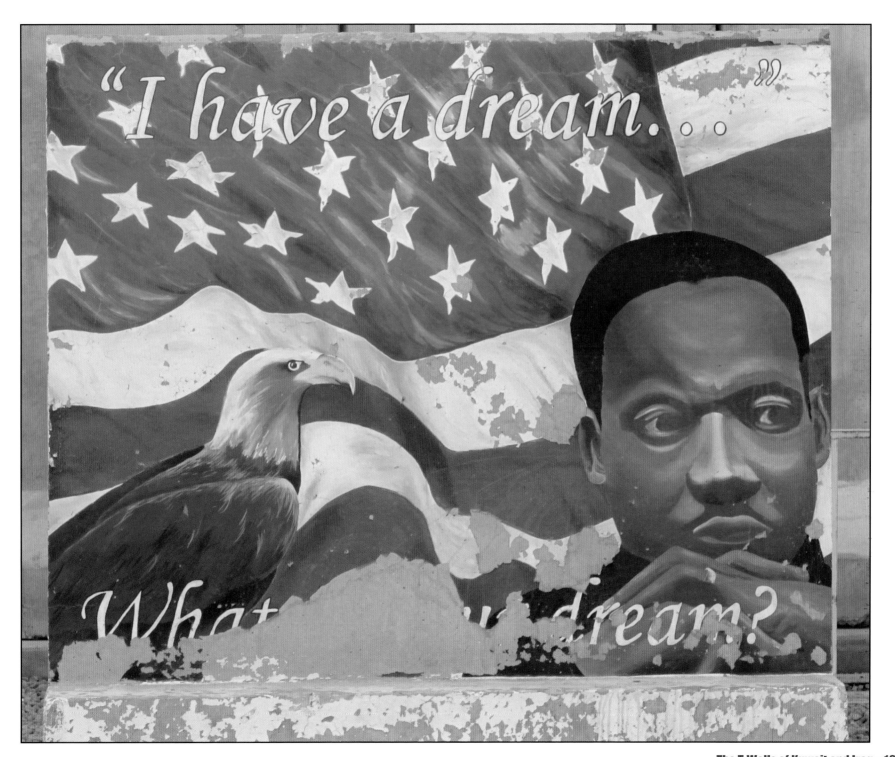

"*I have a dream...*"

What *dream?*

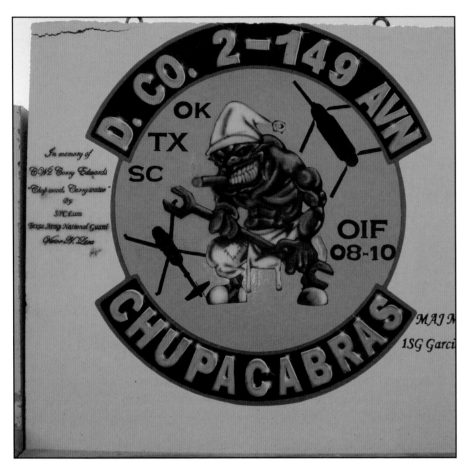

CW2 BARRY EDWARDS

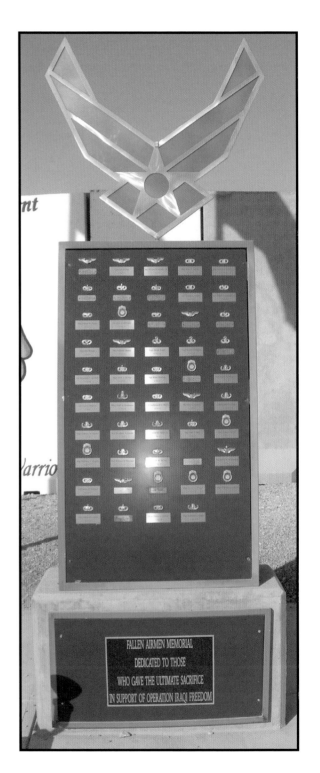

407 AEG

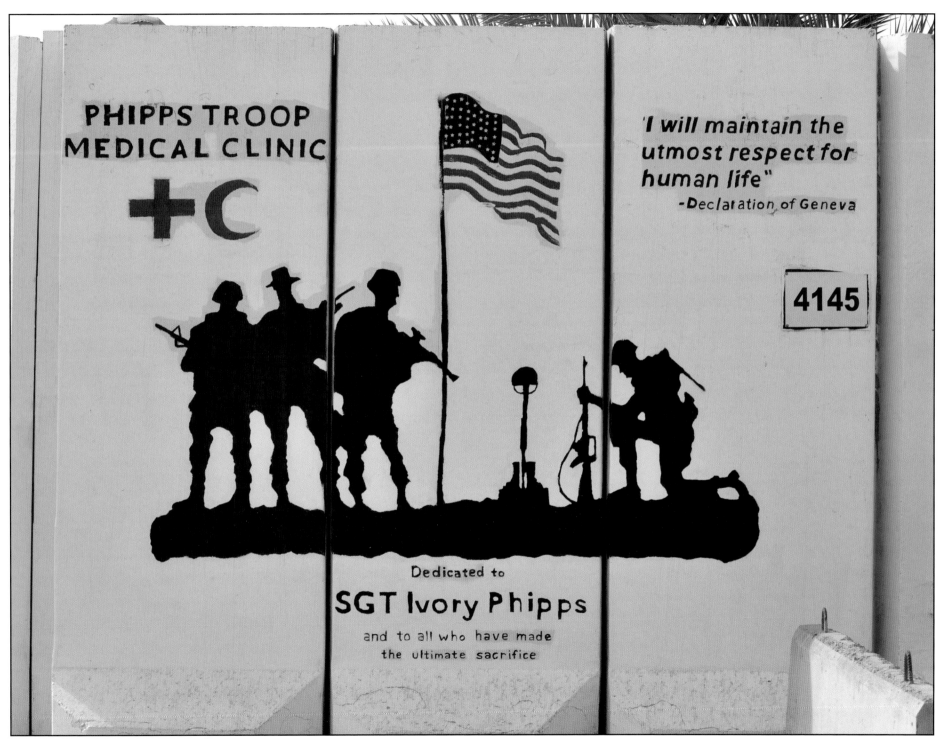

PHIPPS TROOP
MEDICAL CLINIC

"I will maintain the
utmost respect for
human life"
-Declaration of Geneva

4145

Dedicated to
SGT Ivory Phipps
and to all who have made
the ultimate sacrifice

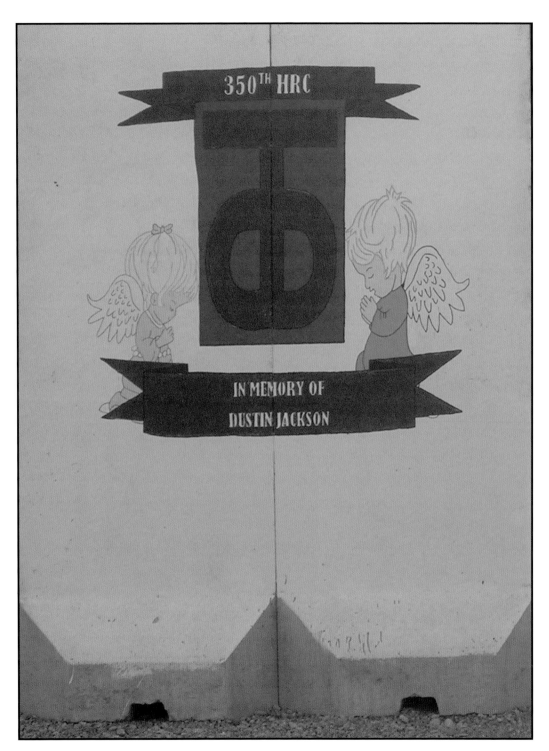

DUSTIN JACKSON

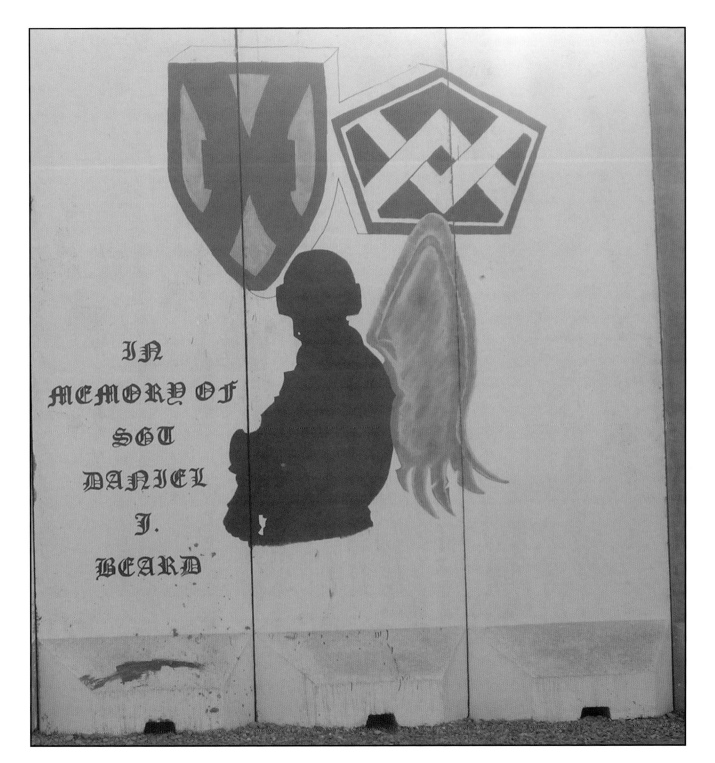

SGT DANIEL J. BEARD

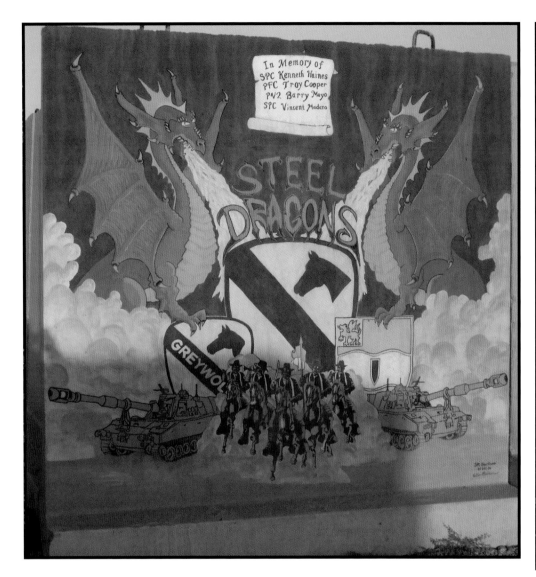

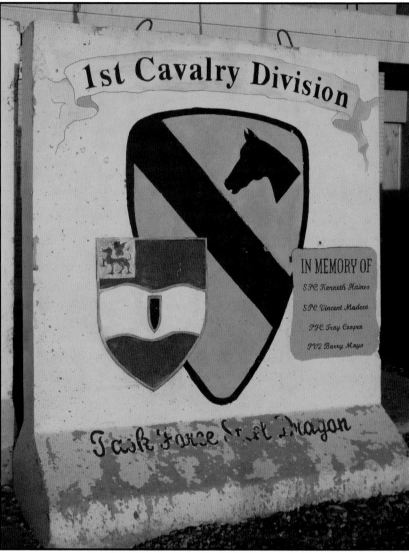

SPC KENNETH HAINES
SPC VINCENT MADURO
PFC TROY COOPER
PV2 BARRY MAYO

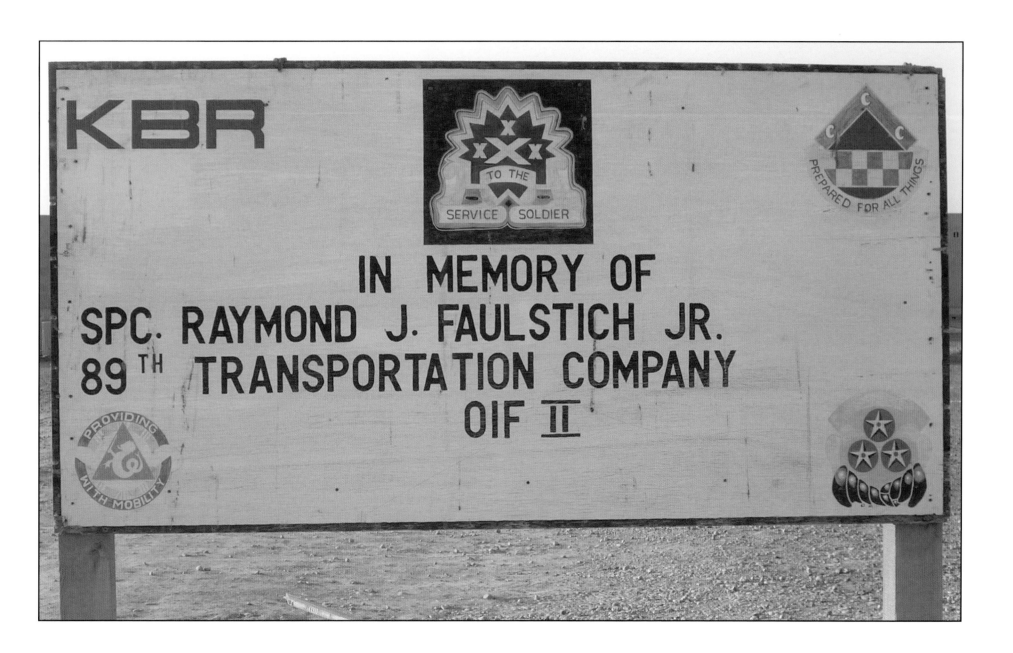

KBR

TO THE

SERVICE SOLDIER

PREPARED FOR ALL THINGS

IN MEMORY OF
SPC. RAYMOND J. FAULSTICH JR.
89TH TRANSPORTATION COMPANY
OIF II

PROVIDING WITH MOBILITY

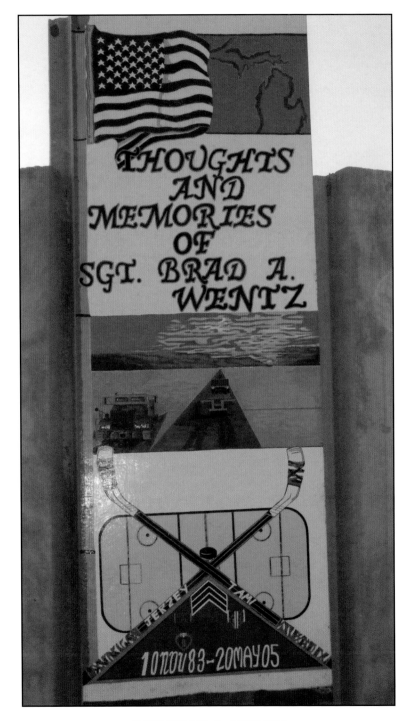

SGT BRAD A. WENTZ   SGT ERICH SMALLWOOD

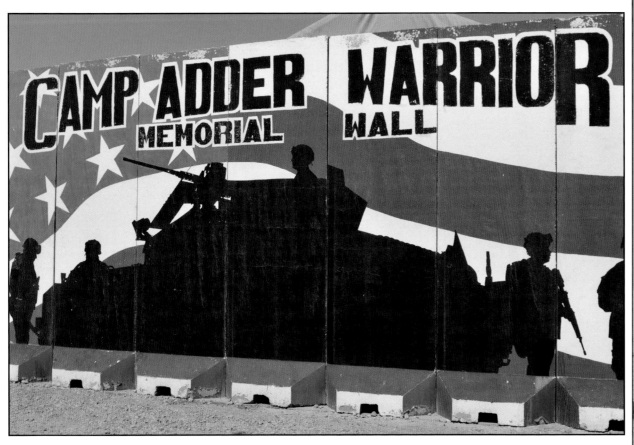

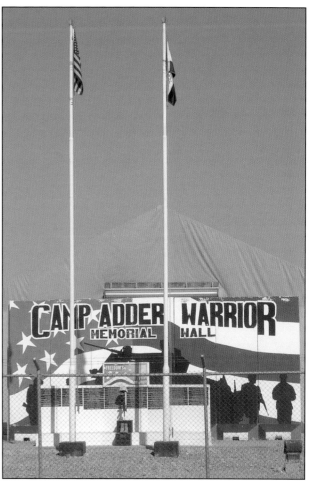

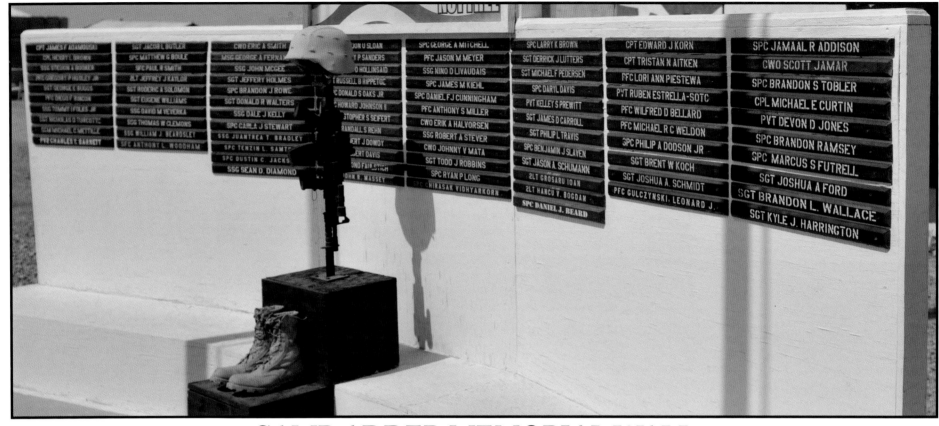

CAMP ADDER MEMORIAL WALL

(visible names)

SPC JAMAAL R. ADDISON
CPT TRISTAN N. AITKEN
SPC DANIEL J. BEARD
SSG WILLIAM J. BEARDSLEY
PFC WILFRED BELLARD
2LT MANCU V. BOGDAN
SPC MATTHEW G. BOULE
SSG JUANTREA T. BRADLEY
SPC LARRY K. BROWN
SGT JACOB L. BUTLER
SGT JAMES D. CARROLL
SSG THOMAS W. CLEMONS
SPC DANIEL F. J. CUNNINGHAM
CPL MICHAEL E CURTAIN
SPC DARYL DAVIS
SSG SEAN D. DIAMOND

SPC PHILIP A. DODSON, JR
PVT RUBEN ESTRELLA-SOTO
SGT JOSHUA A. FORD
SPC MARCUS S. FUTRELL
PFC LEONARD J. GULCZYNSKI
CWO ERIK A. HALVERSON
SGT KYLE J. HARRINGTON
SSG JEFFREY HOLMES
2LT GROSARU IOAN
SPC DUSTIN C. JACKSON
CWO SCOTT JAMAR
PVT DEVON D. JONES
2LT JEFFREY J. KAYLOR
SSG DALE J. KELLY
SPC JAMES M. KIEHL
SGT BRENT W. KOCH

CPT EDWARD J. KORN
SSG NINO D. LIVAUDIS
SPC RYAN P. LONG
SGT DERRICK K. LUTTERS
CWO JOHNNY Y. MATA
PFC JASON M. MEYER
PFC ANTHONY S. MILLER
SPC GEORGE MITCHELL
SGT MICHAEL F. PEDERSON
PFC LORI ANN PIESTEWA
PVT KELLEY S. PREWITT
SPC BRANDON RAMSEY
SGT TODD J. ROBBINS
SPC BRANDON J. ROWE
SGT JOSHUA A. SCHMIDT
SGT JASON A. SCHUMANN

SPC BENJAMIN J. SLAVIN
CWO ERIC A. SMITH
SFC PAUL R. SMITH
SGT RODERIC A. SOLOMON
SSG ROBERT A. STEVER
SPC CARLA J. STEWART
SPC BRANDON S. TOBLER
SGT PHILIP L. TRAVIS
SSG DAVID M. VEYERKA
SFC MIRASAK VIDHYARKORN
SGT BRANDON L. WALLACE
SGT DONALD R. WALTERS
PFC MICHAEL R.C. WELDON
SGT EUGENE WILLIAMS
SFC ANTHONY L. WOODHAM